Bonkers

Copyright © Michelle Holman 2009
Michelle Holman asserts the moral right to be identified
as the author of this work.

All rights reserved. No part of this publication may be reproduced,
stored in a retrieval system or transmitted in any form or by any means,
electronic, mechanical, photocopying, recording or otherwise, without
the prior written permission of the author.

Published by: Michelle Holman
First published 2009
Second edition published 2024

ISBN:
978-1-0670071-3-3 (Printed)
978-1-0670071-2-6 (eBook)

Produced by: Indie Experts Publishing
www.indieexpertspublishing.com
Cover design by Ammie Christiansen
Cover artwork by Katie Fisher
Typesetting by Fast Forward Design
Typeset in 10pt Georgia

National Library of New Zealand Cataloguing-in-Publication Data
Holman, Michelle. Knotted / Michelle Holman

Bonkers

MICHELLE HOLMAN

Chapter 1

Linda Brogan swung the blue convertible around a tight corner.

'Left side of the road!' Jack Millar yelped from the passenger seat, fearing for his safety and the paintwork of his car.

She over-corrected, almost hit the kerb and corrected again.

'Jesus, Linda!' he yelled.

Her insides felt like jelly from the near miss. She hated – *hated* - being criticized. Jack was supposed to adore her, not disapprove – that was her husband, Dan's job. Linda's temper flared along with her insecurities. 'Why can't you drive on the right side of the road in New Zealand like everyone else?'

By everyone else, she meant the United States.

Relieved that she'd slowed down, Jack reached out to stroke her thigh through her trousers. 'Sorry, darling. I just thought you'd done more driving since you'd been here.'

Linda pouted. He didn't know she hadn't driven since Dan and her moved to New Zealand or that she'd never owned a driver's license, here or at home, because she couldn't pass the test. He didn't know she couldn't read and the only reason she could only tell her left from right was because she wore her watch on her left wrist and when she *tried* to write, she used her right hand.

Unlike Dan, Jack wasn't interested in her mind. Their relationship was mostly conducted in bed which was getting boring. Dan definitely had the edge on Jack in that department. She had to coax Jack to let her drive his precious vintage convertible. The thrill of driving fed her reckless, miserable soul.

People who knew she was dumb were shocked when she managed to get a doctor to propose without getting pregnant first. The rest saw how she looked and weren't surprised at all.

Linda remembered the night she met Dan at a party. Remembered him leaning against the wall watching her quietly. His height made him hard to miss but it was the fact he didn't approach her or stare like every other guy in the room that made him stand out. Linda couldn't work out why he was different. She was dressed in a tiny white top and her tightest blue jeans and had the attention of every male in the room and plenty of their jealous girlfriends as well. So why not him?

He was a challenge she couldn't ignore; unlike the girlfriend glued to his side.

Initially, Linda went after Dan to prove a point, to reassure herself she was a desirable, valuable woman. Up close he was gorgeous and shy and smart. *Very* smart. There was a rocky moment when it became clear he saw through her act, that he saw *her*. Linda was hooked.

The early days of their marriage were wonderful. Linda felt cherished and safe, that she'd finally managed to escape her lowly upbringing. Dan came from a nice family and always wanted to be a doctor. He was adored by his patients and wanted to specialize in orthopaedic surgery. Linda spent their money on looking good and creating a beautiful home. Unfortunately, Dan saw filling it with kids as the next step in their story. They hadn't discussed having children before they got married; Dan assumed Linda would want a family and Linda didn't share she had no intention of ruining her figure or that the thought of sharing his love with somebody else terrified her.

Things started to unravel after that. Accepting the position at Auckland's Starship Children's hospital and moving down under was Dan's final attempt to rescue their marriage but it hadn't worked. Linda saw even less of him. She didn't know anyone and rebuffed the overtures of friendship extended by the wives of Dan's colleagues. She was bored and angry and wanted to go home. Dan wouldn't budge.

Linda impatiently shook off Jack's stroking hand. Her rejection of the wives didn't extend to the husbands of Dan's colleagues. The affair with Jack was a last-ditch attempt to make Dan give in, and it didn't work either. He became even more distant. Last night, in desperation, Linda set things up at a barbecue they were invited to so that Dan would catch her with Jack, believing jealousy would bring Dan to his senses and he'd fight for her.

But he walked away. Looked at her in disgust and walked away leaving her to face the shocked, condemning stares of onlookers.

The urge to pee again was a reminder of another consequence of her hasty actions. She wanted to be Dan's wife, not the mother of Jack Millar's kid.

Linda's eyes filled with tears. She'd killed her marriage.

Dumb... dumb... dumb...

There was an intersection with a roundabout up ahead. Linda ignored the sign to give way to traffic and stamped on the gas pedal.

The blue convertible shot across the road. She saw the shocked face of the girl driving the car crossing the roundabout in front of her, heard Jack scream, and felt him make a grab for the steering wheel. She crashed into the door of the other car and shrieked in agony as the front of the convertible crumpled around her legs. There weren't any airbags to cushion her from the impact. Her forehead smashed against the windscreen. And the pain was gone.

☆

The day had already started badly for the driver of the other car. Lisa Jackson's gynaecologist had delivered the news she'd been dreading for years: her endometriosis had finally outfoxed the medical establishment. All the pills she'd taken and the painful, humiliating surgical procedures and suctioning and scraping Janice Millar had tried hadn't worked. The lining of her womb continued to go AWOL each month, escaping to places it had no right to be, leaving Lisa doubled over in agony and held captive by a cupful of fluid most women excreted with nothing more than some tummy cramps and a craving for chocolate.

All that was left was a hysterectomy. Her future was teaching other women's children. She'd never have any of her own.

The sunstrike was typically bad for an early night in March. It was nearly impossible to see out the windscreen, let alone keep an eye on the car in front. Lisa drove slowly, squinting at the white line in the middle of the road. She stopped at the roundabout near her house and checked to the right for traffic. A blue convertible driven by a woman with long, black streaming behind her seemed far enough away to drive on. Lisa turned onto the road circling the flower-crested concrete island at the centre of the roundabout.

Lisa never saw the blue car suddenly accelerate but she

heard the sound of a car skidding as the driver stamped on the brakes to avoid colliding with the convertible when it failed to give way. She heard the squeal of brakes and the blare of car horns and saw the blue car hurtling towards her a split-second before it smashed into the car door.

The violence of the impact and the sickening sound of glass shattering and metal tearing made her scream. The door of her old Mazda caved inwards. Metal shards speared Lisa's right side and tore into her flesh.

And the world stopped.

Chapter 2

Lisa opened her eyes and looked about frantically for the blue car.

Where had it gone?

She touched her right side. It didn't hurt.

She wasn't in her car. She wasn't even on the road. She didn't recognize anything about the place she was in. Where *was* she?

Lisa whimpered. She had a very bad feeling about this.

Surely, she hadn't ...?

Wasn't there supposed to be a bright light at the end of a long tunnel, and voices urging her to head towards it?

She was lying on what felt like a divinely soft reclining chair. She couldn't recall ever feeling so comfortable in her life, in fact, if she took a moment to calm down, she felt warm, safe, and protected.

'Thank Christ!' Lisa mumbled fervently. 'At least I know I'm not dead.'

'We don't say that here, dear,' a female voice remarked pleasantly.

A woman with a blonde bouffant hairstyle reminiscent of a 'fifties lacquered helmet complete with a pink bow was sitting beside her, smiling complacently. She had pink-frosted cupid's-bow lips, blue eyes fringed with thick, black false eyelashes that resembled road sweepers, and a bright green silk scarf knotted about her neck. She sat with her knees primly together and her pink-tipped hands folded on her lap. A pink badge clipped to her white tunic read *Moira*.

She looked like an air stewardess. Lisa and her sister

Sherry were convinced the only people who wore scarves were air stewardesses, bank tellers, supermarket-checkout girls and, of course, porn stars, although why a scarf was necessary when somebody was buck naked and getting it on for the camera was a mystery. They'd come to this conclusion after a hen party when one of the hens decided what was good for the boys would be good for the girls. Lisa and Sherry were so bored they invented the scarf theory to liven things up.

Moira definitely didn't look like porn-star material.

'We don't mind *Good Heavens* or, at a push, *Ye Gods*, but I'm afraid we find blasphemous use of His name upsetting and strongly discourage it,' Moira explained.

Lisa blinked. What the hell was she talking about?

'I heard that,' Moira said reprovingly.

She blinked again. Her eyelids seemed to have taken on a life of their own. 'Where on earth am I? What *is* this place?'

Moira smiled placidly. 'Hardly earth, dear.'

She wasn't making any sense. This did *not feel* right.

Lisa looked about anxiously. She seemed to be in some sort of room, but she couldn't see any walls or windows. The light was soft and she had the impression it was a busy place with a lot of people coming and going, but she couldn't see anybody apart from Moira.

Lisa sat up. She felt *weird*. Her body seemed to just flow into the new position without the usual shift and play of muscle and bone to get it there. Her heart began to pound, or at least it should have. She put her hand on her chest but couldn't feel anything. No vibration. No comforting thuds. The dull ache low in her belly was gone too. She couldn't remember the last time she'd been totally pain free.

'Where am I?' she quavered.

Moira laid a hand on her arm and murmured soothingly, 'You're safe. That's the main thing — you're safe.'

'Who are you? Where's my mum and dad? I was in an accident! They'll be worried about me!'

'We know, dear.'

Something was very wrong. She was twenty-seven years old but right now Lisa needed her parents to make her feel safe.

Moira stroked her arm with a touch as soft as thistledown. It gave Lisa the creeps. She pulled her elbow against her side to avoid the other woman.

'Your parents won't be along until much later.' Moira soothed. 'But there are people on their way to collect you; people you know.'

Lisa decided Moira wasn't dealing with a full deck.

Moira looked offended.

A tall, solid-looking man wearing white trousers and a white tunic suddenly appeared beside them. He had a lot of dark auburn hair, twinkling blue eyes, and he was humming 'Stairway to Heaven' under his breath. His nametag read *George*.

He beamed at Lisa and asked, 'Alright, Lisa?' in a cockney accent.

She gazed at him helplessly. Who was he and was he going to be as weird as Moira? George laughed and winked at her. Lisa winced. So Moira wasn't the only one who could do the Vulcan mind meld.

George turned to Moira and lowered his voice. 'The other one will be coming through in a moment.'

'Yes,' She frowned. 'I just heard. I can't hand Lisa over until somebody arrives to collect her. It's against the rules.'

George's twinkly expression faded. 'We can't just leave

her floating here,' he pointed out. 'Listen ... can you hear that noise? That's the other one. She ain't coming quietly.'

Lisa was eavesdropping unashamedly. Did George just say they couldn't leave her *floating here?*

The sound of a female voice protesting loudly fractured the calm, soft atmosphere. Several figures in white were attempting to usher someone gently past them. Lisa couldn't see what they were walking on or even *if* they were walking. She glimpsed a woman with long, black hair through a gap between the people in white. The woman looked as scared as Lisa felt. She was slapping furiously at her attendants.

'I shouldn't be here!' She shouted in an American accent. 'Take your hands off of me *now*!' She paused. 'How did you do that? I can feel you, but I can't see your hands! Who *are* you people?'

It was reassuring to know she wasn't the only person who was feeling freaked out by this place.

Lisa craned her neck to get a closer look at the woman. She was tall and slender and wore expensive looking silky mauve tank-top and black silk trousers. The white figures fluttered about her, alternately soothing and cajoling. One of them was carrying a baby boy with large, brown eyes. He looked on curiously, apparently unconcerned by the noise.

'Can't you take that child away?' the woman demanded angrily.

'No, Linda. He came with you.'

'Came with me? How could he? I've never set eyes on him in my life!'

Lisa detected an edge of hysteria in her voice.

The group surrounding Linda parted further, giving Lisa a clear view of her face. She had flawless white skin, big clear blue eyes and long black hair. Lisa sucked in a breath. It was the driver of the blue convertible.

She clutched at George and pointed. 'She hit me! In her car!'

He patted her shoulder. 'Don't let it worry you, Lisa. She'll be gone soon.'

Moira tutted. 'Oh dear, this is most irregular. They're not supposed to see each other. Wait here, I'm going to find out where Lisa's grandparents have got to.'

And she was gone.

Lisa gaped. Moira had just disappeared — she had literally vanished – and her grandparents were all dead. She stared at George in alarm.

He looked annoyed and muttered what sounded like 'Silly cow' under his breath before he reached out and patting her comfortingly on the shoulder again. 'There now, don't get yourself all worked up.'

He led her away from Linda and the group surrounding her. Lisa wasn't aware of taking any steps, but she was moving, literally *floating* along. If she weren't so scared, she might have enjoyed the experience. She felt better as the noise retreated; George made her feel safe.

He smiled down at her. 'Might be better to try and not to think about that scarf joke.'

'What scarf joke?'

'I think you know the one I mean, the joke you had with Sherry.'

'How- how did you know about that?'

And how did he know she had a sister called Sherry? Come to think of it, *how* did he and Moira know her name was Lisa?

'I heard you,' George answered as if she'd spoken out

loud. 'Just count your blessings Moira hasn't yet. She tends to listen out for the blaspheming and swearing, but that doesn't mean she won't hear what you think of her scarf if you're not careful.' His eyes started twinkling again. 'How about I tell you a joke?'

Lisa gave a slightly hysterical laugh. 'OK.'

'Good girl,' he said approvingly. 'My dog has no nose.'

She gazed at him in bewilderment. 'How does he smell?'

'Awful.' George flung back his head, laughing uproariously.

Lisa laughed weakly at his ridiculous dad joke. It must be shock.

'Have you ever heard of a racehorse called Dusty Carpet?'

'Um ... no, I don't think so.'

'It's never been beaten.'

Once again, he roared with laughter.

Lisa laughed shrilly. 'George?'

'Yes?'

'Am I dead? Is this heaven?'

He hesitated. 'I'm sorry, mate. There's rules about what I can tell you. I *can* tell you that this isn't heaven. It's sort of like a waiting room.'

'So I'm not dead?'

He sighed and shook his head. 'Can't answer that.'

Lisa regarded him with growing frustration. 'Are you an angel?'

'I haven't been here long enough. I'm ... in training, shall we say?'

She pounced. 'Hah! So you're an angel-in-training?'

'There aren't any angels, Lisa —well, not like you mean.'

Lisa wondered why she hadn't developed a thumping

headache by now. She'd never felt so clear-headed, and so utterly confused.

George began humming 'I'm an Angel in Paradise'. Just her luck to get the only angel in training - or whatever he was - who told bad jokes and hummed. After a few bars, he changed to 'Heaven on the Seventh Floor'.

Lisa jumped when Moira suddenly reappeared. Jesus Christ! The woman was like a bloody jack-in-the-box.

'You really must stop that!' Moira scolded and turned to George. 'A quiet word, please, George?' Her pink Cupid's bow lips were pursed tight as an anal sphincter. Lisa had a feeling Moira wasn't a fan of her, or of George's little medley of hits either. She leaned closer to eavesdrop on their conversation.

'It has been decided one of them will be going back,' Moira said sotto voce.

'Which one?' George didn't attempt to lower his voice. Lisa suspected he was making sure she could hear.

'Lower your voice!' Moira hissed. 'I think it will be the *other one*.'

'*Her?* I've seen her life play. Why should she get a second chance? She made her poor husband's life a misery.'

'That's not for us to decide! I know you're new, but you must understand there are rules that must be obeyed.'

'Rules,' George grumbled. 'It's wrong that the bad 'un gets another go round and the good 'un stays back.'

'That's none of your business,' Moira insisted. 'You stay with Lisa until word comes through and then escort back whomever is chosen.'

She disappeared again.

George was frowning. Lisa watched him. What did it mean that one of them had to go back? *Go back where?* She tried to form the words to ask but her mind felt like a scrabble board missing the letters.

'Will you be alright if I leave you for a minute? I'll come right back.'

Lisa shrugged. 'OK.'

George disappeared.

She didn't understand why she suddenly felt so calm. She didn't know where she was or what had happened to her since she'd been hit by the car, and she was in the company of people who could vanish and reappear and read her thoughts. Her biggest concern was that her family would be worrying about her. Apart from that, she was in no hurry to leave George and his jokes.

Her recliner reappeared. Lisa settled into it gratefully. Soon, she'd wake up, at home, in bed. It would great if the visit to her gynaecologist had been a dream too.

George returned. Lisa waited patiently while he stood beside her thinking. Finally, he said, 'Sometimes rules need to be broken.'

'What do you mean?' she asked warily. 'George, you're not going to do anything that'll get you into trouble with Moira, are you?'

He grinned. 'Not a lot she can do about it, is there?'

Lisa found herself on her feet again and George's big hand in the small of her back. He started to hum, 'Heaven Must Be Missing an Angel' as they drifted away from the calm, soft light towards a brighter one.

She was reluctant to leave the oasis of peace behind her. 'Where are we going?'

'Somewhere you should be. Just close your eyes, Lisa, love. Close your eyes . . .'

She was floating down a long tunnel, in the opposite

direction this time, past all the other people she sensed around her but couldn't see. She popped out of the tunnel into bright lights and noise and saw her sister, Sherry standing in the middle of a corridor in her police uniform. She was struggling with another officer Lisa recognized as Dillon Taylor. Dillon been her boyfriend before the endometriosis took over her life.

Sherry was looking furious and desperate at the same time. Dillon wore the mask-like expression of somebody in deep shock hanging onto their self-control by their fingertips. He gripped Sherry tightly by the upper arms and told her repeatedly that she couldn't go in there.

Lisa reached out as she went by but couldn't stop. Her fingertips grazed Sherry's forearm, but Lisa couldn't feel her. 'Sherry!'

Sherry stopped struggling and turned sharply towards Lisa, a puzzled expression on her face. She looked at Dillon and demanded, 'Did you hear that? It sounded like Lisa!'

Lisa opened her mouth to try again when a tremendous force seemed to lift her up and fling her at the double doors behind Sherry and Dillon. She screamed, convinced she was going to smash into them and was suddenly she on the other side.

There were people in blue scrubs clustered around somebody on a trolley. Bags and plastic containers of fluid hung from poles attached to the bed and monitors flashed and beeped. A woman wearing a blue apron was guiding an x-ray machine out of a doorway opposite. Lisa felt herself being sucked towards the bed. She was going to crash into the people and the person on the trolley. She flung up her arms and covered her face.

★

There was something in her throat and she was choking on it.

Lisa tried to raise her hands to claw at her mouth, but they seemed to be weighed down. She could feel something wrapped about her forearms, stopping her from lifting them. She couldn't get at the thing in her mouth, and she couldn't scream for help because of it. Inside her head, she cried out for George, but his warm, reassuring presence was gone.

There was a rush of activity around her, female voices speaking quickly, issuing orders.

'– coming round – '

'– give her a bolus and get her under again – '

Just before she began to slip away, Lisa heard someone say, 'Better let her husband know she's come round.'

She hoped they would think to call her parents when they called the other woman's husband.

☆

There were so many dreams. At least, Lisa thought they were dreams until she realized that the people who spoke to her were real. Sometimes she opened her eyes and looked at them before falling asleep again.

It was a strange twilight world. The lights were bright, and the people touching and talking to her wore dark-green uniforms and didn't speak quietly. They were kind in a brisk sort of way. Lisa wanted to ask them if they could read her mind, but she was too tired and couldn't stay awake. Part of her expected to see George and Moira, but this place wasn't imbued with a wonderful sense of peace, and she hurt everywhere.

Gradually, Lisa became more aware of her surroundings. Whenever she woke, she was lying in bed, and she was never alone. She guessed she must be in hospital and the voices and belonged to the nurses looking after her. Lisa began to recognize some of their faces and the routine of bed baths and turns from her left side to her right.

'Don't want you getting any bedsores, do we?' one of them said by way of explanation.

Her throat really hurt. It was so sore she avoided swallowing, but the nurses kept making her sip water through a straw, explaining they wanted to get rid of her drip. What drip? Who cared about that when her throat felt as if somebody had taken a piece of sandpaper to it?

Her head hurt too. It felt as if it had swollen to twice its size, and there seemed to be something wrong with her right leg, too. Apart from that, Lisa was content to let them do what they wanted, provided she could fall back into the deep, dreamless oblivion of sleep.

Sometimes a man came to poke and prod her. He forced her to open her eyes and pay attention. Lisa didn't like him. She tried to do as he asked, but the lure of sleep was seductive, and she let herself slip into it and away from his demands.

'Time to get her out of here and onto the ward,' Lisa heard him say as if she were a car that had broken down in an inconvenient place. 'Let's get her moved.'

Chapter 3

A plump nurse with dark-brown, curly hair said, 'My name's Nancy and I'll be looking after you today.'

She placed a small, white plastic bulb attached to a lead in Lisa's hand. 'Here's your call bell. I've safety-pinned it to the sheet so you won't lose it. I'll be popping in and out all morning. Once you've had your bath, we'll get you up in a chair for an hour or so.'

The doctor who poked and prodded had got his way.

Lisa had been transferred along a bewildering series of corridors and in and out of elevators until she reached a room with a window and bright sunlight that hurt her eyes. The nurses were different, and they didn't stay with her all the time.

Being left alone made her feel anxious. After wanting nothing more than to be left in peace, she now felt like a baby abandoned by its mother. Nancy's maternal figure in its white uniform represented security.

The bath and hour sitting in a chair exhausted Lisa. She found out her right leg felt heavy because it was encased in a plaster cast from the knee down. When it came to plaster casts, Lisa was a pro; she'd been born with a left club foot and spent endless months in and out of plaster. The cast brought back memories of photos she'd seen of herself as a baby with her leg in plaster after operations to correct the deformity.

As for her head, it had gone from feeling like it was stuffed full of cotton wool to pounding as if the entire cast of *Riverdance* were rehearsing inside her skull. It was hard to speak; her mouth didn't feel like it belonged to her. It felt *odd*. Her lips felt fuller, and her mouth seemed bigger. When she ran her tongue over them, her chipped upper incisor was perfectly smooth. It took several tries before she managed to tell Nancy that her head hurt. Her voice came out in a croak and her lips felt like they were made of stiff rubber when she tried to form the words.

When the nurse suggested a couple of Panadol, Lisa stared at her in disbelief. Surgical removal of her head was more what she'd had in mind.

Nancy gave Lisa two tablets and a loan of her sunglasses for the rest of the day. Lisa sat in the chair, holding her head and looking like one of the Blues Brothers while Nancy and another nurse named Chris stripped her bed and changed her nightdress.

'Why does my throat hurt so much?' she asked hoarsely.

'It's from the tube you had down your throat when you were in Intensive Care,' Nancy explained as she threaded Lisa's arm into a nightdress.

Lisa felt her meagre supply of energy dwindling. 'Intensive Care?'

'Yes. You were on a ventilator for nearly a week. The tube in your throat connected you to the machine.'

A machine had been *breathing* for her?

The nurses put her back to bed when her hour in the chair was up. Lisa was embarrassed by the personal nature of the things they were doing for her. She wondered where her mother and father were. 'My mum and dad? Where are they?'

Nancy shook her head. 'I don't know about your mum and dad, Linda. I thought all your relatives were in the States.'

Why would her parents be in America? They wouldn't have flown off on holiday while she was so sick. Where were Sherry and her brother, Ben? And why had Nancy called her Linda? Lisa decided she must have misheard.

'I thought we could wash your hair later today; it must feel horrible after all this time. Your husband brought in all your toiletries. You have some beautiful stuff, Linda.'

Lisa stared at Nancy's departing back as she rushed off muttering about plastic bowls and towels.

There it was again — she'd called her Linda. And husband? Had Nancy said *husband?*

Her heart began to thump. When she put her hand against her chest, Lisa could feel it vibrating and thudding beneath her palm. It felt nothing like it had in the waiting room when she'd been feeling so frightened. She was definitely alive, but why was Nancy calling her Linda, and why on earth did she think she had a husband?

Linda. Linda. *Linda.*

Lisa gasped. She touched her hair and froze. It felt tangled and dirty but what concerned her the most was that it felt straight.

Straight.

She had straight hair.

She pulled a strand from behind her ear and was amazed to discover that it was long enough to reach the end of her nose, and she was downright shocked when she saw it was black.

Jet black.

A car accident and a week in intensive care couldn't do that. It couldn't take a mop of short, unruly blonde curls, straighten them out and turn them black. Could it?

Lisa smoothed a shaking hand backwards to a limp

ponytail resting at the nape of her neck. Her hair would have grown in a week, but not this much.

Something was *very* wrong.

She noticed her hands and began to hyperventilate. They were long and elegant and some of the fingers had those acrylic nails Sherry liked to treat herself to. And her left foot — the one not encased in plaster — was too far away to be *her* foot. Her legs weren't that long. Her family affectionately called her the runt of the litter because she was only five feet two inches tall.

Nancy returned carrying a blue plastic bowl and towels. 'Right, I'll just get your sponge bag out—'

She noticed Lisa's white face, dropped the bowl and towels on a chair and hurried to the top of the bed. 'Linda? Are you feeling dizzy? I'm just going to lower your head.' She reached for the lever at the side of the bed.

'No!' Lisa clutched her arm. 'Please, Nancy, please get me a mirror! I need a mirror!'

Her eyebrows shot up. 'A mirror?'

Lisa nodded desperately, still clinging to her arm.

Nancy hesitated and checked her pulse. 'Are you sure you're not feeling faint?'

'No!'

But Nancy wouldn't bring a mirror until she'd checked Lisa's blood pressure. 'I don't want you getting all upset about the way you look,' she warned with a faintly disapproving look. This wasn't the reaction she expected from a woman who'd been dragged back from death's door. 'You're hardly going to look a million dollars when you've been unconscious for a week.'

She reluctantly passed Lisa a small hand mirror.

Lisa strangled the slim handle in her fingers, terrified of

what she might see.

'Well?' Nancy prompted. 'Do you want to see yourself or not? I won't have time to wash your hair if we don't get a move on.'

Taking a deep breath, Lisa raised the mirror.

Despite the bruising and unhealthy grey tinge of the skin, the face she saw was lovely. Jet-black hair parted in greasy strands across a smooth forehead. Large, blue eyes stared back at her. The face had high cheekbones and a long, narrow nose above a lush, pink mouth.

It was the face of the woman she had seen in the waiting room.

The face of the woman driving the blue convertible.

The woman called Linda.

George had put her back into the wrong body.

☆

Nancy didn't wash her hair. Instead, she called the doctor who prescribed something to calm her down and make her sleep.

It was evening when she finally woke. The only light in the room was from her overhead lamp, which somebody had tilted towards the wall so it wouldn't shine in her eyes. Lisa guessed that Nancy had done it; she'd been so kind when Lisa had broken down and sobbed. Nancy held her hand and stroked her hair until she fell asleep. 'There now, sweetheart. We'll soon have you looking your old self. You're a beautiful girl, but what's really important is you're alive.'

By then, Lisa had run out of sobs, so the tears just trickled down her face and into the pillow. How could she explain to a practical, sensible soul like Nancy how ironic her comment was in the circumstances?

She was alive, but inside another woman's body. How could something so unbelievable have happened? Lisa suspected George had disobeyed the rules and sent her back instead of Linda. She'd stolen Linda's life. Although that didn't seem so wrong when she considered that it was the other woman's reckless driving that had killed her in the first place.

Killed her? What was she thinking? She was here, *alive*. In the wrong body perhaps, but still *alive*.

I'm going mad. I'm going stark, raving mad, Lisa thought miserably. Tears begin to well again in her swollen eyes.

A faint sound near the bottom of her bed halted her plan to indulge in another crying fit. She raised her head listlessly to check where it came from.

A man sat in one of the orange plastic chairs that were standard hospital issue. Lisa couldn't see him properly because of her puffy eyes and the low light.

'You're awake,' he said in a deep voice with a pronounced American accent. Getting to his feet, he took the few steps needed to bring him alongside her and into the pool of light from the overhead lamp.

Lisa stared up at him and blinked.

He was very tall and dressed in a dark-green polo shirt and dark-grey chinos. His thick, dark hair needed cutting; it flopped onto his brow and curled over the collar of his shirt. It looked untidy, as if he had a habit of running his hand through it. He eyed her cautiously. He seemed to be waiting for her to say something.

Faced with yet another strange face in a day full of strange faces and experiences, Lisa was at a loss. She thought he must be one of the doctors — on a better day she would have been delighted to get one this good looking. But she didn't want to hear anything more that might add to her problems. Instead, she lowered her eyes and followed the impressive length of his legs from his belt buckle all the way down to his tasseled grey shoes.

'How do you get a pair of trousers to fit?' she said slowly in the voice that didn't sound like her own. She looked back up at him. 'Did the shop sew two pairs together?'

He stared at her in shock for a couple of beats before giving a reluctant laugh. It sounded harsh and cracked in the middle, as if he hadn't done it in a long time. 'I buy my clothes at a tall men's shop in the city.'

He collected the chair from the bottom of the bed and came to sit beside her. Close up, she saw that his eyes were grey, and he looked tired and haggard.

'How are you feeling?'

Lisa eyed him thoughtfully, wondering where he was going to fit into the puzzle. She realized the calmness she felt wouldn't last. It was just her mind shutting down after everything that had happened today. She was numb. Frankly, she'd given up caring for the moment.

'My head hurts. My leg hurts. Oh, and they stuffed some suppositories up my backside this afternoon. Apart from that, I'm bloody marvellous.'

She could tell she'd shocked him again. He tried to laugh and failed. His expression was troubled, as if he couldn't figure something out. Lisa regarded him sympathetically. She felt like telling him she couldn't figure it out either.

'Do you know who I am?' he asked.

'No.' Lisa stared back listlessly. 'Do you know who I am?'

'Uh huh.' He tilted his head as if he were listening to her carefully. 'You don't recognize me at all?'

She tried to shake her head but changed her mind when

pain stabbed her in the temples. 'No. Why? Are you famous?'

He smiled fleetingly, showing the white even teeth Americans seemed to be blessed with, usually thanks to their love affair with orthodontics. 'I'm Dan,' he watched her closely. 'Dan Brogan.'

Tears pooled in her eyes. Lisa was amazed she had any left. 'Nice to meet you, Dan.'

'Sssh. Don't cry,' He snagged a couple of tissues from the box on the locker and handed them to her.

'Am I s'posed to know you?' Lisa asked wearily after she'd blown her nose.

'Mmm hmm.'

'Are you one of my doctors?

He shook his head.

She decided to take the plunge. 'Who do you think I am, Dan?'

He seemed fascinated by her voice. Lisa got the feeling it intrigued him just as much as what she was saying.

'Don't you know who you are?'

'Oh, *I* know who I am,' She was beginning to slur with tiredness. It was hard shaping words with Linda's mouth. 'It's just a matter of who everybody else thinks I am.'

Dan Brogan frowned. 'OK, you've lost me.'

'Tell me who you think I am!' She cried in frustration, then wished she hadn't because it made her head throb.

'You're Linda,' he said quietly. 'Linda Brogan.'

Lisa stared at him in dismay.

Brogan.

Maybe he was Linda's brother.

'Are you and Linda related?' She guessed that the way she was referring to Linda in the third person was adding to his confusion.

'I'm your husband, Linda.'

Lisa gaped. 'My *husband?* But I'm not married!'

'I'm afraid you are,' He insisted quietly.

Lisa suddenly noticed he was wearing a wedding band. 'No, you don't understand! I *know* it sounds mad but I'm *not* Linda! My name is Lisa! Lisa Jackson! I was put back in the wrong body by mistake. . .' She trailed off.

Dan stared at her in silence.

So now they'd lock her away with all the other nuts.

Well done, Lisa.

He dragged a hand through his hair and gripped the back of his head. 'How about we talk about this tomorrow?' he suggested at last. 'I'll talk to Rod Cameron, your neurosurgeon, and tell him how you feel. OK?'

Lisa was too shell-shocked to answer.

'Don't be too hard on yourself, Linda. You've spent the last week in ICU with a head injury. It's hardly surprising you feel confused.'

Lisa gave a cracked laugh that ended on a sob. 'You can say that again.'

He reached out to give her hand a comforting pat. They both jumped at the unexpected jolt the contact gave them. Linda Brogan's husband snatched his hand back and didn't seem to know what to do with it for a few moments. Eventually he shoved it into the pocket of his chinos. 'I'll come back and see you tomorrow.'

Lisa didn't bother to answer.

☆

Dan walked blindly down the corridor from Linda's room, his mind frantically searching for answers. Brain injuries weren't his specialty, but he knew enough to know it wasn't unheard of for people injured as seriously as Linda had been to experience some memory loss. The logical, educated part of his mind could accept this; he knew her recovery might be prolonged and incomplete. If the part of her brain responsible for speech had been damaged it could explain why she appeared to be finding it difficult to talk. She sounded nothing like herself. In fact, she spoke with the long, flat vowels of a New Zealander.

Linda never made self-deprecating jokes, so her remark about the suppositories was out of character. The one about his trousers too. She used to make cracks about his rumpled appearance, but her remarks had long ago stopped being given jokingly.

He felt as if he was the one who'd sustained a head injury. The woman in the bed looked at him as if he were a stranger; his heart squeeze when he saw the bruised, frightened look in her eyes. Linda worked hard to project an image of supreme self-confidence; Dan was one of the few people who knew the demons and low self-esteem that tormented her and how she fought back by manipulating the people around her. It was just one of many reasons their marriage had failed. Dan hadn't forgotten what a consummate actress she was. A part of him wondered what she was up to this time. Was she fooling them all now?

The head injury must be the cause of her memory loss and bizarre claims. It *had* to be, unless he wanted to start believing her story about being put back in the wrong body.

It was either the head injury or something Dan had known for a long time. That his wife was a compulsive liar.

Chapter 4

Dan was born and raised in Boulder, Colorado, and attended medical school at the university. He met Linda Mulholland while he was a resident at a hospital in Los Angeles. He was twenty-nine and she was twenty-two.

The pair couldn't have been more different. Dan was quiet and most comfortable watching from the fringes, but it was hard to go unnoticed when, apart from his younger brother, he usually towered over everyone else. His family and close friends knew he was painfully shy, which was why he could come across as gruff, particularly when it came to girls. It wasn't that he didn't like them — far from it — he was as preoccupied as the next man with the female sex and, well, sex in general.

Because he tended to stand back and watch, he often noticed things about girls that passed his friends right by. It was his powers of observation that made him a good doctor and valued member of the Emergency Room team. Dan didn't feel the need to brag about himself, largely because he thought he was pretty ordinary. He didn't understand that his big body and looks attracted women, and the fact he was a doctor certainly didn't detract from his charm. But what made them stay was his ability to listen. *Really* listen.

And that he never repeated what he heard.

'Hey, Brogan! Is it true you managed to get Samantha into the sack? Theo said he saw you going into her apartment last Thursday night and your car was still there in the morning.'

Dan would shrug and say vaguely, 'Thursday night?

Samantha? I thought that was the night I played poker at Mike's.'

As he was notoriously forgetful about anything other than his work, his friends usually gave up in frustration.

Dan had a reputation among the females of his acquaintance for being the real thing — the strong, silent type. Although he might be forgetful, he certainly wasn't stupid. He quickly realised that it didn't pay to tell women that the reason he stayed silent was because he didn't have the answers to their problems, or at least, none they'd want to hear. After observing many of his buddies shoot themselves in the foot by offer advice and watch their girlfriends disappear into the sunset, he came to the conclusion that the wisest course of action was to keep his mouth shut and nod sympathetically in the right places. It worked. Dan kept his head down, took women out and enjoyed their company, in and out of bed.

'Dan, you're such a rarity. You *know* instinctively that women are from Venus and men are from Mars, and I bet you've never even read the book.'

No, he hadn't. With his nose constantly buried in medical texts, it was doubtful he'd even heard of it.

Linda erupted into his life at a party. She was dressed in a tiny white top and tight blue jeans that emphasized her stunning cheerleader's body. She was one of the few people besides Dan who remained sober; the only thing he saw her drink the entire night was Pepsi.

'Holy cow!' one of his friends mouthed reverently when she sauntered into the room. It just about summed up the reaction of every man there, much to the annoyance of their dates.

Linda was clearly aware of the attention she was

generating and loved it. Dan noticed her habit of stroking the ends of her shiny black hair idly across her lips, neck — or the tops of her breasts — when she spoke to a guy. The poor sucker went from a state of semi-arousal to rock-hard in the time it took to imagine being that lucky strand of hair. Linda giggled and apologized when somebody pointed out what she was doing, explaining it was an unconscious habit she really needed to break.

Some unconscious habit, Dan thought, sipping his beer. She was so beautiful she almost made his eyes cross. Every man at the party wanted her, and she played them off expertly one against the other the entire night while Dan leaned against the wall with a beer in one hand and the other in the pocket of his jeans, watching her. She appeared to avoid any guy who was even slightly inebriated, as if the booze bothered her.

As the night wore on, she looked across at him more often, a puzzled expression on her face. Dan was the only guy in the room who hadn't made a move on her. He'd only drunk two cans of Budweiser because he had to work in the morning. He wasn't trying to be strong and silent that night either; it was more that he couldn't imagine this extraordinary creature was (a) real and (b) could be remotely interested in him.

Eventually, Linda flounced across the room and leaned against the wall beside him. 'Don't you talk, big guy?' she demanded.

Dan stared down at her for several long moments. She was even more gorgeous up close.

Linda reached up to wave a manicured hand in front of his face. 'Hello? Anybody in there?'

His nostrils filled with the musky scent of her perfume.

He frowned and drew back, his awkwardness growing as he imagined making a fool of himself in front of this girl.

'Don't,' he said abruptly.

Linda froze, her hand in mid-air. It wasn't the reaction she was used to.

'Don't?' she repeated uncertainly.

'Sorry,' Dan muttered miserably. 'Didn't mean to be so rude.'

'Oh,' she laughed, her expression brightening. 'That's OK. *I* was rude.'

She lifted a strand of her hair and began stroking it just above her right nipple. Dan forced himself to keep his eyes on her face while the zipper on his jeans suddenly became way too tight.

Her blue eyes were bright with mischief. 'What's your name?'

'Dan Brogan.'

He scanned the room nervously. There was no sign of Sally, his date.

'Brogan? Hey! You're Irish too! My name's Mulholland. Linda Mulholland.'

From the corner of his eye, Dan watched Linda stroke her hair across her nipple. It puckered against the thin, stretchy fabric of her white top.

'Maybe we're related,' she suggested.

His brows rose in disbelief. If she'd been a member of his family, he was certain he *and* his brother would have known about it.

She continued to eye him appraisingly. 'And what do you do, Dan?'

Make a fool of myself at parties, he thought miserably, scanning the room again for Sally. 'Bartender.'

'Oh,' She looked disappointed and dropped her hair.

'Do you have to do that thing with your hair? I mean, it isn't as if the guys aren't already looking.'

Her mouth formed an O of surprise.

'What thing with my hair?' she snapped.

'You know what I'm talking about,' Dan muttered, regretting his outburst. He'd just broken his golden rule about never offering a woman advice.

Sally entered the room and didn't look too pleased when she spotted him with Linda. She fought her way through the crowd to reach them, wrapped her hands around Dan's arm and pressed herself against his side.

'Hi, Linda,' she said coolly.

Linda stopped glaring at Dan long enough to reply tonelessly, 'Hi, Sally. How are you?'

'Pretty good.'

Sally snuggled closer to Dan, unknowingly nudging him closer to Linda so her breasts were now pressed against his other arm. He closed his eyes briefly, a man torn between heaven and hell. The heaven of a pair of breasts snuggled either side of him and the hell of the owners of the breasts looking like they wanted to sock each other in the eye. How had that happened? He suspected things might get nasty if he didn't intervene.

'Sally?' he asked.

'Yes, sweetie?' She glared at Linda.

Dan winced. *Sweetie?* Sally was overdoing it a bit. 'I think we'd better hit the road.'

'Of course, honey,' she smirked at Linda. 'I'd forgotten you have an early start at the hospital in the morning.'

'The hospital?' Linda repeated sharply. 'You're a bartender at a hospital?'

Sally frowned. 'Dan's not a bartender. He's a doctor.'

Linda stared at Dan.

Dan stared at Linda.

She chased him relentlessly for the next three weeks until he gave in, a man more than happy to go to this particular scaffold. He was completely smitten, although he did his best to hide it, sensing the best strategy was to keep Linda on her toes. As soon as she had the upper hand, she'd try to walk all over him. But she was charming, funny, unpredictable, and very, very sexy.

'Would you have been interested in me if I'd been a bartender?' Dan asked the first time they slept together.

Linda considered her reply but decided to answer him truthfully because she'd learned that he could spot a lie a mile off. 'I would still have wanted to go to bed with you.'

'Thanks a lot,' he replied dryly.

He was lying on his back with Linda draped across him, her long hair spilling across his chest and abdomen.

She pressed a kiss into his belly, smiling when his muscles clenched in response. 'You're welcome, Doctor Brogan.'

'But apart from going to bed with me?' Dan persisted, toying with her hair.

She pursed her lips. 'I would have dumped you. I didn't fight my way out of a trailer park to slip right back again.'

Dan respected her honesty.

He'd known Linda about two months when her mother was admitted to the hospital where he worked. Linda had never mentioned her family. At the time Dan wasn't overly bothered because they were still in the early stages of their relationship, only getting out of bed long enough to go to work, eat and catch an occasional movie. He discovered

Linda's mother had been admitted because a colleague involved in her care was having trouble contacting Linda, who was listed as Betty Mulholland's next of kin. The colleague contacted Dan because he knew Linda was his girlfriend.

Linda was reluctant to see her mother, explaining they'd never been close. 'I haven't seen her in almost two years.'

Coming from a close-knit family, Dan found this hard to understand. He couldn't imagine falling out with his parents and brother so badly that he wouldn't speak to them for two years. He was almost sorry he'd passed the message on. 'I'll come with you if it'll make you feel better.'

Linda accepted reluctantly. 'You might as well find out sooner rather than later what I come from,' she said resignedly.

Dan knew ten seconds after entering Betty Mulholland's hospital room that she was suffering from delirium tremens due to alcohol withdrawal.

She began to complain bitterly the moment Linda stepped over the threshold, her nicotine-stained fingers shaking as they plucked at the covers on her bed. 'So you decided to show your face? Think you're too good for your own mother now you've landed some hotshot doctor?'

Judging by the hostile expression on Linda's face, Dan guessed she'd seen and heard it all before. It explained her aversion to alcohol.

Betty had probably once been as beautiful as her daughter, but booze and bitterness had wiped away all traces. She was a thin, withered husk of a woman, old before her time, with hard eyes, and she was out for her daughter's blood. She looked Dan over the way he imagined a female praying mantis did just before it bit off the male's head. 'I always told you the only thing you had going for you was your looks,' she sneered. 'Sure as hell wasn't your brains!'

Dan glanced uneasily at Linda. Her face wore a blank expression, as if she was accustomed to tuning out her mother's vitriol.

Betty continued malevolently, 'She's dumb as a post, y'know. Always in the bottom of the class at school. Had to do fifth grade three times over. Never graduated.' She gave a cracked laugh. 'At least *I* managed that! You can say what you want about me, Miss High and Mighty, but at least I'm not *dumb!*'

Linda pushed past Dan and ran out of the room.

Dan stared at Linda's mother, struggling to believe a parent could speak to their child the way Betty had spoken to her daughter.

He walked slowly over to the bed. Bracing his hands on either side of the bedcovers covering Betty's skinny legs, he thrust his face close to hers and growled, 'Listen to me you crazy old bitch. If you ever so much as spit in Linda's direction again, I'll make it my business to make you sorry.'

Betty shrank back against the pillows. 'You can't threaten me! I'll get you fired for saying that! I'll ... I'll get you struck off! Nurse!' she shrieked. 'Nurse! There's a madman in my room! *Help!*'

Dan knew the nurses who worked on the floor and that Betty Mulholland spent much of the day yelling and abusing the staff. He didn't expect they'd be along any time soon to rescue their patient. He straightened and waited. When Betty stopped yelling to draw breath, he took the opportunity to say, 'As long as we understand one another, Mrs Mulholland. Hopefully we won't be meeting again.'

As he left the room Betty began to yell again, using

language that would have put a sailor to shame.

Linda was waiting in the car park leaning against Dan's car, her arms wrapped about her waist and her eyes shaded by sunglasses.

Dan's heart contracted when he saw the way her shoulders were hunched defensively, as if she was waiting for a blow. He stopped in front of her, trapping her between him and the car. 'You OK?'

She shrugged and looked off into the distance. 'Sorry about that,' she said stiffly. 'I don't know why I let you come with me. You really didn't need to hear that.'

He grunted. 'Forget about me. What about you? Is she always like that?'

Linda looked at her feet. 'Pretty much. But I'm used to it.' She frowned at her pink-tipped toes peeping out of delicate, high- heeled sandals. 'What took you so long?'

'There were a couple things I wanted to clarify with your mom.'

'Clarify?'

Dan hesitated. He felt justified in what he'd said to Betty Mulholland, but he didn't feel particularly proud of himself, a guy his size threatening a wizened little old lady, even if she did have a mouth like a sewer. He decided an edited version of the truth was the best way to go. 'I told her I'd take it personally if she ever hurt you like that again.'

Linda jerked her head up, making the silver hoop earrings she wore bang against her cheeks and her sunglasses slip down her nose. She gazed at Dan incredulously. 'You what?'

He sighed and swiped his palms across his face. 'I told her I'd make it my business to make her sorry if she did anything to upset you again. I couldn't stand by and let her get away with treating you like that. You don't deserve it.' He said gruffly.

Linda stared at him. 'Don't I?' she asked in a wobbly voice.

Dan groaned when she began to sniff and the tears started sliding down her face. 'Linda ... hey, I'm sorry! She's your mother and all but damn it! I couldn't let her talk to you like that—'

She stopped him mid-sentence by winding her arms his neck so tightly she almost strangled him. 'That is the most wonderful thing anybody has ever done for me!' she bawled.

On the ride back to her tiny apartment, Linda said hesitantly, 'She's right about one thing, you know.'

Dan gave her an are-you-serious look.

'I *am* dumb.'

'No, you're not.'

'Yes, I am!' she insisted vehemently. 'I *am* dumb, Dan! I ...' Her voice dropped to a whisper. 'I can't read.'

Dan was stunned. He'd noticed Linda only ever looked at magazines and would entice him away from a book if he picked one up. He'd put it down to the fact she was a person who thrived on action. Linda was not a particularly relaxing person to be around, but she was fun and keenly intelligent, always noticing things about people and places and asking lots of questions. It was one of the few traits they shared.

'Did you miss a lot of school when you were young?' he asked, feeling as if he were navigating a minefield blindfolded.

'Oh no,' Linda laughed bitterly. 'We moved around a lot, but Betty always put me in school. It was her drinking time.'

'But you can't read?'

She stared out the window. 'I can read for a little while.

If I do it for too long, I get dizzy and the words start to wriggle around on the page. I did really well at school until fifth grade because I could kind of cover it up. It took me three times as long as the other kids to do my homework, but I made myself do it. I liked being in my bedroom instead of downstairs listening to Betty slurring and swearing.'

Linda paused for so long that Dan thought she had stopped. 'When I started fifth grade, Betty had a boyfriend who came to live with us. They were always fighting and things were so bad that I couldn't even get away from the noise in my room, so . . .' She shrugged. 'My grades went down and I kept on repeating fifth grade again and again and *again*.'

Dan gripped the steering wheel tightly, wishing it was Betty Mulholland's scrawny neck. 'Linda,' he said gently, 'what you've described sounds like dyslexia.'

She flinched and snapped, 'I *know* what it's called, Dan.'

'Lots of famous, successful people—'

'Yeah, yeah, I've heard all about them! Thomas Edison, Albert Einstein, Leonardo da Vinci, Alexander Graham Bell, Walt Disney.' Linda glared at him. 'If I wanted to invent the freakin' phone or do a remake of *Snow White* I'd be really thrilled.' She turned away to look out the window. 'I'd be happy if I could just tell my right from my left without having to use a secret code.'

'What secret code?'

Linda sighed and held out her hands. 'You know how I tell my left from my right?'

He shook his head.

She held up her left hand. 'I wear my watch on my left hand and I write with my right hand.' She shot him a challenging look. 'Oh, by the way, I can't actually tell the time. The watch is just for show. That's why I'm always late to everything.'

★

Even if Dan hadn't been besotted with her, he wouldn't have been able to dump Linda like she expected him to following her revelations. He was by nature a rescuer. He'd been the kid who brought home stray dogs and injured birds and always tried to include the littlest and least popular kids in the games at school. It was no surprise to his parents when he chose medicine as a career.

'Yeah, a doctor or a missionary,' his brother, Glenn remarked when Dan applied for pre-med. 'Except the no-drinking rule would have been a killer when it came to missionary work. And if it was a toss-up between nuns and nurses, the nurses would win every time.'

Their mother, Molly, was a regular attendee at the local Catholic Church and took offence at her younger son's remarks. 'Missionaries do wonderful work in very difficult places around the world.'

'I'm sure Dan has given the missionary position a lot of thought, Mom,' Glenn replied solemnly.

'Glenn,' Kell Brogan growled warningly, struggling to keep a straight face.

His wife looked suspiciously between them, demanding, 'What? *What?*'

Linda's upbringing couldn't have been more different from Dan's. Betty Mulholland's tender ministrations and Linda's ongoing sense of failure due to her dyslexia made her develop a toughness that wasn't always attractive. Her natural mistrust of people made them dispensable if they didn't play the game her way.

Dan made it clear from the beginning that he expected

there to be only two people at a time in their relationship. 'You screw around on me or lie to me and I'll walk away. Do you understand?'

'I understand,' Linda said slowly. 'But does that mean I can expect the same in return?'

'Absolutely.'

He knew it went against her natural instincts, but she badly wanted to believe him. Dan gave Linda the stability she had been looking for all her life.

'I'm not going risk losing the best thing that's ever happened to me, Dan,' she assured him, stepping into his arms. 'I love you.'

Chapter 5

Despite Dan's assertions, he was so head over heels in love with Linda it would have killed him to walk away. Some his friends tried to dissuade him from marrying her. One friend at the hospital even tried to warn him off. 'Linda Mulholland is bad news, Dan. She's checked out every resident in a twenty-mile radius and she's determined to marry one of them.'

Dan ignored the friend, but he was shaken when his mother, with her staunch religious convictions, asked why they didn't just live together for a while before getting married. 'After all, everyone else is doing it.'

Linda's introduction to his family wasn't an outstanding success. Her defensive attitude combined with an attack of nerves at meeting her future in-laws made her appear brittle and uncaring. The Brogans never saw the sweet, funny, loving woman Dan knew.

'She's very pretty,' Kell said.

'She's very tall,' Molly offered.

'Sleep with her, but don't marry her,' Glenn advised bluntly.

The two brothers didn't speak again until just before the wedding when Glenn stood up as Dan's best man.

Linda was hurt and resentful. 'Your family doesn't like me.'

'They don't know you. Give them a chance.'

They got married six months after they met. Betty Mulholland was not invited.

Everyone agreed that Linda made a breathtaking bride

in a wedding gown of ivory lace and a long, gossamer-fine wedding veil attached to a tiny satin cap at the back of her gleaming black hair. Dan paid for the wedding dress because she'd set her heart on it and couldn't afford it.

Linda loved being a doctor's wife. She quit her job as a nail technician and enrolled in adult-education classes that she never completed. Dan made the mistake of finding out about the many reputable teaching programmes for dyslexia in their local area.

'I am *not* attending any more of those dumb classes!' Linda yelled. 'I've been through all of them at least twice and they don't work! They *never* work!'

'But, Linda, you can't have tried them all. What about the Irlen method?'

'Oh great! Is that the one where you wear dorky glasses with pink lenses?'

'Who cares what you look like if it means you can read and write?' Dan yelled back, finally losing patience.

Linda burst into tears. 'Don't shout! Please don't shout at me!'

She'd been so indoctrinated by Betty that all she had of any value was her looks that Dan might have been speaking Zulu for all the impression he made. Linda was so frightened of looking stupid or unattractive, she refused to even consider the idea of glasses. In her opinion, being beautiful was all that made her lovable.

Dan learned to accommodate her dyslexia. He read everything he could find on the subject and grew increasingly frustrated as he became convinced her problem was not insurmountable. It wasn't a lack of skill on Linda's part, but a lack of will. But he didn't have the faintest idea how to break through the habits and beliefs of a lifetime. He bought her a waterproof digital watch so she never needed to remove it and always had a reference point to tell left from right. He made sure she always carried her mobile phone so he could remind her if she had to get to something on time. As time went by, he became less of a husband and more of a parent.

By the end of their first year of marriage, Linda realized that being a doctor's wife meant long hours alone and sleep broken by the phone ringing to call Dan back into the hospital for an emergency.

'I never see you!' she complained. 'I'm bored out of my skull!'

'What did you expect, Linda?' Dan retorted. 'When you married me, you married the job. We come as a package.'

When he suggested they start a family, she looked at him as if he were mad. 'You want me to sit at home on my own all day with a *baby?* What if it turns out like me instead of you? That's just what we need — another dummy in the family.'

Dan couldn't argue with her on one point: his hours at the hospital meant he'd be an absentee father, which wasn't what he wanted.

He eventually chose paediatric orthopaedics as his specialty. Gradually, Dan began to gain a reputation as one of the best young orthopaedic surgeons around. He was fascinated by the work being done using Ilizarov splints, a type of surgery where a special frame was attached to bone with pins and screws that were turned regularly, causing the healing bone to grow. It had been used with great success on children who in the past would have walked with a limp for the rest of their lives. Dan was so gifted at successfully operating on difficult cases that, despite his youth, he started getting calls to operate on children from out of state and began writing papers for medical journals. Although his star was on the rise, watching kids deal with pain and long months of rehabilitation kept him humble and his feet firmly on the ground.

Linda became increasingly frustrated and bored as the years passed. Dan was her life. She was an intelligent woman but her only purpose in life was to cook his meals, look after the house and go shopping. She was jealous of Dan's success and began accusing him of having affairs with his more attractive female colleagues. At social functions, she was barely civil to them. With hindsight, Dan could see that Linda had been a time bomb just waiting to go off.

When he saw an advertisement for a surgeon at a children's hospital in Auckland, New Zealand, specializing in the Ilizarov technique, Dan applied and was jubilant when he was hired. He hoped that a change of scene would allow Linda and him to start again.

'You expect me to leave my friends and my house to go to some tinpot little country at the bottom of the world?' she demanded incredulously.

'It's only for a couple of years tops, and it's a great opportunity,' Dan insisted. 'I don't think you realize how lucky I am to get this job at my age.'

'For *you*, maybe. But what about me?' she raged.

He regarded her stonily. 'I'm damned if I do and I'm damned if I don't when it comes to you, Linda. You keep saying you hate being on your own so much; well, this will mean a reduction in my working hours. I'll have my own team and we'll have more time together.'

'I've heard it all before,' she sneered.

'Well, you can always stay here. Suit yourself.'

Dan walked out of the house and spent the night at a drive-in, watching a movie he couldn't recall. It was the first time he'd ever walked out on Linda. She was badly shaken when he returned home in the early hours of the morning and flung herself at him as he walked through the door, sobbing, 'Don't leave me! You mustn't *ever* leave me!'

He held her close. 'Honey, I don't want to be apart from you, but you make it so damned hard, If I thought giving up my work would make you happy, I would.'

Linda raised her head from his chest and said sharply, 'No! Don't ever stop being a doctor.'

Dan loved New Zealand. The population was small with a million of them living in the biggest city, Auckland. It had a subtropical climate and straddled a narrow isthmus between two harbours. The Manukau harbour to the west had black-sand, surf beaches and a gannet colony and was fringed by the lush rainforest of the Waitakere Ranges. Dan was entranced the first time they went hiking there; the bush was so thick and unique with its prehistoric-looking tree ferns it wouldn't have seemed out of place to see a dinosaur go lumbering by.

In stark contrast, the Waitemata Harbour to the east had white sandy beaches, calm waters, and the bonus of quick access to the Hauraki Gulf with its multitude of tiny islands. Many Aucklanders owned a boat, and the two harbours were their playgrounds, gigantic paddling pools where they could swim, surf, boat, dive, and fish.

Dan loved the ocean and the easy-going lifestyle. They rented a house on the North Shore right above a beach, which gave him ample opportunity to indulge his love of water sports. He bought windsurfers for himself and Linda, and mountain bikes to tackle the hilly streets surrounding their home.

Linda hated New Zealand. She hated that the seasons were different, which meant Christmas was in summer and her birthday in June was in winter. She couldn't get used to people driving on the left- hand side of the road and was nearly run over because she forgot to look the opposite way crossing the street. It annoyed her when she kept getting into the wrong side of the car, and she soon tired of windsurfing, biking or hiking, so Dan ended up going alone. She complained that Auckland wasn't so much a city as a big town and that the only decent shopping was across the Harbour Bridge in Parnell and Newmarket.

Dan failed to understand how anybody could be miserable when they were surrounded by so much beauty. They had a nice home, enough money, and he wasn't working the insane hours he had in the States, which meant they could spend more time together. He watched fathers playing with children on the beach and wondered why it couldn't be him. Eventually he just stopped listening to Linda.

He thrived on his work at the hospital and got along well with his colleagues, who appreciated his surgical skills and modest, self-deprecating charm. And, as always, he loved the kids.

When Linda decided she was homesick, Dan refused to budge. 'I can't leave, Linda. I've signed a contract.'

'So? Contracts can be broken.'

'I won't do that.'

He'd come to realize Linda would never be happy — certainly not with him. But whenever he raised the subject of them separating, she panicked and insisted she loved him and couldn't live without him. Dan suspected it was the lifestyle he provided that she couldn't live without.

They met another American couple at a cocktail function held at the hospital for a retiring member of the surgical staff. Janice Millar was a gynaecologist working at the main hospital up the hill from the children's hospital. She was a plain woman who'd spent most of her life struggling with shyness. Dan felt an instant affinity with her.

Janice clearly adored her husband, Jack, who was involved with one of the yachting syndicates competing to win the America's Cup. Jack Millar was charming and unfaithful to his long-suffering wife. Linda was enthralled by the glamour he exuded and the witty stories he shared about competitive yachting. Dan listened to Jack drop the names of the billionaires financing the syndicates and decided he was full of bullshit, a phony. Janice looked embarrassed, but Linda lapped it up.

From the moment Jack set eyes on Linda, he pursued her relentlessly. Bored and feeling neglected despite the extra hours Dan spent at home, Linda was a plum ripe for the picking. Those extra hours together had hammered home the unpalatable fact that she had little in common with her husband and that the longer they were married, it was becoming harder to get Dan to give in to her whims and tantrums.

Dan had no idea his wife was having an affair. He was simply relieved she seemed happier and didn't sulk or throw tantrums when he walked through the door at the end of a long day. What finally alerted him was the way Linda would hang up the phone when he walked into the room, or the line would sometimes go dead if he answered a call.

His suspicions were confirmed when he caught Jack fondling Linda's breasts beside their host's swimming pool at a barbecue in March, about eight months after they'd arrived in New Zealand. Linda was giggling and egging him on when Dan came on the scene.

The pain in his chest made him feel as if it were going to burst open. Although he'd long ago realized his marriage was over, he was devastated to finally have proof. Dan saw Linda watching him over Jack's shoulder as he bent to kiss her breasts. Her face was clearly visible in the moonlight, her expression gloating. Dan felt physically ill. He suspected Linda had seen him coming and wanted to be discovered.

She slapped Jack on the shoulder. 'Jack! Jack! Stop it! We have company!'

Jack was shocked when he saw Dan watching them from just a few feet away. 'Shit!' He yanked his hand from beneath Linda's top.

Dan's initial reaction was to beat Jack's face in. His expression made Jack backed into Linda, who tripped and would have fallen into the pool if she hadn't grabbed his back.

'Watch it!' she snapped angrily.

Dan stepped forward to pound Jack and stopped. Linda looked excited, as if she were enjoying the situation. He felt bile burn the back of his throat. 'Jesus,' he whispered. '*Jesus.*'

Jack held his hands in front of his face, shying away from a blow that didn't come. 'Don't hit me, Brogan! You'll fucking kill me with those fists!'

'Hit him!' Linda screamed and shoved Jack towards her husband.

Jack stumbled sideways to avoid Dan. He looked at her incredulously. 'Shut up, Linda!'

She turned on Dan. '*What's the matter with you? Don't*

you care?'

'You're welcome to her.' He turned and walked away.

He was vaguely aware of the shocked audience of people gathered in the doorways leading into the house at the other end of the pool. All he wanted to do was to get away from Linda and Millar and find a place where he could breathe fresh air.

'You bastard!' Linda screamed. 'You bastard! You can't just walk away from me!' Then more shrilly, 'Dan! Dan! *Come back!'*

He didn't go home that night. Instead, he spent the night at the hospital in one of the rooms reserved for the registrars and house surgeons.

☆

The next time Dan saw Linda was the following evening. She was lying in the resus room in the Emergency Department at Auckland Hospital, her clothes tangled beneath her where they'd been cut from her body.

Linda and Jack Millar had been involved in a car accident not far from the home she shared with Dan. She was speeding and didn't have a driver's license. The young woman driving the other vehicle died in the Emergency Department. Jack escaped with cuts, bruises and a concussion. Linda had a broken leg and a head injury because she wasn't wearing a seatbelt. She stopped breathing in the emergency room, and it was touch and go as they struggled to revive her and stabilize her condition.

Dan watched from the end of the bed, numb and disbelieving. When one of the doctors told him Linda had suffered a miscarriage, he stared at him blankly, grappling with the implications.

The swelling in Linda's brain was severe enough for the

ICU doctors to contemplate taking her to theatre to relieve the pressure. Instead, she was put on a ventilator and into a drug induced coma to allow the swelling to subside.

As he sat beside Linda's bed watching the rise and fall of her chest and hearing the *swish swish* of the ventilator, Dan thought about the miscarriage.

They hadn't made love in months. He wasn't the father of her baby. The knowledge hurt way more than seeing Linda in Jack's arms. Dan was sure the pregnancy had been an accident. Linda had always relegated the subject of children to later, until he'd given up asking her to consider it.

He felt as if he was functioning on autopilot. He found himself observing his wife as a patient, noting her injuries, and applauding her progress, but his emotions weren't engaged. At no point did Dan wish for her death. His mother, father and brother all offered to come, but he declined, knowing they'd see through his act and guess the true state of his marriage.

He kept a lonely vigil by Linda's bedside, talking to her, encouraging her to get better and wake up. It was during these hours that he came to a decision. He would take care of Linda and help her back to get back on her feet, and then he'd let her return to the States and sue him for divorce. Linda would do her utmost to ruin him financially, but he was willing to take the risk. He just wanted some peace. At least there weren't any children involved; he would never have been able to hand them over to Linda, whose only parental role model was Betty Mulholland. Linda would have used any child they had as means to get back at him.

Dan considered himself beyond hurt. A part of him wondered where the funny, bright, tender girl he'd married had gone. He'd made the mistake of thinking he could rescue her. It had taken him eight years to understand that Linda couldn't be rescued and that anybody who tried ran the risk of being destroyed in the process.

But, as usual, Linda was not going to be so easy to put aside. It wasn't a surprise when one of her doctors called to say she'd asked for a mirror and reacted badly when she saw her face.

'I had to sedate her. She's sleeping now, but I thought you should know before you came for your usual visit tonight.'

'Did she ask about the baby?'

The doctor assumed he was speaking to a grieving father and replied sympathetically, 'No. She hasn't mentioned it.'

Linda's first request had been for a mirror. Her appearance meant the world to her. As for the baby, there was always the possibility she'd forgotten she was pregnant. She had a great capacity to ignore what didn't suit her.

Dan was convinced his feelings had died where his wife was concerned and yet he'd been moved by the woman he'd encountered tonight, with her strange accent and sad, puzzled eyes. This Linda didn't seem to care that her hair was greasy, and her skin was pasty, or that the leg not in plaster was covered in dark fuzz.

She just looked lost.

He wouldn't abandon her. She had nobody else and the best way for her to regain her memory - if she *had* truly lost it - was to be around familiar people and things.

I'll treat her like a patient, Dan decided as he headed towards the hospital car park.

It was the best he could offer.

Chapter 6

Nancy wouldn't take no for an answer when Lisa tried to get out of having her hair washed the next day. 'It must feel awful!' she insisted.

Lisa shrugged, sunk in despair at the hopelessness of her situation. 'Who cares? It's only hair.'

Nancy eyed her knowingly. The nursing team were aware of the latest developments in Linda Brogan's case, that she'd lost her memory, didn't recognize her husband - the rather scrumptious American orthopaedic surgeon who worked at the children's hospital - and that she wanted to be called Lisa.

'I'd lie,' Chris, a fellow nurse, insisted after the morning handover. 'If I woke up and found out that he was my husband, I'd say yes, he's mine, I'm his and when are we going home?'

'Thank you, Chris,' the charge nurse observed dryly. 'I'm sure I don't need to remind any of you about patient confidentiality. Particularly when the patient happens to be married to a senior member of the paediatric surgical staff.'

Nancy thought Linda looked depressed, which concerned her. It had been decided that the same group of nurses would care for her so she got used to seeing familiar faces. She had an appointment with the psychiatrist and a CAT scan was scheduled for later that day to check for any new bleeding in her brain.

'Do it for me,' Nancy cajoled, pulling back the covers on the bed and pushing a wheelchair closer. 'You're making the place look untidy.'

Lisa allowed herself to be wheeled to the shower. She was impressed when Nancy sat her on a plastic chair with holes in the bottom and managed to hose her down with the shower head without getting the plaster cast wet.

'You're brilliant, Nancy. You didn't even put a plastic bag over my cast. The nurses always put one on when I was little, and they still got it wet sometimes.'

Nancy draped a towel over Lisa to keep her warm and began to wet her hair. 'Why did you have a cast?'

'I was born with a club foot. I had lots of operations and plaster casts to correct it from when I was a baby...'

Her voice trailed away. That was *her* history. Not Linda Brogan's. She peeped at Nancy, but she was busy pulling plastic bottles from the bags she'd carted down to the shower on Lisa's lap.

'What's all that?'

Nancy peered at the back of the bottles. 'Well, *this* one says it's a Pre-Rinse and *this* one says it's a Shine Application.'

'Can't you find one called shampoo and one called conditioner?'

'Probably, but not with those names.' Nancy gave the bulging plastic bag by the wall a nudge with her toe. 'I don't go in for all this expensive stuff. I'm more of a supermarket-special girl myself.'

You and me *both*, Lisa thought. Hair washing Linda Brogan-style had obviously been an event. She must have set a whole day aside to use everything in the bottles.

They settled the dilemma by implementing their *eeny-meenie-miny-mo* problem-solving skills.

While Nancy toweled her hair dry, Lisa inspected her new body. Linda had been blessed with one of those bodies that wouldn't have looked out of place in a *Sports Illustrated* calendar. She had mile-long legs, gently curving hips and a surprisingly generous set of boobs for such a slim woman. She was nothing like Lisa, who had a chest which could have doubled as an ironing board.

'Do you think these are real, Nancy?'

Nancy peered over Lisa's shoulder. 'Are what real?'

Lisa pointed. '*These.*'

Nancy blinked. 'Your boobs?'

'Yeah.' Lisa lifted one with a forefinger and searched beneath it. 'Can't see any scars.'

'Doesn't mean they're not fake,' Nancy replied when she'd got over her surprise. 'They use a new technique where they thread the prosthesis up through the umbilicus so there aren't any scars.'

'*What?* You mean they insert them through your belly button?'

Nancy nodded and began to towel her back.

'I don't believe you. How would they fit?'

'They put them in empty and fill them up when they're in place.'

Lisa thought about this for several moments. 'Bit like inflating a car tyre.'

Nancy snorted. 'You can only really tell by feeling.' She stepped in front of Lisa and peered at her breasts. 'They look real. You could always ask your husband — he'd know.'

Lisa tugged the towel over herself. She could imagine the look on Dan Brogan's face if she asked him about her boobs, or rather, about his *wife's* boobs. She changed the subject. 'Nancy, do you know if I've ... er ... if I've had a ... period since I've been in hospital?'

Nancy was busy shaking out another one of Linda's silk

nightdresses. Lisa eyed it with distaste. She preferred the comfort of the oversized T-shirts she wore to bed.

'No, you haven't had a period since you've been in hospital.' Nancy paused. 'Why do you ask?'

Lisa felt the tension uncoil in her belly. 'No reason.'

Perhaps there was a silver lining in this particular cloud, and the long hellish years of suffering might be over. Hopefully, when Linda's body finally had a period, it would be the same as most other women's and nothing like the agony Lisa suffered each month. She was vaguely surprised that Nancy was so emphatic that Linda hadn't had a period and put it down to the intimacy of the nurse–patient relationship. Right now, the nurses and doctors knew far more about this body's functions than she did.

Linda's husband made a brief appearance when the physiotherapist was putting Lisa through her paces on her crutches. She was sweating profusely with her tongue stuck out the side of her mouth, a sign she was concentrating hard. Lisa didn't see the amusement on Dan's face at her intent expression or that the sash on her pink silk robe was trailing on the floor behind her. Her hair lay across her shoulders, shining and clean from her shower. She kept blowing irritably at her fringe, which hung in her eyes.

Dan nodded a greeting to the physiotherapist and picked up the trailing sash. When Lisa executed a clumsy turn to head back towards her room, she found him standing there holding it like a leash.

'I'm telling you now,' she panted, 'I don't fetch sticks or chase balls.'

He laughed, wound the sash into a ball and pushed it into one of the pockets on the front of her robe. His hand brushed against her thigh through the thin material. 'You're doing real well.'

Lisa was startled by the casual intimacy of the gesture until she remembered he was Linda Brogan's husband; he'd done a lot more than touch her thigh in the past.

He was wearing charcoal-grey trousers, a pale-green shirt and a dark-grey jacket which made him look even taller than usual and his grey eyes darker. He would have seemed imposing if it weren't for the grey tie with a big yellow Tweetie Bird he wore.

Lisa nodded at the tie. 'Like the tie.'

'Thanks.'

Nancy and Chris said he was known as 'Dr Dan' at the children's hospital, instead of 'Mr Brogan' as befitted his surgeon status, and that the kids loved him. Lisa guessed cartoon ties would be a big hit with them.

Chris wriggled her brows. 'The kids aren't the only ones who love him.'

'Chris!' Nancy rolled her eyes meaningfully in Lisa's direction.

'It's OK, Nancy,' Lisa said drily. 'My memory might be shot but there's nothing wrong with my eyes.

'Amen to that.'

'Chris!' Nancy snapped.

Lisa smiled. The nurses helped keep her sane and distracted her from the mess she was in.

☆

Oblivious of his pin-up status among the female staff, Dan followed Linda as she slowly made her way back to her room with the physio in close attendance. She was uncomfortable when he touched her leg through her robe. Her eyes widened, and she blinked up at him like a deer caught in the headlights of a car. He mustn't relax and succumb to the puckish charm and offbeat sense of humour that Linda had displayed since she woke up. He needed to remember she was still Linda, equipped with a deadly arsenal of weapons she could unleash at any moment. More importantly, if she was to be believed, right now she saw him as a stranger.

After promising to visit later that night, Dan headed to Linda's room to collect the bag of dirty laundry from her locker. As he crouched in front of the locker, he replayed the sound of her voice. Her vowels were even flatter than when she first woke up. Dan was perplexed that his Californian-born wife sounded more and more like a Kiwi. Was she unconsciously mimicking the nursing staff? At any rate, Linda didn't sound like Linda anymore.

He wasn't going to be fooled by the odd accent and strange sense of humour. In the early years of their relationship, Linda used to laugh a lot and made jokes but never at her own expense. Dan was even more disturbed by what the nurse looking after Linda had shared when he asked how she'd been this morning. He was positive she didn't have a club foot as a child. If she had, she'd have scars from the surgery, and he knew exactly what to look for because it was the type of corrective surgery he performed down the hill at the children's hospital.

Why would she lie about that?

Nancy, the nurse, also mentioned that Linda asked if she'd menstruated since she'd been in hospital. Dan wondered grimly if Linda wasn't nearly as amnesiac as she liked to pretend. Had she remembered she was pregnant before the accident? Nancy said she didn't ask about the baby, but it meant nothing. The woman he'd married still existed inside the woman recovering from her injuries.

☆

Linda's husband came to visit again that night, bringing fashion magazines and more skimpy nightdresses. He'd changed into a dark-green T-shirt with some kind of a bird on the front, faded blue jeans and a battered brown leather jacket, and kept brushing back a strand of hair that flopped across his brow. Lisa suspected he was overdue for a haircut, and it wasn't at the top of his to do list.

She'd woken from a long afternoon sleep feeling depressed and homesick and haunted by the thought of her family grieving for her. How were her parents coping? And Sherry and her brother, Ben? They were a close family; they'd be devastated by her apparent death.

When Dan shrugged off his leather jacket, Lisa saw the front of his T-shirt properly. It was decorated with a big, brown kiwi wearing a smug smile beneath the tagline "*I'm a little kiwi who eats roots and leaves*". She smiled to herself and wondered if Dan knew exactly what he was wearing on his chest to his place of work. The saying was a Kiwi classic, but Lisa had her doubts that *root* was a euphemism for sex in America.

She pointed at his T-shirt. 'Does...um...root mean the same thing in the States as it does in New Zealand?'

He glanced down at the front of his shirt and back up again. 'I don't know. What does it mean in New Zealand?'

Lisa cleared her throat awkwardly. 'It means having sex.'

'You don't say?' Dan studied the front of his shirt and nodded. 'Guess I did the right thing sending one to my brother for his birthday, because he's the biggest bed-hopper in the state of Colorado.'

She threw one of the magazines at him. 'Why didn't you just tell me instead of letting me make a fool of myself?'

He ducked. 'And spoil the fun? When my mother saw Glenn's shirt, she told me I was dreaming if I thought he'd ever become a vegetarian.'

They looked at each other and grinned.

Dan picked up the magazine and placed it with the others on top of the locker. 'I brought some of your favourites.'

'Thanks,' Lisa said politely.

She glanced disinterestedly at the glossy magazines. She'd never been all that interested in fashion and makeup, leaving that side of things to Sherry. She liked nice clothes, but Sherry was the clotheshorse of the family. Looking at fashion magazines full of stick thin models posing in outlandish clothes wasn't her cup of tea. As her endometriosis got worse, she had to give up being a full-time as a primary school teacher and settle for working as a relief teacher so she could take time off when she was sick. She loved teaching and reading. The last book she read before the accident was Jane Austen's "Emma". It was part of her personal library of favourites which she ready at least once a year. She considered asking Dan to bring a copy but doubted she was up to reading a novel.

Lisa watched him crouch down in front of the bedside locker. The hems of his jeans rose to reveal a pair of unmatched socks, one brown, one dark green. Her smile faded as he began placing clean underwear and nightdresses inside the locker. It was embarrassing watching a stranger handling her underwear and even worse when it occurred to her that he must be responsible for washing them as well.

'I'll do that!' She leaned over the edge of the bed to snatch a G-string from his hands and almost fell on top of him.

Dan managed to catch her just in time. 'That was stupid,' he said sharply and lifted her back against the pillows.

Lisa shrank away from him. She was starting to enjoy the feel of him touching her way too much. 'Doesn't Linda own a single pair of normal knickers?

'Normal knickers?' He looked confused. 'What do you mean?'

'I think you call them panties. Does she have any normal panties?'

He aimed a thumb at the locker. 'What are those?'

'They're G-strings, or ... what do you call them? *Thongs!* They're *thong*s!' Lisa cried triumphantly.

'You don't like thongs?' Dan was a big fan himself.

'I don't know how anybody in their right mind could,' Lisa winced. Probably not the smartest thing to say right now. 'They feel like anal floss.'

His look of incomprehension indicated he wasn't just at sea; his ship was sinking. 'Anal floss?' He watched her brows lower and added hastily, 'I'll see what I can find at home.'

'Thank you, and while you're at it, do you think you could bring me some big T-shirts to sleep in instead of these skimpy nightdresses?'

His mouth tightened. Linda *loved* sexy nightwear and lingerie.

'T-shirts?' Dan repeated brusquely. 'You don't own any *big* T-shirts.'

Everything Linda owned was tailored or fitted. She wasn't the type to hide her assets.

'What about you?'

'You want to know what I wear to bed?'

Lisa glowered at him. 'Do you have any old T-shirts I could borrow?'

'I guess so.' Dan shrugged and sighed. 'I'll bring you some tomorrow.'

'Thanks.'

He stood uncertainly by the bed for a couple of beats before going to collect the orange plastic chair and lowering his long frame into it. 'How are you feeling?'

If one more person asked her how she was feeling, she was going to scream. Lisa wished she could tell the truth. Something along the lines of: 'I feel really confused and pissed off. I'm in the body of another woman, and it's injured. I have to pretend that I've lost my memory when I haven't lost it at all, I just don't have the one everybody thinks I should have. And to top it off, the original owner of this body is responsible for killing me.'

When she didn't answer, Dan tried again. 'The results of your CAT scan were good.'

Lisa gazed morosely at the plaster cast which was beginning to itch like hell. 'They tell me there's a brain in there after all.'

It was just the sort of comment Linda would make. 'And you saw Dr Fergusson, the psychiatrist?'

She recalled the hour she'd spent with the psychiatrist after lunch. 'Now he really *is* nuts.'

She'd never met a psychiatrist before, let alone been examined by one, which was what Dr. Fergusson had been doing only he didn't use hammers to test her reflexes or shine lights in her eyes. He introduced himself as Craig before settling into the orange chair with the appearance of staying for some time. All the other doctors were in a hurry except him. He looked about thirty-five, with light-brown hair and indecently long eyelashes that kept getting caught on the lenses of his glasses and making him blink. Lisa was curious to see what he'd do. It would be nice if he didn't start out by asking her how she was, but she didn't hold out much hope.

'Bored?' he asked.

She blinked. 'Well ... yes, I am as it happens.'

Craig propped an ankle on the opposite knee, leaned back and cupped his head. 'Hospitals are boring places, especially when you're not sick enough to not notice and not well enough to leave. I've never been too keen on them myself.'

'How can a doctor not like hospitals?' Lisa snuck a look at the ID tag clipped to the pocket of his jacket. Was he really a patient or visitor masquerading as a doctor?

He unclipped the plastic card and offered it to her. 'It's OK. I am the real thing.'

She blushed and mumbled something about never doubting it.

Craig returned his ID to his jacket. 'You still seem unconvinced. What were you expecting?'

Her head was beginning to ache, and she wasn't buying his amiable fool act. 'A couch? A watch to hypnotize me? Some of those black-and-white cards I'm supposed to tell you look like people having sex?'

Now he'd think she was a sexual deviant as well as nuts. She imagined him telling Dan Brogan. *Ahhh!*

Craig seemed to take pity on her. He changed the subject. 'The nurses tell me you don't remember anything before waking up in hospital. Would you agree with that?'

He might not be wearing a white coat, but he still had the authority to lock her up if he decided she was bonkers. 'I don't remember being Linda Brogan,' she hedged.

'Can you tell me the first thing you do remember?'

Falling down the steps at the front of the house when I was almost two and splitting my mouth, Lisa thought and touched Linda's mouth. It bled everywhere and I have a small scar on my bottom lip as a reminder. Or at least I *used* to have a scar on my bottom lip. Her eyes filled with tears. She shook her head and whispered, 'No. No, I can't tell you the first thing I remember.'

He waited while she blew her nose and wiped her eyes before asking gently, 'Do you remember Dan Brogan?'

Lisa shook her head miserably.

Craig suggested antidepressants.

She refused to take them.

'Don't dismiss them out of hand, Linda. You *are* depressed, which is hardly surprising considering what you've been through. It's frightening to wake up not knowing who you are.'

She looked at him glumly. *But I do know who I am.*

'I'm confident you will regain your memory.'

I never lost it.

'But in the meantime, it's important you take each day as it comes.'

You sound like my mother.

'I think it would be a good idea if we meet regularly.'

To check if I need locking up.

'Keep a notepad nearby. If you remember anything at all, jot it down.'

If I jotted down even half of what's going on inside my head, you'll be measuring me up for a straitjacket.

'Craig?' Lisa asked, desperate to stop the flood of questions and advice.

'Yes?'

'Why don't you get some contact lenses? What *is* driving

me bonkers is watching you get your eyelashes caught on your glasses.'

He blinked rapidly in surprise, which only made the problem worse. Sighing irritably, he removed his glasses and rubbed his eyes with his thumb and forefinger. 'I've tried contact lenses, but they irritate my eyes after a couple of hours.'

Lisa made a sympathetic noise. 'Why don't you trim your eyelashes?'

'I tried. But I had to take my glasses off to do it and I nearly took my eye out with the scissors.'

She shuddered.

He replaced his glasses and smiled. 'You're very good at that, aren't you?'

'What?'

'Changing the subject.'

Lisa was relieved when he left, promising to visit again in a couple of days.

She was startled from her reverie when Dan asked, 'Did talking to him help?'

'He was very nice but he can't help me.' She studied her cast, feeling hopeless. 'I don't think anybody can.'

Except George. He'd know exactly *why she was feeling the way she did.*

Despite the lectures Dan had been giving himself, he felt his heart tugged by her look of utter desolation. It reminded him of the day she told him she was dyslexic. He had to make sure he didn't get suckered again. 'Why do you say that?'

Lisa saw Dan was wearing the same expression as Craig Fergusson when he was trying to get inside her head. That was nobody's business but *hers*.

She changed the subject by blurting out the first thing that came into her head. 'Are these real or fakes?' She pointed at Linda's breasts.

Dan's brows shot under his untidy hair. She was asking him about *her breasts?* The same breasts that he'd kissed and fondled countless times? That he could picture in exquisite detail if he closed his eyes? He felt a surge of anger. This was the Linda he knew, the Linda who used her body to divert attention from a subject she didn't want to pursue, but in the past, she hadn't been so heavy-handed about it.

'Pardon me?' he asked coldly.

She dropped her gaze and mumbled, 'Nothing.'

He reminded himself that whatever he might think of her, she was still recovering from serious injuries and didn't deserve to be punished for what had happened in the past, a past she said she couldn't remember.

'Why do you think your boobs are fake? Do they feel different?'

Lisa wished she'd never asked.

'Different to what?' she retorted. 'I was the original Miss Two Backs before ... all this ... happened.'

Dan took a breath and counted to three. 'They're not fake. Fakes feel different.'

'For whom? The feeler? Or the feelee? Hang on while I pop under the covers for a quick grope.' Lisa made a show of sliding under the sheet and thrashing about. She reappeared above the covers, and she glared at him. 'Sorry, the results were inconclusive. *How* would I know what implants feel like? I said I was flat-chested before, not a lesbian!'

Dan laughed and Lisa's stomach did a little flip. He needed to do it more often. He was gorgeous when he relaxed and came out of his shell; all the strain and worry disappeared from his face. She felt guilty when she realized that she was the cause of most of it. Me *and* Linda, she decided shrewdly, wondering what the relationship between Dan and his wife had been like.

She crossed her arms. 'How do they feel different?'

'They just do.'

Lisa raised her brows. 'Done a lot of research on the subject, have you?'

'Some. Why?' Dan dropped his gaze. 'Did you want a second opinion?'

They locked gazes. Heat uncurled in the pit of Lisa's belly. She fought the urge to uncross her arms.

'Sorry, I shouldn't have said that.' Dan said stiffly.

She rubbed her hands nervously up and down her upper arms. 'It was a *joke*, Dan. We were *joking* with each other.'

He watched the slide of her hands, heard the whisper of her palms brushing against her skin and got abruptly to his feet. 'You need some sleep.'

He replaced the chair at the end of the bed.

Lisa didn't want him to go. 'I'm not tired.'

'I am,' Dan replied brusquely. 'I'll see you tomorrow.'

'Oh. OK,' she replied forlornly and watched him head to the door. 'Night.'

He didn't reply.

Chapter 7

Dan brought Lisa a supply of his T-shirts. She loved them; they were so big they covered her from shoulder to elbow and neck to knee. If Dan found it unnerving seeing her wearing his clothes, he kept it to himself.

At first, he brought his best T-shirts until Lisa told him she meant it when she said she wanted *old*. She preferred the ones he'd brought her since. Dan didn't share that he thought his old jogging T-shirts molded her curves way better than her slinky satin nightdresses ever had and he had to work hard to hide his appreciation.

Linda's leg was healing well, and Lisa was moving around on crutches without help. The doctors and nurses began making noises about Lisa going home. The only home on offer was Dan's. Lisa dreaded leaving. She'd been so busy trying to make sense of her bizarre situation she hadn't thought about what would happen next. She was on an emotional rollercoaster. One moment convinced she could handle what had happened to her, that after coming so close to dying she needed to grab this second chance with both hands. The next moment plunged into despair, longing for her family, and trying to imagine a future living the life of another woman with a man she didn't know.

She couldn't fault Dan. He was a gentleman: kind and patient, but distant. It made Lisa wonder about the state of his marriage to Linda. It didn't seem natural for a husband to be so polite around his wife. He wasn't affectionate and avoided touching her unless he had to. Lisa didn't think this was entirely out of consideration for her memory loss. She sensed Dan regarded her as a responsibility and hadn't liked his wife.

She had nothing but time on her hands to think about that and why Linda didn't have any visitors apart from him. She must have made some friends since she got here so why hadn't they visited? The last thing she wanted was a visit from somebody from Linda Brogan's past but that didn't stop her feeling curious about Linda. When she'd asked Dan if Linda had any friends, he gave her a look that bordered on hostile.

'Who did you want to visit?' he asked coolly.

Lisa regretted asking and shook her head. 'Nobody. Forget I ever said it. I was just being curious.'

A couple of days later, a large bunch of pink roses arrived.

Mary, the ward clerk, placed them on the windowsill. 'There's no card. Perhaps your husband sent them.'

When Dan arrived later, straight from the children's hospital and still dressed for work in a dark suit, blue shirt and Lilo and Stitch tie, Lisa asked if he'd sent the roses.

He studied them. 'Nope. Why do you ask?'

'There was no card with them.'

He looked as if he wanted to tip them into the rubbish bin. 'A secret admirer, I guess,' he said flatly, drawing a puzzled frown from Lisa.

Mary tapped on the open door. 'Lisa? You didn't fill out your menu for tomorrow.'

Dan and the ward staff had started calling her Lisa, even if it was just to humour her.

Lisa was grateful for the interruption. She dug her hands and good foot into the mattress and boosted herself up the pillows. 'I've been lazy. Nancy or Chris always does it for me.' And true to form, the hospital food was revolting. There was never any meat on the plate.

Lisa felt annoyed when she saw how Mary looked at Dan like he was a Christmas present she wanted to unwrap somewhere nice and private. He was supposed to be Linda's husband. It was rude to ogle him whenever he made an appearance. Sometimes Lisa felt like a teenager with a crush when Dan came into the room, or she heard his voice. It made her even more awkward around him.

Mary handed over the menu, all the time smiling at Dan, and departed.

It was the first time Lisa had to write anything since she'd woken up. She didn't notice the tension on his face as she took the menu.

'Have you got a pen I can borrow?'

She was perplexed when he hesitated and reluctantly handed over a pen.

Lisa studied the menu and blinked. There were three columns that must be for breakfast, lunch, and dinner. She raised the paper and peered at it. For some reason, breakfast looked like *dreakfast* and dinner looked like *binner*. The longer she stared at the words, the less sense they made; in fact, they began to wriggle about, and the white spaces between the black print began to form patterns like rivers trickling down the page.

'What the...?'

Dan tried to take the menu from her. 'I'll do it for you.'

Lisa eluded him. 'No! This is amazing!'

'Linda, you'll only get upset. Let me do it for you.'

He fell silent when he saw Lisa's face. She looked like she was having an epiphany.

She pressed the menu against her chest and his old blue Nike T-shirt and cried excitedly, 'Linda was dyslexic, wasn't she?'

★

Dan didn't know what to make of the next half hour.

Linda kept referring to herself in the third person. Try as he might, he still thought of her as Linda and had to work hard to remember to call her Lisa. Whenever he messed up, she would give him such a disappointed look he felt as if she'd caught him stepping on a kitten.

She kept firing questions at him. When was she diagnosed? How was she affected? Did she suffer with nausea? With motion sickness? Was she accident-prone (she rolled her eyes) and best of all: what educational programmes had she attended?

The roses had been bad enough, but Dan struggled to keep his cool. 'You attended lots of them when you were a child.' He wasn't telling her anything she didn't already know.

'But none of them worked?'

He chose his words carefully. 'You weren't keen on them.'

'What about as an adult?'

He stopped trying to sweeten his answers. 'You refused.'

Lisa looked appalled. 'How did she cope?'

'She - *you* - didn't.'

She started snatching up the magazines on her locker that she'd ignored and began peering at the print. 'This is amazing! I've always wondered what it was like for the kids I taught.'

Dan clenched his jaw. '*What* kids, Linda?'

'I'm a teacher,' She flipped through the magazine, not caring for once that he'd called her Linda. 'Primary school. There's usually some children in each class with learning disabilities — dyslexia, dyscalculia, attention deficit disorder but I never really understood until now what they saw. *Look!*' she stabbed at the page with a finger. 'That's *was,* isn't it?'

Dan angled his head to see. 'Yes.' He gazed at her in disbelief. "Was" and "saw" were words dyslexics often struggled with. Linda had always tripped up on them. 'How did you do that?' he demanded.

She dropped the magazine, picked up the menu and pointed. 'And that's *dinner* and that's *breakfast?*'

Reversing Bs and Ds were also common perceptual errors.

Dan stared. 'How did you do that?'

Lisa looked the most animated he'd seen her since she'd regained consciousness. 'Have you heard of Scotopic Sensitivity Syndrome?'

He nodded silently, the skin prickling over his scalp. He'd never spoken to Linda about SSS, because she wouldn't have wanted to know. She was still speaking to him. 'Pardon me?'

'I said: have you heard about the Davis Dyslexia Correction Method?'

He thought about all the books on dyslexia he'd read over the years in the hope of finding some way he could help her and snarled, 'Of course I have!'

She looked hurt. 'Sorry.'

Dan sighed and rubbed his eyes. 'I shouldn't have snapped at you.'

'I know this is hard for you, too.'

There was an awkward silence.

Dan could see she was bursting to ask him something. Lisa could never be accused of sulking the way Linda had done in the past. 'What is it?'

'Could you arrange for me to see somebody before I go home? To get some help?' she picked up speed as her enthusiasm overflowed. 'Flash cards with pictures are a good way of learning sentence organization and how to recognize words.' She grabbed the pen. 'How's my writing?'

Dan felt like he'd been run over by a truck. 'A few sentences at a time. You suffer with dyscoordination when you write and your—'

'My handwriting drifts off the page.'

Lisa began to slowly write her name in the space at the top of the page, the tip of tongue appearing a couple of letters in. She tilted her head to accommodate the wavering, downward passage of her writing.

Dan's metaphorical truck threw itself into reverse and backed over him.

Linda was *attempting* to write. With an audience. She *wanted* to talk about her dyslexia and knew things she'd specifically avoided talking about in the past. But most unsettling, she was writing with her *left* hand. And the name she was laboriously printing wasn't Linda Brogan.

It was Lisa Jackson.

He sat in the plastic chair, his hands hanging limply between his spread knees, and shook his head wearily.

'Dan?'

'What?'

'Do they have meat on this menu?'

'You're a vegetarian, Linda.'

Her mouth set in the stubborn line he was coming to recognize, a rebuke in her eyes at being called Linda. 'In a pig's ear I am,' she muttered.

Dan slumped back in the orange chair.

'Do you eat meat?'

'Yes,' he replied heavily. 'I do.'

'Good.' She held out the pen. 'Can you tick some meat? Please?'

Dan studied her pale little face and her bright eyes watching him so trustingly and slowly reached out to take the pen. He began to tick everything with meat. 'You've been a vegetarian for eight years, Linda.'

'I'm afraid this herbo just fell off the wagon.'

'Herbo?'

What the hell was she talking about?

'Herbivore.' She explained and seemed to deflate.

The vivacity and sparkle disappeared leaving her looking tired and listless like she did when Dan first walked in. He wondered what had punctured her bubble of happiness and wished he hadn't reacted so negatively. But it was damned hard not to react that way when your wife of eight years suddenly does a one-eighty on a personal issue she's tried to hide from her entire life *and* insists she eats meat when she only just tolerated cooking some for him a few times a week.

He couldn't take any more surprises and came up with his usual excuse to leave, 'You're tired.'

Lisa nodded and slid down in the bed. Her expression was so bleak Dan had to fight the urge to scoop her up and hug her.

'I'll let you get some sleep.'

She closed her eyes and turned her face into the pillow. 'Goodnight.'

'Night.'

Dan watched her for a couple of beats before reaching over to dim the bed light.

On the way out, He dropped the menu off at Mary's desk

and headed to the staff carpark feeling every bit as desperate and lost as Lisa seemed to be.

☆

Lisa tried not to cry, but the tears came anyway.

It was the herbivore joke that did it. She wished she could tell Dan how she and Sherry called vegetarians "herbivores", and Sherry would demand, 'Do I *look* like a caterpillar?' if the subject of becoming a vegetarian ever arose. They had nothing against vegetarians until Ben's uptight, non-meat-eating girlfriend, Brenda arrived on the scene. She gave them a bad name.

The loneliness and misery Lisa felt thinking about her sister threatened to crush her. Whenever she hit rock bottom, she used the excuse of sleep to get rid of anybody. Dan always took the hint and left.

Time was running out. She couldn't stay in the hospital forever.

What, then?

☆

Nothing had added up since Linda regained consciousness.

When she first woke up, she'd struggled to form words and her speech was hard to understand. Dan thought there might have been some damage to the part of her brain responsible for speech, but the CAT scans showed there wasn't any bleeding or swelling in the area. When she finally did speak it was with a New Zealand accent and her speech was casually sprinkled with local expressions. She didn't care about her appearance; so long as she was clean and fed, she was relatively happy. She talked about having corrective surgery for a club foot as a child. And now she had written a stranger's name using her left hand. Linda was right-handed.

Dan felt like an astronaut launched into space without training and spacesuit. He didn't know what to do or how he was supposed to be. He liked the new Linda more than the old one. But the bunch of roses reminded him of what she'd been capable of in the past. They would have come from Jack Millar; the cowardly bastard just wouldn't leave it alone.

He'd orchestrated bumping into Janice Millar at the hospital so he could pass on the news that Linda had suffered significant memory loss from the accident. It was one way to make sure Janice's husband heard about it. He'd considered going to the house and confronting Jack but knew that this time he would have ended up taking the guy apart and Janice and her kids didn't deserve that. He was sorry to see how thin and anxious she looked when he spoke to her. Dan could sympathize, knowing that your spouse was unfaithful hurt.

Lately, he'd been thinking a lot about the young woman who died. He didn't know her name but did know she lived not far from Linda and him and that she'd been twenty-seven years old, two years younger than Linda.

The police told him that much when they came to see him. They wanted to interview Linda, but so far, her doctors' explanations of her mental state and loss of memory had held them off. They were worried about how she would deal with knowing that her reckless actions had resulted in someone's death when she was obviously so depressed.

If he thought there was anything to be gained for the dead woman's family, Dan would have considered letting the police speak to Linda. She'd have to face up to what she'd done sometime. There would be a coroner's case and, at the very least, Linda would get a fine and community service for driving without a license. The reason she might get off so lightly was because it seemed that the other woman should have given way to Linda and might have contributed to the accident. Millar was at fault too. He should never have let Linda drive without checking she had a driver's license.

Despite Dan's assurances that thousands of people with dyslexia passed their license every year, Linda wouldn't even consider sitting it back home. She either caught cabs, rode a mountain bike, or walked when he wasn't around to drive her. They used to enjoy mountain-biking together when they first met, but gradually Dan's work commitments made it was something they shared less often and Linda got a gym membership instead.

'You're not interested in the same things as me,' she complained.

Dan made the mistake of snapping, 'What you mean is, I don't want to get acrylic nails or talk about how many butt crunches I can do or which hem length is in this season.'

Attacking Linda's intelligence was the worst thing anyone could do to her. He tried to apologize, but she wouldn't listen. She expected Dan to be perfect. It was his job to make her feel better, not the other way around.

His thoughts returned to the woman who died. He tried to imagine his life ending when he was only twenty-seven. Tried to imagine the pain and devastation her parents must have felt at having to bury their child. She'd sustained serious head injuries and a lacerated liver and bled out before she arrived in the Emergency Department.

And Linda survived.

Dan wondered if there really was anybody up there with

a plan. He was glad Linda survived but he wondered how big a hole her passing would have created compared to the one that might have been left by the death of the other woman.

★

Lisa needed her parents. But it was impossible to see them and they wouldn't have recognized her anyway. Craig Fergusson tried again to get her to take anti-depressants and again she refused. There wasn't a drug big enough to take away the pain inside her.

Dan always left her enough loose change to buy a morning paper and a phone card for the public telephone by the elevators outside the ward. Lisa wondered who he thought a woman with amnesia would call, while Dan wondered why a woman who struggled to read would want to buy the *New Zealand Herald*.

The day before Lisa was due to leave the hospital, the need to speak to her family became overwhelming. She hobbled the length of the ward to the telephone. Once there, she could hardly push the buttons to dial her home number because her hands were trembling so badly. It rang for such a long time that Lisa was about to hang up when she heard her mother's subdued voice say, 'Hello?'

She let out a great, shuddering sob and clung to the receiver, unable to speak.

'Hello?' her mother repeated, sounding slightly irritated.

Lisa gulped. 'Mum?'

There was a long pause.

'Who is this?' her mother demanded shrilly. 'Who are you?'

Lisa wailed softly. '*Mum!*'

Her mother's voice cracked. 'Who are you? Why are you

doing this?'

There was the muffled sound of voices in the background. Lisa could hear her mother saying, 'It sounds like Lisa! It sounds like Lisa!'

Her father came on the line, spitting furiously, 'Who are you? I swear I'll get this call traced and make a complaint to the police! Is this your idea of a joke?'

'Dad!' Lisa sobbed, clinging to the plastic canopy above the telephone for support. '*Dad! Please* don't hang up!'

There was a shocked silence then her father moaned, 'No! Oh no! Please leave us alone!'

He hung up and Lisa slid to the floor whimpering like an animal with the telephone receiver still in her hand.

A passing visitor found her and rushed to get a nurse. They wheeled her back to her room and called Dan, who left his registrar to finish the ward round he was doing and hurried up the hill to the main hospital.

☆

Lisa was curled up on the bed as tightly as the plaster cast would allow her when he went into her room after a rushed explanation from the nursing staff. She didn't appear to be aware of anything or anybody and was crying desperately.

'Linda?' Dan said softly, making his way around to the far side of the bed so he could see her face. 'Linda, honey? What's wrong? Who's upset you?' He sat on the side of the bed and stroked the tangled black hair from her brow.

She continued to cry hopelessly. '*Please* stop calling me Linda.'

'OK.' He continued to stroke her hair.

'What am I going to do?' she whispered, staring at the wall opposite. '*What* am I going to do?'

Dan's heart clenched. He'd rarely seen such utter desolation in a human being and in his profession, he'd seen plenty of pain.

'Who did you call?' he asked gently.

'My ... my family.'

He frowned. 'Your family? You mean your mom? In the States?'

She pushed his hand away. 'No! I mean *my* mum and dad! *Here!*'

Dan tried to keep his expression neutral. She wasn't making any sense.

Lisa covered her face with her hands and wept.

'Please don't,' Dan implored. He slid his arms beneath her and lifted her against his chest. She struggled briefly and then relaxed against him when he began to rub her back.

Lisa listened to the steady beat of his heart and succumbed to the comforting stroke of his hand. Her sobs subsided and her tears stopped soaking the front of Dan's shirt. She clutched the material, unknowingly scratching him with what was left of the unfamiliar acrylic nails.

Dan winced but continued to stroke her. He thought she'd gone to sleep, but when he checked he saw her eyes were still open. He gently eased her back against the pillows and bent over her with a hand braced on either side of her waist.

'Everything will be OK,' he looked into her swollen eyes. 'I promise I won't let anything bad happen to you.'

Lisa stared up at him, a faint frown etched between her brows. 'Thank you,' she said in a voice clogged with tears. 'You've been so kind. I do appreciate it, Dan.'

'I'll come and see you as soon as I've finished my ward rounds. You'll be OK until then?'

She nodded, noticing for the first time that he was in his work clothes.

As he got up, Dan discreetly palmed the phone card from the top of the locker and slid it into his trouser pocket. Who could Linda have called who would upset her so much? Apart from Betty Mulholland, the only person he could think of was Jack Millar.

☆

The next morning, Dan made separate appointments to meet with Rod Cameron the neurosurgeon, and Craig Fergusson. He needed to run some things by them before he took Linda home, although it was doubtful that they could tell him anything new.

'Before the accident Linda was right-handed,' he explained to Rod. 'Now she's left-handed and her speech has changed radically. I'm the first to admit this isn't my specialty — I'm a bone man — but from what I've seen of the CAT scans, she's recovered remarkably well.'

'I can't explain the changes, but in the greater scheme of things does it really matter?' Rod asked. 'Your wife is alive with full motor and sensory function, and she should eventually regain her memory from before the accident. Isn't that what counts?'

Dan understood the neurosurgeon thought he was being an ungrateful pain in the ass. He had patients who would never recover and had to explain to their families their brains had died, and it was the machines they were hooked up to that kept their bodies functioning. Linda was a success story.

Dan headed to the office he shared with two other surgeons at the children's hospital to meet with Craig Fergusson. They'd struggled to find time in their hectic schedules to meet before Linda was discharged. Fortunately, they had the office to themselves when Craig arrived. He knew Craig a lot better than he knew Rod Cameron and was far more open about his fears for Linda. He explained about the changes in the way she spoke, the lack of interest in her appearance, and her change in diet.

'She insists she isn't Linda and that her name is Lisa Jackson.'

'It's interesting that she's chosen to call herself Lisa, it's very similar to Linda. Do you have any idea who Lisa Jackson is?' Craig asked.

'No,' Dan had a hunch but didn't want to follow up on it. 'After years of refusing to talk about her dyslexia, she's suddenly an authority on the subject, asking me to bring her flash cards and coloured filters to see if they'll help her to read.'

Craig listened sympathetically. 'That sounds positive. I can't explain much of what you've told me, but the depression would explain her lack of interest in her appearance.'

'Not when we're talking about my wife, Craig. Linda was obsessed with her appearance. She felt her looks were all that validated her as a person.' Dan paused and added grimly, 'Linda was the kind of woman who would have taken time out to fix her lipstick if she was bleeding to death.'

'You speak about her as if she's gone.'

'Perhaps she has.'

Craig watched him thoughtfully. 'How are you coping? This isn't an easy situation to deal with, especially with the added pressure of work.'

'I'm fine.' Dan picked up a paperclip from his desk and began to straighten it. 'Did you hear what happened after she made a telephone call the other day?'

'Yes.' Craig let his eyes wander across Dan's desk. It was a mess, but the cleaning staff knew better than to tidy it. The only time they had seen nice Dr Dan lose his temper was when somebody tried to dust his desk. 'She wouldn't tell me who she called. Did she tell you?'

'She said she called her family but the only family she's got is her mother in the States and Linda hates her and lost touch with her years ago.'

'So you're her only family?'

Dan nodded and continued straightening out the paperclip. 'Do you think she could be suicidal?'

'No. She's too grateful to be alive. What's happening when you take her home? Are you going to take some leave?'

Dan dropped the paperclip. 'I can't. I have some procedures booked that I can't hand over to my registrar. Some of the children have been waiting months for their surgery, I can't just up and go on vacation. But I'm worried about leaving Linda at home alone.'

'I thought you said that your mother offered to come and stay?'

'My mom would come, but Linda and her never got on.'

'This is different. They might now.'

Dan shook his head. 'I don't want to take the chance.'

Craig blinked, removed his glasses, and put them back on again scowling.

'Why don't you wear contact lenses?'

'Because I can't, that's why.'

'Then why don't you have laser surgery? I can give you the name of a good surgeon.'

Craig shuddered. 'I don't do knives and human flesh. Why do you think I became a psychiatrist?'

Dan looked amused. 'Well cut your goddamned eyelashes or something.'

'That's what your wife told me to do.'

The amusement slid from Dan's face. 'What the *hell* am I going to do, Craig?'

'Does she have any friends you could ask to help out?'

'No.'

'You know how it works, Dan,' Craig said. 'The more Linda associates with people from her old life, the better the chances are of her regaining her memory.'

'Yeah, I know how it works.'

'So at the moment, you're it.'

'Yeah,' he agreed bleakly. 'I'm it.'

'And if she wants to be called Lisa, call her Lisa.'

Chapter 8

Something Dan hadn't discussed with Craig was the physical attraction that had developed between him and Linda – no, *Lisa*. It had come out of left field, catching him by surprise. Linda had long ago ceased to be attractive to him; he could appreciate she was beautiful, but she made him think of a mouth-watering dish that tasted rotten. Their relationship had deteriorated in the months prior to her accident to the point where he hadn't wanted to touch her.

Dan took a seat in his customary chair at the end of the bed.

He noticed that - as usual – Lisa wasn't using her crutches and hadn't tied her robe properly and the sash was trailing on the ground.

Lisa noticed that - as usual - he was wearing mismatched socks, and today his tie was decorated with SpongeBob SquarePants.

He cleared his throat. 'When you come home . . .'

Lisa was about to climb onto the bed. She stopped and looked at him uneasily. Any talk about going home made her nervous. She'd much rather talk about Sponge Bob than going home. She pointed. 'Where did you get that one?'

Dan stood up and picked up the end of the sash. He reached around her to thread it through the belt carrier on the opposite side and began to tie it. 'In a shop and stop changing the subject.'

Lisa balanced on her good leg with her hands held out at her sides for balance. His chest was a few inches from her face and his knuckles were against her navel. She sucked in her belly, inhaled the smell of warm, spicy man, and felt her pulse rate accelerate from a jog to a hundred-metre-sprint. She kept her eyes on the front of Dan's shirt, hoping he couldn't tell.

Dan realised it had been a stupid idea to rescue the sash and even more foolish to tie it. 'Where's your crutches?' he demanded testily.

'On a walking holiday in Scotland.'

He couldn't help it. He laughed.

Her hair was tied in two fat braids that brushed the tops of her breasts. Dan thought she looked adorable. His eyes dropped to her soft, pink lips. He watched them part as she inhaled slowly.

'When I come home?' she prompted softly.

What the hell was he doing?

Dan dropped the sash, stepped back and crashed into the edge of the table straddling the bed. 'Do you want me to take any laundry home?' he said shortly.

'No, thanks.' She made a performance of straightening the table.

'When you come home,' he continued gruffly, 'I won't be able to take any vacation at first, so you'll be on your own a lot. But I'll arrange to take some time off as soon as I can.'

Lisa looked horrified. 'Don't do that! I don't need you to look after me, I'll be just fine.'

Well, that sure as hell put him in his place, Dan thought sourly. 'I guess we'll cross that bridge when we come to it.'

'Yes. When we come to it.'

☆

Sherry Jackson was furious. Some sick bitch had called her mother, pretending to be Lisa.

'I'll get the call traced,' she told her father as they stood together in her parents' kitchen. 'I'll find out who it was and—'

'Leave it, Sherry,' Brian interrupted wearily. 'Just leave it.'

'But what if they phone again? What if—'

He held up his hands to staunch the flow of angry words. 'If they phone again, I'll let you know. But for now, I just want to try and forget about it.' He glanced through the kitchen doorway at his wife sitting at the dining-room table, staring out the window and chain-smoking. 'Making a fuss won't help your mother at the moment.'

Sherry tried to swallow her fury and frustration. It was her inability to put things right that was causing her the most pain now. First it had been the shock and disbelief that Lisa had been in a car crash not far from their family home, followed by the news at the hospital that she'd died about fifteen minutes before Sherry got there.

When she closed her eyes at night, Sherry saw the shell-shocked faces of her mother and father as they walked slowly along a corridor in the Emergency Department followed by two of her fellow officers. They looked like zombies, their arms hanging limply by their sides and their eyes empty after confirming that the body in the room they'd just left was that of their daughter, Lisa Louise Jackson.

Ben went straight in to see Lisa when he arrived at the hospital. He came out crying so hard it was difficult to understand him. 'Go'n ... go'n ... see her, Sherry. She's ... she's still warm.'

But Sherry didn't want to see Lisa's dead body. Instead, she went scouting to find out where the driver of the other car had been taken.

A nurse answered the question as she hurried by. 'The driver of the other car is in Resus Room One, officer,' She saw Sherry's uniform and assumed she was just another one of the police officers who regularly attended the busy city Emergency Department. 'An officer is already there.'

Sherry checked the whiteboard and saw the name *Linda Brogan* scribbled in red felt-tip pen in the space for Resus Room One.

The nurse had her eyes fastened on a point further along the corridor behind Sherry. 'Mr Brogan?'

Sherry followed her gaze and saw a very tall, dark-haired man dressed in surgical scrubs striding towards them. A blue surgical mask dangled from his neck. He noticed Sherry's uniform and looked at her questioningly, obviously wondering if she was waiting to speak to him. When Sherry continued to stare at him without saying anything, he turned his attention to the nurse. 'Where is she?'

'Resus Room One. I'll show you the way.'

'How is she?' Sherry heard him ask as they hurried away.

He had an accent. Linda Brogan's husband was an American surgeon.

She sped along the corridor after them, intent on getting inside RR1 and doing ... what? Her steps faltered as the door to the room swung open to admit Brogan and the nurse, and Dillon Taylor, a fellow police officer and friend, came out.

He stopped when he saw her. 'Sherry? What are you doing around here?'

Sherry noticed the way he held his hands out at his sides as he stepped towards her. When she tried to slip round him, Dillon caught her and held her tightly while she struggled break free.

'Sherry! You *know* you can't go in there!'

'Is she alive, Dillon?' She wrenched herself from his hands. 'Because Lisa's *dead!*'

The news rocked him. He and Lisa had been an item for two years, before her endometriosis got so bad that she'd broken the relationship off. If it hadn't been for that, Sherry and the rest of the Jackson clan had expected Dillon to be joining the family.

He shook his head slowly. 'She can't be.'

'*She is!*' Sherry hissed. 'And she's still alive? The Brogan woman?'

'They're still working on her.' He grabbed her again when she tried to push past him. 'You can't go in there, Sherry!'

Just then, Sherry thought she heard Lisa call her name and felt a light touch on her arm. She looked to her right but there was nothing there. Absolutely nothing. She felt a rush of air as if something was speeding past her in the direction of the resus room doors.

Dillon caught her as she wobbled on her feet. 'Sherry? Are you OK?'

'Did you hear that?' she whispered. 'It sounded like Lisa.'

Ashen faced, he snatched Sherry against him and carried her along the corridor and away from the room.

☆

Sherry studied her mother through the kitchen doorway. Last Christmas Jill Jackson finally managed to give up smoking after twenty-five years. Her children had nagged her about stopping for years, but it wasn't until Lisa, sensing that their mother was wavering, came home with a packet of cigarettes and began smoking that Jill finally gave in and kicked the habit.

'You're a lousy smoker,' Sherry remarked after watching

Lisa cough and splutter her way through her first cigarette.

'You mean there's such a thing as a good one?' Lisa gasped, eyes watering from the smoke.

Sherry had to admire her tactics and wondered why she hadn't thought of it. Lisa knew their mother wouldn't be able to stand the thought of her smoking.

'How could you be so stupid?' Jill cried shrilly. 'Damaging your health!'

Lisa lit a fresh cigarette from the burned-down butt of the last one. 'What's the difference between me and you?' She was wearing an old pair of their grandmother's gloves to prevent her getting nicotine-stained fingers. 'You think living with Nicotine Jill hasn't done something to my lungs?' She pounded her chest. 'Inside here is twenty plus years of your nicotine. I decided to cut out the middleman.'

It was a low blow. Their mother always smoked outside the house and wore a guilty expression, like a junkie getting a fix, while she was doing it.

By the fourth cigarette, Lisa had turned green. 'Sher, I don't know how long I can keep this up. I think I'm going to be sick.'

'Make sure you do it in front of her.'

Thankfully, Jill gave in before Lisa was halfway through the fifth.

Sherry and Ben had made bets on how long she'd hold out. Ben won.

'If one of us had tried it, I would've given much longer odds,' he told Sherry. 'But you know how Mum and Dad are about Lisa.'

They were *all* protective of Lisa. Sherry was old enough to remember her coming home from the hospital as a skinny, premature baby with a feeding tube in her nose, and later in plaster after the operations to correct her club foot.

The endometriosis had been the final straw. Lisa couldn't seem to get a break. It wasn't fair that she and Ben were tall and strong and so healthy they hardly ever even caught a cold while Lisa was small and fragile looking.

But she wasn't a wimp. One of their parents' favourite stories was about the day Ben started school. Lisa, who was two years older, towed him into his classroom by the hand and introduced him to his new teacher, saying solemnly, 'Mrs Davies, this is my little brother, Ben. He's just starting school today and he's a bit shy.'

Mrs Davies repeated the story to Jill Jackson, describing how tiny, elfin Lisa with her mop of blonde curls and blue-grey eyes scarcely reached her 'little' brother's shoulder. 'But I didn't dare laugh at her. She was deadly serious.'

Sherry swallowed the lump in her throat. Lisa might have been small and not always in the best of health, but she had more guts than just about anybody Sherry knew. She angry that Lisa's death had sent Jill straight back to her old habit. Lisa would have been so disappointed.

She sighed. They were all trying to find something to ease the pain of losing her. Their father hid in his garden pretending to work on his plants, but whenever Sherry went to find him, he was sitting on the wooden bench beneath the five-finger tree staring at nothing, a pair of pruning shears forgotten in his hand and an expression of such utter desolation on his face it made Sherry want to cry. He'd aged since Lisa's death. Sherry and Ben were worried about how frail he looked It was one of the reasons she backed down about tracing the call.

'Did you see the pictures the school sent us?' Brian asked. 'The ones the children did for Lisa?'

'No.' Sherry tried to smile. 'I'll have a look at them before I go.'

Lisa's losing battle with endometriosis got so bad in the last three years it had taken over her life. She broke up with Dillon and joked with Sherry about her celibate state. 'I think my reproductive system has probably got a sign on it saying condemned.'

Sherry rarely suffered so much as a tummy-ache when she got her period, and actively disliked kids, while Lisa suffered horribly most months and would have made a great mother. It wasn't right.

And it wasn't right that Linda Brogan had survived and was about to go home with her rich, surgeon husband. Sherry had kept tabs on Linda through her police contacts. She knew the Brogans lived in one of the houses high on the cliffs overlooking the beach, about a five-minute drive away from the Jackson house.

Ben told her to back off. 'Mum and Dad have enough to deal with at the moment without you doing something stupid.'

'I'd just like to see her face-to-face and tell her exactly what she's done to us,' Sherry replied bitterly. 'I want her to suffer too.'

'What makes you so sure she isn't suffering?'

'She's alive! Lisa's dead!'

'That's right. *She* has to live with what she did for the rest of her life.'

'How can you always be so fucking forgiving, Ben?' Sherry demanded angrily. 'Don't you hate Linda Brogan?'

'Of course I do!' he yelled. 'I want to kill her for what she's done!'

Sherry dropped her gaze. She was the yeller in the family,

not Ben.

'There's nothing we can do for Lisa now,' he continued more quietly. 'It's Mum and Dad we need to think about. Let the police and justice system go after Linda Brogan.'

Sherry hadn't told Ben or their parents that Lisa hadn't given way at the roundabout and might be partly to blame for the accident. Instead, she wound her long, strong arms around his back and hugged him tight.

Ben hugged her back, a troubled expression on his face. He knew his big sister. She wouldn't let it drop.

☆

Sherry carried a cup of tea through to the dining room and placed it by her mother's elbow. In her opinion the benefits of tea were vastly overrated. She'd spent the week after Lisa's death having well-meaning people force-feed her the stuff, only to find herself leaping for the tea caddy whenever a fresh outbreak of emotion seemed imminent from anybody in the near vicinity.

Her mother didn't appear to notice the cup of tea.

'Cup of tea, Mum.'

Jill smiled brightly. 'Thanks, love.' She didn't even glance at the steaming brown liquid in her favourite rose-decorated teacup on the table beside her.

Sherry wondered how her mother would react if she suggested they swap wine for tea and get drunk instead. Or maybe she should just start spiking the tea? It couldn't be any worse than the diet of cigarettes, sleeping tablets and cold tea her mother existed on at the moment, or that ghastly blank-eyed, bright smile.

Jill reached for a cigarette. 'The stonemason called.'

Sherry went behind the table and opened another window.

'Sorry, love.' Jill sucked smoked into her lungs and blew it out the side of her mouth away from Sherry.

'That's alright,'

Why was she lying? Her mother was going to smoke herself right into a hole next to Lisa if she wasn't careful. The thought of her sister in the cold, hard ground at the cemetery made Sherry feel ill. Ben agreed with her that Lisa would have wanted to be cremated, but their parents couldn't face it.

Jill was still talking.

'Pardon, Mum?'

'I said Lisa's headstone is ready. We can have it laid next week.'

'Oh. That's good.'

Like Lisa would have given a damn.

It was important to her mother and father. They visited the cemetery several times a week, it had become a pilgrimage for them. Ben visited sometimes too but Sherry hadn't gone back since the funeral.

'It's a lovely stone. Beautiful marble. And we picked out that lovely picture of Lisa on the beach last Christmas. You know the one I mean?'

'Yes, I know the one.'

Jill nodded. 'I think she would have liked it.'

She would have hated it, Sherry thought savagely. She would have hated *all of it*.

A white pickup truck pulled up outside the house. Ben climbed out, closely followed by his fiancée Brenda.

Sherry suppressed a groan. That was all they needed: a visit from Ms Glum.

Brenda was miserable *and* miserly. She'd changed their little brother from a happy-go-lucky, fit extrovert into an overweight, serious-minded worrier. Last year, Lisa caught Brenda in the two-dollar shop buying Ben's birthday present. Relations had been strained between them ever since.

Sherry and Linda had nothing against vegetarians until they met Brenda. She gave the movement a bad name. Sherry started calling her a herbivore and the name stuck. Brenda was the only person Sherry knew who could take something fun and find a reason why it shouldn't be and ruin it for everybody else. She'd spent the previous Christmas sitting at the dinner table with a disapproving expression on her miserable face while the rest of the family, Ben included, enjoyed barbecued fish and steak. Brenda partied with two lettuce leaves and a cherry tomato for company.

'You're in trouble tonight, Benny boy!' Sherry directed a meaningful look at Brenda, who sat hunched in her seat on the deck nursing the same glass of white wine she'd been given on arrival.

As usual, Ben leapt to Brenda's defense. 'Aw, she's alright.'

Sherry stared at him in puzzlement, wondering for the thousandth time just what he saw in Brenda. But that was Ben: saviour of lost causes, underdogs, and vegetarians.

Brenda had come into her own when she helped plan Lisa's funeral. She positively glowed and came up with some lovely ideas. It was Brenda who thought of releasing helium balloons as the hearse departed from the church and giving the children plastic bottles of bubbles to blow. Sherry's throat still clogged every time she remembered the sight of the balloons and bubbles soaring off into the sky. It was probably the only thing Lisa would have liked about her funeral.

Brenda had slipped back into her old ways since then. Sherry suspected what really pissed Brenda off was her inability to get Ben and his family to feel sorry for her anymore. Compared with Lisa's death, her problems were a mere blip on their collective horizon. Poor Brenda had been upstaged by a dead woman and she didn't like it. Sherry wished she could tell Lisa so they could laugh about it.

As she watched through the window, Ben opened the front gate and came up the pathway to the house, pausing to chat to their father who was doing some pruning. With a jolt, Sherry realized that all Brian did these days was prune old and dying vegetation. As far as she knew, he hadn't even bothered to put down spring bulbs, which he did every autumn regular as clockwork. She looked at his greying head and felt a tug of fear; he looked so old and frail.

Ben came into the house like a breath of warm, fresh air, his arms thrown wide to dispense hugs and comfort. He had the same blue-grey eyes as Lisa and their mother, but dark hair like Sherry. Brenda trailed behind him, her mouth pinched and her eyes watchful.

He smothered Sherry against his chest. 'How're you, PC Plod?'

She gave a token squirm of protest before snuggling against him. 'Shite.'

'That's what I like to hear.' He cupped her face in his hands and waggled her head from side to side. 'Where's Mum?'

'In the throne room.'

Ben sighed. The dining room had been renamed because their mother had taken it over. At first, she lay on her bed staring at the ceiling, until Ben managed to prise her out of the bedroom. Sherry thought it was about time they kick-started Jill into action again, but worried they'd run out of rooms.

'You really shouldn't make fun of her,' Brenda piped up sanctimoniously. 'She might hear you.'

Ben ignored her, which cheered Sherry up immeasurably. She'd noticed it happening more often since the funeral, and again wished Lisa was here to see it. When Ben went to the dining room to speak to their mother, Sherry turned to Brenda and said pleasantly, 'Brenda?'

'What?'

'Why don't you stick your finger up your arse and spin on it?'

Brenda's eyes nearly popped out of her head.

Sherry smiled and sauntered into the dining room feeling much better. Brenda did have her uses after all.

Ben was standing over their mother, her cigarettes and lighter in his hand. 'Enough, Mum.'

'What?' she quavered, her eyes filling with tears.

'You know what,' He waved the packet of cigarettes in front of her face. 'Lisa would be ashamed of you.'

Jill looked shocked. She'd become accustomed to being handled with kid gloves and Ben was the last person she would have expected to play the heavy with her. Sherry, yes, but not her kind, easy-going son. The mention of Lisa's name made her tears spill over. 'I can't *help* it! I know I shouldn't but ... but... it helps.'

Ben lowered his bulky frame into the chair beside her. Sherry eyed him anxiously. Had he put on more weight?

'Mum, you have to start doing things again,' Ben insisted, his gaze unwavering.

'But—'

'No buts. It's been a month now; Sherry and the neighbours can't do the shopping and cooking forever.' He placed a gentle hand on her back. 'You've still got Dad. And us.'

Jill pressed her palms against the tabletop and gulped. 'It's ... so ... *hard*.'

'I know,' Ben said softly. He glanced at Sherry, who was leaning against the doorframe between the kitchen and dining room, her face as pale as the white linen cloth spread on the table. '*We* know.'

'She was my baby,' Jill whispered brokenly. 'I feel like somebody has cut off a part of me. I feel crippled.'

Ben put his arms around her.

Sherry studied her baby brother. Since Lisa had died, she'd seen a side of him she never knew existed. Thank God, somebody had finally taken the bull by the horns and told the truth, and that for once, it didn't have to be her. She should have been braver and done it. After all, she was the eldest. She could almost hear Lisa snorting at that piece of logic.

Her mind returned to the nagging issue of Linda Brogan. She would be living right around the corner soon. Right within reach. She *had* to see Linda Brogan.

Chapter 9

The day finally arrived for Lisa to leave the hospital and go home with Dan Brogan. Despite his regular evening visits, Lisa knew about as much about him now as she did the night she woke up to find him sitting at the bottom of her bed. She'd have struggled to describe Dan if anybody had asked her what he was like.

The best she could have come up with was: a) Reliable. The few times he'd missed his evening visit he phoned to apologize and she never ran out of clean underwear; b) Kind. She'd drenched him in tears and snot on at least two occasions; c) Patient. He'd put up with her mood swings and confusion without batting an eyelid and tried to remember to call her Lisa; and d) Distant as the moon.

It reminded Lisa of a warped patient–doctor relationship, and she'd come to realize that that was exactly the way Dan treated her — as a patient. It was odd, considering she was supposed to be his wife and that Linda Brogan was an extremely beautiful woman. Even cooped up on the ward with a limited amount of contact with the outside world, Lisa had noticed the attention that Linda attracted, particularly from men. The first time a man saw Linda, he stared, and if he was young and cocky enough, he'd try to strike up a conversation. The shy ones blushed and retreated or started mumbling if Lisa spoke to them.

She might have found it amusing to live as one of the Linda Brogans of the world for a day or a week. She'd have been lying if she said it wasn't a buzz to look in the mirror and see that drop- dead gorgeous face staring back at her.

Even with greasy hair, a few spots and a bogie hanging out of one nostril, Linda Brogan would still have managed to look amazingly good.

The cow.

And becoming the owner of such a spectacular set of breasts when she'd always been flat as a board had at first also seemed only fair. If she had to come back in the wrong body, it might as well be one with all the attributes she missed out on the first time around. But within a few days, she'd had enough of their uncanny ability to get in the way. Linda's boobs had a mind of their own. They bumped against the sides of her arms, and if Lisa clamped her arms together, they retaliated by trying to launch themselves out of the front of her nightdress like a pair of mountaineers determined to summit. It was impossible to go without a bra anymore without risking stopping traffic or spiking herself in the nose with a nipple if she moved too fast.

One thing Lisa did enjoy was Linda's height. Going from five feet two to five feet nine was a joy. Even stooped over on crutches, Lisa could reach things she couldn't before the accident, and it was wonderful to not always be looking up people's nostrils when you spoke to them. Now they looked up hers.

She was nervous about leaving the hospital and its routine. Nervous about leaving Nancy and Chris and the other nurses she'd come to know so well. Nervous to be going home with a strange, silent man who considered her to be his wife even if he did go out of his way to not touch her. Dan had never once touched her with the casual affection most husbands and wives shared, although a couple of times lately she'd caught him looking at her breasts with what could only be called a distinctly male look of appreciation on his face. The only time he voluntarily touched Lisa was when she was upset or needing help. It didn't take a rocket scientist to work out that all had not been well in the Brogan marriage. And Lisa's brief exposure to Linda in the waiting room after the accident had revealed that she hadn't been the sweetest of individuals.

For the time being, Lisa had given up trying to convince people she wasn't Linda Brogan. She wanted to get out of the hospital, and even oddballs like Craig Fergusson probably weren't too keen about releasing patients back into the community who seemed to be barking mad, plus she wasn't fooled by Dan Brogan's air of calm reserve. The man was shrewd and extremely observant.

He had collected up the last of his wife's cosmetics, shampoos, and lotions the night before she was due to go home. 'What do you want me to leave for tomorrow?' he asked, standing amid the last of the multitude of bags he'd hauled in over the past couple of weeks.

Nancy and Lisa were aghast when they just seemed to keep coming, but Lisa suspected Dan was as confused as the next man when it came to the mysteries of female grooming and had simply emptied the entire bathroom cabinet. How could he know Lisa was only a couple of steps ahead of him when it came to understanding which pot of gunk went where? Sherry was the one who was big on cosmetics and stuff.

She looked at the smart Louis Vuitton makeup case and bulging plastic bags stacked against the opposite wall and shrugged. 'Beats me. Take your pick.'

Whenever she made comments like this, Dan would give her one of his penetrating looks that always made her feel nervous. It was as if a buzzer indicating an incorrect answer in a game show went off in her head. *BA BAH!*

Lisa tried to get ahead of the game. She pointed at random. 'You can take those and... that one.'

Watching her narrowly, Dan hooked his fingers through the handles of the carrier bags and nudged one of her selections with his foot. 'This one?'

Lisa nodded emphatically. 'Yes.'

'That's your hairdryer.'

BA BAH!

She studied the bag and him cautiously. 'My hairdryer?'

He nodded. 'Uh huh.'

She reconsidered. 'You're right. Leave it. It's great for blowing down my cast when it gets itchy.'

He stared at her.

BA BAH!

Lisa gazed back anxiously. Wrong again.

'What about those?' He nodded at the pink roses on the locker.

A second bouquet of roses had arrived, again without a card, and once again Dan's response had been stony.

'See if the nurses would like them.'

'You're sure?'

She nodded.

'I'll see you tomorrow evening around six.'

He departed juggling bags and the vase of roses.

After he'd gone, Lisa hopped along to the television room on her crutches and tried to lose herself in an episode of *Shortland Street*. Her fellow patients, who now considered themselves experts on the hospital system, gathered together at night to criticize or praise the medical soap as they saw fit.

'Call that an enema?' an elderly woman cried scornfully

as Lisa lowered herself into the seat beside her. 'What good would that little thing do? The one Chris gave me this morning was *twice* the size of that.'

Lisa stopped herself from sharing that Chris had only ever given her a couple of suppositories and they'd worked just fine. She shuffled her bottom to the edge of the battered, floral sofa and felt about for her crutches. *Institutionalized.* That's what she'd become. She hadn't realised until now.

A man with a Zimmer frame and a hip replacement piped up from the corner. 'I remember when I had my bowel resection in the 'eighties,' There was a competitive light in his milky eyes. 'Those were the days when they *really* gave you a good clear-out. They hooked me up to a drip through my nose.' He pointed at his beaky nose in case anybody wasn't sure what he meant. 'They flushed bags and bags of that saline stuff through me while I sat on the commode for the entire afternoon.'

The woman sitting next to Lisa looked annoyed at being outdone. 'Haven't put you off, have we, dear?' she asked as Lisa struggled to her feet.

'No, just tired,' Lisa lied, exiting as quickly as she could.

'That's youngsters for you,' she heard the elderly man remark as she hopped away. 'They've got no stomach for things.'

☆

At six o'clock the next evening, when Dan arrived to collect her, Lisa was sitting in the television room with the last of her bags packed on the floor beside her. Her hair was pulled back in a long, shiny ponytail. She wore a simple, pale blue long- sleeved peasant top over a matching muslin skirt. Lisa was no expert on clothes, but she sensed what she was wearing cost a small fortune.

She'd been visited that morning by the orthopaedic surgeon, who professed himself happy with her progress, and her plaster cast had been replaced with a much lighter acrylic one. There was a variety of colours to choose from, and Rob, the plaster technician, had talked just about everybody needing a replacement into having a blue-and-white one to show their support for the Auckland rugby team.

The Jacksons were keen Blues supporters. 'How're they doing?' Lisa asked.

'Great!' Rob exclaimed. 'They'll win the competition this year.'

'I've been in here so long I'd forgotten all about it.'

'Well, you don't want to miss the game tonight,' He wound a sticky cobalt-blue acrylic bandage around her leg. 'They're playing away to Canterbury. Should be a good game. Do you have Sky?'

'I don't know.'

He looked at her oddly but seemed willing to forgive her for being weird because she was a fellow supporter. Being so pretty didn't go against her either.

Dan raised his brows when he saw the cast. 'Were they all out of purple and green?'

'Don't you like it? I thought it went with my outfit nicely.' Lisa turned her leg from side to side to admire her new cast. 'Anyway, who cares? Go the Blues!'

'Go the Blues?' he echoed.

Lisa put his confusion down to not being a local, and explained patiently, 'They're the Auckland rugby team. There's a big game tonight.'

He regarded her wearily. 'I know who the Blues are,

Lisa.'

She checked the clock on the wall of the television room while Dan disappeared to find a wheelchair. Her nerves were jittering and clanging like an orchestra tuning up. At last, she was leaving the hospital. She was terrified. Concentrating on something safe and familiar like a rugby game was comforting.

Dan returned with the wheelchair. 'I'll take your things down first and then come back for you.'

'OK.' She tried to ignore the knot of tension in her belly. 'Dan?'

He looked up at her questioningly as he transferred the last bags onto the seat of the wheelchair.

'Do you have Sky?'

'Yes.'

Lisa checked the clock again. 'We should make it back to your place by seven-thirty, shouldn't we?'

Dan hated the way she referred to home as *your place*. 'What's so important about being back by seven-thirty?'

'The rugby match starts at seven-thirty.'

He released the brake on the wheelchair with unnecessary force. Linda had never shown an interest in men's sport and certainly not in the sports of the country she was visiting under sufferance. She didn't appear to be regaining any of her lost memory; in fact, she was just getting more and more weird.

'Sorry,' Lisa muttered. 'If you don't want to watch it, that's OK. Forget it.'

Dan realized he was scowling. He didn't want to frighten her, to make a difficult situation even worse. This had to be a hell of a lot harder for her than it was for him; she was going home with a stranger. But so was he.

He reached for his most reassuring bedside manner. 'It's OK. I was going to tape it and watch it later. We can watch it together if you like.'

When it was time to leave, Lisa clung to Nancy, unable to prevent the tears falling.

'You'll be fine, sweetie, just fine,' Nancy patted her back soothingly.

She'd grown fond of the strange American girl in the past couple of weeks. She was sweet and funny and incredibly brave. She glanced at Dan Brogan waiting patiently a discreet distance away and lowered her voice further to say, 'You have a good man there to take care of you, and I'm *sure* your memory will eventually come back.'

Lisa couldn't speak for the tears clogging her throat. The nurses were all buzzing about the nurses' station exclaiming over the huge bunch of flowers and food basket Dan had brought them as a thank you.

'Thank you,' she when she finally detached herself from Nancy and hopped over to join him. 'That was a really nice thing to do.'

'It was the least they deserved.'

'We'll miss you, Linda!' Mary the ward clerk cried, staring all the time at Dan. Of all the staff on the ward, she was the only one who still sometimes called her Linda. And the only one who made no effort to hide her crush on Dan.

Lisa exchanged a wry look with Nancy, who rolled her eyes and laughed. As usual, Dan seemed oblivious to the female interest he generated.

The old man on his Zimmer frame and the elderly lady from the previous evening stopped to admire the flowers.

'Good luck, luvvie,' the woman said. 'Do you have far to go?'

'The North Shore.'

'Oh, good. You'll be home in time for *Shortland Street*.'

'Yes,' Lisa watched the pair limp away and turned to Dan. 'Get me out of here.'

He was relieved she'd stopped crying. 'Why?'

'I'll tell you later.' She refused to use the wheelchair. 'No. I want to walk out.'

When they reached the lower ground floor, Dan led her to a wooden bench by the entrance and sat her down with her crutches propped beside her. 'Will you be OK to wait here while I get the car?'

Lisa listened to him with half an ear. She was too busy looking about her. It was a beautiful evening, darkness just beginning to fall. She had been in hospital for an entire month. After weeks of being inside, she shivered and lifted her face to the gentle breeze. The air smelt fresh and clean, not air-conditioned, and lifeless.

Dan hesitated. 'You're cold.'

'A little bit,' she closed her eyes. 'But it's OK.'

He watched her for a few moments. 'What are you doing?'

'I haven't felt the wind on my face in so long.' She opened her eyes and smiled up at him. 'It's *good* to be alive,' she whispered.

Dan swallowed; moved by the depth of emotion in the simple words. 'I'll get the car,' he headed towards the car park.

Lisa was impressed when a sleek, silver Diamante pulled up. She whistled when Dan came to help her in. 'Nice wheels, Doctor.'

The surprises just kept coming. Linda had always called his choice of cars boring. She much preferred Jack Millar's bright-blue convertible and never understood that Dan's height and convertibles weren't compatible. He didn't know what prompted him to speak up. Perhaps it was just one surprise too many for one night or that he'd spent the day in surgery and was tired.

'You always thought I pick boring cars,' he retorted. 'You much preferred the blue convertible.'

Lisa felt her light, happy mood evaporate, and the accident begin to replay inside her head. Her heart started to thump as she lowered herself into the car. Her fingers fumbled ineffectually when she tried to fasten her seatbelt. Eventually she gave up and looked up at Dan with a haunted expression on her pale face.

'Yes,' she whispered. 'I remember the blue convertible.'

Startled by her admission, he stared intently at her in the semi-darkness of the car interior. 'You do?'

'Yes.' Her breathing was shallow and she was trembling.

Dan was torn between regret at her distress and excitement that she remembered something. Her hands were balled into fists and pressed them against her breastbone. He reached for them. 'Easy, easy now,' He gently eased her hands down to her lap. 'Slow your breathing down.'

It took Lisa a few tries before she could do as Dan asked and it would have taken a lot longer if he hadn't been so reassuring and treated her like one of his patients. She relaxed into the car seat and would have stayed that way if she hadn't become aware that his large, warm hands were covering hers and resting right against her pubic bone with nothing but a wisp of muslin and a pair of Linda Brogan's skimpy, lacy knickers between them.

Lisa looked up into Dan's face and felt a wave of such

unadulterated lust and longing that she had to clamp her thighs together to stop herself from guiding his hands between them. She pressed herself back against the seat to keep from reaching for his mouth with her own.

Dan released her hands and straightened abruptly, trying to wipe the heated feel of her from his mind. He didn't want to remember how she looked naked and open to him, or how close he'd come to flattening his palms and running them down the length of those long, beautiful thighs. Was it just one of Linda's tricks because she realized she'd slipped up by admitting she remembered something?

Reaching over, Dan took the two ends of the seat belt and clicked them in place, ignoring the way Linda flinched when he touched her, and his gut clenched when he felt her soft skin and smelt her clean, floral scent. She didn't seem to like any of her favourite perfumes anymore. Remembering what his wife had been capable of before her accident had the effect of pouring ice water on his state of arousal. Dan started the car and headed onto the road and across Grafton Bridge.

Lisa sat beside him in tense silence, her humiliation rapidly overtaken by despair that she wasn't going home to her parents but to a strange house with this reserved, watchful, distrustful man who seemed to hide so much of himself away. For all she knew, he could be some sort of a criminal. She was ashamed to admit that a few moments earlier, if he'd said he wanted to have sex with her right there and then, she would have agreed wholeheartedly. On second thoughts, maybe not in front of the hospital.

As the car travelled along the road, Lisa felt her heart rate pick up and her breath catch in her throat again. Dan was driving sedately, cautiously even but it made no difference.

'I don't think I can do this,' she blurted when they stopped at the traffic lights to Karangahape Road. 'I don't know you! I don't know anything about you!' Her voice was edged with hysteria.

Dan glanced at her with concern. The lights went green. He drove across and pulled to the side of the road. 'Linda . . .' he began in his calmest doctor's voice.

'My name is *not* Linda!' Lisa shouted. 'I am *not* your wife! My name is Lisa! *Lisa Jackson!*'

She fumbled for the door handle and stumbled from the car, almost falling face down on the footpath. Righting herself, she staggered onto the footpath and began to hop down the street.

Swearing, Dan leapt out of the car and into the oncoming traffic, causing angry drivers to lean on their horns. Slamming the door shut, he slid across the front of the car and ran after Lisa, who was making surprisingly rapid progress for a woman with a broken leg and no crutches.

'Linda! For crissakes come back! You'll hurt yourself!'

His long legs ate up the distance between them.

She hopped on doggedly, shouting over her shoulder. 'My name is Lisa, *not* Linda! *Bugger off!*'

Once he'd caught up with her, Dan remembered to click the electronic locking device in the direction of the Diamante and followed along behind her, his hands in the pockets of his suit jacket. He was furious that he hadn't seen it coming.

It was just like Linda to throw a tantrum to deflect attention from her earlier lapse. But the desperate note in her voice and the damp patch beginning to appear on the blue muslin shirt between her shoulder blades wasn't an act.

In the past, Linda always made sure that when she pulled one of her drama-queen stunts she looked good.

Dan felt confusion, concern and finally, amusement. He strolled behind her, trying not to laugh at the sight of his oh-so-elegant wife, hopping along one of the busiest streets of Auckland city, clutching at shop fronts for support and swearing a blue streak. '*Bugger off?* That's a new one. Usually it's fuck off.'

Lisa paused to glare at him through her fringe as she clung doggedly to the front of a shop and snarled, 'It can be in the present, too, if you push your luck, smart-arse!'

People rushing home from work were eyeing them curiously.

'Are you alright, love?' an older woman paused to ask Lisa uncertainly, keeping a wary eye on Dan.

'No!' Lisa pointed at him. 'He's *following* me!'

'Oh dear,' The woman fidgeted from one foot to the other, a bag of shopping weighing down each hand. She looked about hopefully, as if expecting a police officer to materialize.

'I'm her husband.' Dan said.

'*He is not!*'

'Linda.' Dan sighed and shook his head. He was beginning to enjoy himself.

'*My name is not Linda!*'

The woman looked swiftly between the two of them and plonked one of the shopping bags down. She fished her mobile phone from her handbag. 'I'm calling the police.' She peered at the phone, tilting it this way and that to see the screen. 'Oh, this thing!'

'If you push the red button, the screen will light up,' Dan suggested helpfully.

Lisa glared at him. How dare he be so cavalier about this?

A small crowd of onlookers had gathered to watch.

'This thing is a waste of time. The kids insisted on buying it for me last Christmas, but I can't get the hang of it.' Lisa's rescuer jabbed at several buttons. 'What button?'

Dan leaned closer and pointed.

'Oh!' She beamed at him when the small screen lit up and then frowned. 'What's that?'

He tilted his head to look. 'You've got messages.'

'I have?'

Lisa shook her head in disbelief. 'I'm still not coming home with you.'

'Fine.' He leaned against the window next to her. 'But you'll have a long wait for the police. They're pretty busy on a Friday night.'

The woman regarded him suspiciously. 'How do you know?'

He nodded in the direction of the hospital. 'I'm a surgeon at the hospital. I deal with the police a lot.'

You're a doctor?'

Dan nodded. The woman put her phone away.

Lisa was furious. So *what* if he was a doctor?

A man spoke up from their audience. 'I know you. You operated on my granddaughter's arm last year when she fell off the trampoline. You're Dr Dan, aren't you?'

Hearing he worked at the children's hospital sent his approval rating skyrocketing even further with the would-be mobile phone rescuer.

Lisa watched in disbelief as Dan proceeded to have a chat about the progress of the man's granddaughter since her operation and the dangers of trampolines and skateboards.

She was exhausted from her frenzied hop down K Road. She felt stupid and ungrateful. Dan didn't deserve to be treated like this; the situation wasn't easy for him. But it wasn't for her either. And he needn't look so bloody relaxed about it.

She pushed away from the window, got her balance and began to hop back in the direction of the car.

Dan snapped to attention. 'Where're you going?'

'To fly a kite! Where the – the *fuck* does it look like I'm going?'

Lisa's former champion bristled as she hopped by. 'Swearing never helped anything!'

Grandad eyed Dan sympathetically. 'Looks like you have your hands full there.'

Lisa struggled on before collapsing against a streetlight, panting and vaguely aware Dan was bidding the members of their impromptu get-together goodnight. She didn't look up when he reached her side. Instead, she hugged the cold metal lamppost and watched the cars rushing past filled with people on their way out to enjoy Friday night or home to their families and the beginning of the weekend. The thought made her bottom lip wobble.

'Linda?'

Lisa stiffened.

'I mean Lisa.'

'What?'

'I'm sorry I upset you.'

She pressed her cheek against the cold metal post and sighed. 'I'm sorry you had to chase me.'

Dan studied her drooping figure. 'Are you sure you can make it back to the car?'

Lisa looked along the street to where the Diamante was inexpertly parked on the side of the road. 'We'd better get back before somebody comes around the corner too fast and hits it!'

'Do you want me to carry you?' he asked carefully. 'Just this once? It'll be a lot faster.'

The fight had gone out of her. She nodded wearily. He picked her up and set off in the direction of the Diamante.

Lisa tucked her face against his neck, felt his stubble against her cheek and the steady thump of his heart beneath her breast. He stiffened when she snuggled against him but she didn't care. She needed this. She needed *him*. The warmth of his big body and the faint scent of the spicy aftershave he wore calmed her. She was glad he was a person who was comfortable with silence. She'd acted like a fool. Dan Brogan might be a stranger, but right now, he was all she had.

Chapter 10

Lisa couldn't decide if she was happy or sad that Dan didn't drive through Browns Bay to get to his place. If he had, he would have driven through the roundabout where the accident had occurred and past her parents' house.

She imagined what home would look like right now. The lights would be on in the lounge, and her brother Ben's ute would be parked in the driveway. They always got together on the night of a Blues match to share a few beers, eat potato chips, and argue about the referee's calls and who should or shouldn't be in the team. Jill cooked big dishes of lasagna or paella, Sherry and Lisa supplied the salads or vegetables, and Ben and their father brought wine and beer. Would they be doing that tonight? Or would they be too sad to get together? Lisa wanted to wail with grief. She should be going home to her family and telling them she wasn't dead.

She barely noticed when Dan finally turned into a driveway and parked inside a double garage. When he turned the ignition off, they sat in awkward silence for a few moments, neither one knowing what to say.

'This is it,' Dan said at last. 'Home.'

Lisa didn't answer.

After switching on the garage lights and organizing her crutches, he led the way through the laundry and into the main house, turning on lights as he went. He stopped in the living room and gestured towards a large, deep sofa upholstered in a rich sky-blue fabric.

'Have a seat while I bring in the rest of your things. Can you make it down the steps?'

Lisa looked at the three wide wooden steps leading down into the room and nodded.

Dan disappeared and returned with her things which he carried through the living room to the other end of the house.

The room looked as if it belonged in a spread from Home and Garden. It was decorated with impeccable and expensive taste. The blue sofa had a twin, and two large chairs covered in a blue-and-white-checked fabric occupied opposite corners of the room. Soft peach mohair blankets were draped invitingly across the back of them. A glass-fronted wooden display unit was tucked in a corner beside a fireplace with a marble hearth. A trio of black wrought-iron candleholders in different sizes and topped by fat, white candles were grouped at one end of the mantlepiece and taller candlesticks stood on the pale bricked hearth. A beautiful mirror with a beaten bronze frame hung on the wall above.

When Dan returned, Lisa was sitting in the middle of the sofa looking out the glass doors that occupied the entire wall facing onto the back garden. A full moon hung low in the sky, spilling a swathe of light across the sparkling darkness of the sea beyond. Lisa realized the house was set on the cliff overlooking Browns Bay.

'Nice view,' she remarked politely.

'Yes.' Dan went to look out the windows, his hands tucked in his trouser pockets. 'It was the view that made us buy it.'

She watched him silently. It was the first time he'd mentioned himself and Linda without trying to make it sound as if he meant *her*. Maybe she was making some progress.

He turned back to her. 'Are you hungry?'

She shrugged. 'Not especially. I'm knackered more than anything.'

He seemed amused by her choice of words. 'Do you want to go to bed?'

Her gaze flew to his face.

'I meant *alone*.'

'I *know* what you meant,' Lisa sighed. 'Look, I'm sorry I've been such a drama queen.'

Dan's brows rose as if she'd made the understatement of the year. 'Don't mention it,' he replied wryly. 'I enjoy chasing women around the streets of Auckland.'

She smiled reluctantly. Did *anything* faze him? Her gaze snagged on the clock on the mantlepiece. 'Oh hell!'

He looked at the clock. 'What?'

'The game!' She struggled to her feet, nearly tripping over the glass-topped coffee table in front of her. 'It's going to start in a few minutes!'

'The game? You mean the rugby?'

'*Yes!* Is that the TV?' She gestured impatiently at the entertainment centre.

That was how Lisa spent her first hours in Dan's house, stretched out on the big blue sofa with one a peach-coloured blanket over her knees while Dan sprawled in a wing chair by the fireplace. He'd come up with a bowl of potato chips and a can of beer for himself. Lisa was surprised when he didn't offer her one. So far, he'd been the soul of politeness.

Dan caught her looking at his beer. 'Did you. . . would you like one?'

'Yes, please.'

He retraced his steps to the kitchen, feeling utterly bewildered.

Lisa felt like a social pariah. She'd never have picked Dan as having a problem about women drinking but it showed how little she knew him. She and Sherry enjoyed a beer when they watched rugby. Their mother only ever drank sherry which her kids thought was how Sherry got her name. They were convinced Jill overdid it at their parents' wedding reception and when Sherry turned up almost nine months to the day after the honeymoon, Jill named the baby after the cause of her downfall. Jill insisted it wasn't true, but they noticed their father always smirked and refrained from commenting.

It was a standing joke in the family. Lisa and Ben like to take turns coming up with possible variations on Sherry's name.

'You could have been Bundaberg if she'd been drinking rum,'

'Or Jack Daniels if you'd been a boy,'

'Johnnie Walker.'

'Remy Martin.'

'Harvey.'

'Harvey?' Sherry scoffed.

'Harvey's Bristol Cream.'

'Hey, Dad? What brand of sherry was Mum drinking at your wedding?'

'I did *not* get drunk on sherry at my wedding!' Jill insisted.

Brian always ruined things by winking and smiling.

Sherry whacked Ben with a rolled-up newspaper to get him to shut up and threatened to whack Lisa with a rolled-up newspaper if she didn't shut up too.

Lisa was deep in thought when Dan returned with her beer. He stood in front of her holding a glass of beer, scowling at her obvious unhappiness and his inability to find a rational explanation for Linda's about-turn on alcohol consumption.

She noticed his expression and asked, 'I'm allowed one, aren't I? I mean, it won't hurt my head or anything, will it?'

He shook his head and silently handed over the beer.

What had she done wrong now?

'You didn't need to put it in a glass. I don't mind drinking it out of the can.'

'Of course you don't.' Dan retorted grimly.

He flung himself into the armchair, clasped his hands on top of his head and stared grumpily at the television.

Lisa fought the urge to stick her tongue out at him.

Dan sat through the Blues match in shell-shocked silence, feeling like he was in the middle of some bizarre dream and couldn't wake up. He spent more time watching the woman stretched out on his sofa than the game. *Lisa* got right into the match, munching potato chips, and polishing off two beers, one straight from the can. She chugged them down like a pro. He was relieved when she refused another, saying two was her limit.

'I get drunk easily. Two glasses of wine and I fall asleep too.'

He swore if she started belching and smashing beer cans on her forehead, he'd load her into the car and take her back to the hospital.

Then there was the rugby.

The only time Linda had paid any attention to the national sport was when she saw the All Blacks on television and started drooling at how buff they were. Dan suspected she was trying to make him jealous, but he'd given up caring about Linda's pathetic digs. Frankly, he didn't give a rat's ass any what she thought of his body anymore.

Lisa knew the game. She knew the rules. She howled at the ref for dumb calls. She cringed at a ball knocked forward, and nearly fell off the sofa when the opposition weren't penalized for a head-high tackle.

'Did you *see* that?' she yelled.

By then he'd given up pretending to watch the game and had his chin propped on his fist watching her instead.

'That was definitely head-high! He should have awarded a penalty! It was right in front of the sticks. Three points missed! You *dickhead!*' she shouted when the referee came into shot.

Dan watched her with a mixture of fear and fascination. Who was this woman?

Lisa thought he disapproved of her shouting and bad language and apologised. 'Sorry. I get a bit carried away when I'm watching a game.'

'Uh huh.'

Auckland lost to Canterbury.

'It must have been the home advantage.' She scowled. 'And a referee who forgot to wear his contact lenses.'

'They outplayed them, Lin—'

She fixed him with a look. 'We're not going through all that again, are we?'

Dan dug his thumb and forefinger into his eyelids.

Lisa reached for the remote and turned off the television.

He blinked. How did she manage to get hold of it? Everybody knew the guy got the remote control.

'I can't pretend to be somebody I'm not and I'm *not* your wife. I don't know the first thing about her.' She frowned. 'Except she owns lots of beauty products.'

'That's insane!' Dan snapped. '*You are Linda!* Look!' He

snatched up a gold-framed wedding photo from a side table, stomped over and thrust it under her nose. 'That's one of us on our wedding day. It's *you* for crissakes!'

Lisa reached out slowly and took the photograph. Dan and Linda were standing beneath an archway of roses. He was wearing a tuxedo and she looked exquisite in an ivory fairytale dress with a tiny little hat fastened to the back of her black hair with a long veil attached. Dan looked young and handsome, and nothing like the careworn, forbidding man glaring at her. He looked *happy*.

She cleared her throat nervously, hoping she was as good a judge of character as she liked to think. They were in Dan's house, not the hospital. He was a large, extremely powerful man. If he lost his temper, there was no one to call on.

'I know I look like Linda, Dan, but please believe me. I'm not her.' Lisa wiggled her fingers to draw his attention to the appalling state of the acrylic nails on her fingers and joked weakly, 'Would Linda have let her nails get into this state?'

She sucked in a breath and cringed when Dan suddenly ploughed his hands through his hair.

He noticed and said stiffly, 'I may be angry but I'm not going to hit you.'

There was a long silence during which Dan replaced the photo on the side table and came to sit at the other end of the sofa. He set his elbows on his spread knees and studied his clasped hands. He'd taken off his jacket and tie at the beginning of the game. The top two buttons of his dress shirt were undone. His throat and neck were brown and strong.

Lisa turned her gaze away and said softly, 'I'm sorry, Dan. For both of us.'

He shook his head and frowned at the carpet. 'None of

this makes any sense. You've had a serious head injury. You've *lost* your memory.'

'But I *haven't*. I haven't lost it at all. I remember my entire life. It just isn't your wife's life.' She sighed. 'Oh, I wish I could make you understand . . .'

He lifted his head, fixing her with cool, grey eyes. '*Please*,' he urged. '*Do.*'

Lisa's heart stuttered in her chest. 'I'm scared ... to tell you.'

'Why?'

'Because ... because I know how crazy it will sound, and if you throw me out I have nowhere to go.'

His expression softened slightly. 'I'm not going to throw you out.'

'You'll just get Craig Fergusson to lock me up instead.'

He smiled faintly. 'It's not as easy to lock people up as you might think, Lin— Lisa.'

She smiled back and shivered.

'Are you cold?'

'A bit. I'm tired, I guess.' Lisa felt drained. She didn't have the reserves to deal with all this emotion and the beer was making her sleepy. 'I'm truly not trying to avoid your questions. I'm just not up to having this conversation tonight, I really need to go to bed. Can we talk about it tomorrow?'

He nodded reluctantly. 'I'll show you your room.'

☆

When Dan opened the door to the bedroom, Lisa gasped at the size of the bed. 'Crikey! It's like your trousers! Did you get the shop to put two beds together?'

He laughed quietly. 'We had it made in the States. I always hang out of the bottom of beds.'

Lisa frowned. 'This is *your* bed.'

'It's OK,' he said quickly. 'I've been sleeping in the spare room for ... a while.'

'Show me.'

'What?'

'Show me where you're sleeping,' She began to hop back along the hallway.

'Lisa!' Dan followed. 'It doesn't matter.'

'Yes, it does. How big is the bed you're sleeping in?' She pushed open a door two along from her bedroom. 'This is it, isn't it?'

He came up behind her and looked sheepishly at the mess in his bedroom. 'Yes.'

The room was cluttered with medical texts and paperbacks stacked on the bedside tables and spilling onto the floor. A cane laundry hamper stood in one corner, a pile of dirty clothes towering over it with the lid balanced precariously on top. The wardrobe doors stood open to reveal badly hung clothes and shoes piled up haphazardly on the shoe rack. A collection of mugs and plates were scattered across the top of a beautiful wooden chest of drawers, and there was a queen-sized bed with a navy-blue duvet cover hiding beneath more books and clothes. The bed was far too small for him.

Lisa laughed. 'You messy pup!'

He tried to reach around her to close the door.

'Nope!' She braced her arms on the doorframe, leaned forward and stuck her butt out to stop him. 'I haven't seen it all yet.'

Dan closed his eyes against the delicious feel of her beautiful ass snuggled against his zipper and said through gritted teeth, 'Yes, you have,' He didn't care who she thought she was, she still had his wife's beautiful body. He solved the problem by hooking an arm around her waist and lifting her clear of the doorway.

'That's cheating!'

'So sue me.' He set her down on the carpet.

Lisa stopped laughing when she saw his grim expression and allowed him to shepherd her back to the other bedroom.

He showed her the bathroom between their bedrooms. 'We share access but if you lock the door, I promise not to barge in on you.'

She managed a nod. Could this possibly get any more awkward?

'Can you manage OK with . . .?' He gestured to her blue skirt and top.

'Definitely,' she said shortly.

'Good,' he replied curtly. 'Goodnight, then.'

'Night,' Lisa turned her back and hopped towards the dressing table opposite the bed.

Stubborn little witch, Dan fumed as he stalked along the hallway to his bedroom with its doll-sized bed.

Prick, Lisa thought. *Miserable* prick.

She studied the monster-sized bed wretchedly. She'd get lost in it. It was the size of a rugby field; her bedroom at home was smaller than his bed.

Please, please, don't let me sleepwalk.

Chapter 11

Lisa did sleepwalk.

She'd done it ever since she was a child. Whenever she was upset or frightened, she went walkabout in her sleep. Her family were experts at turning Lisa around and putting her back to bed without waking her. Generally, she only did it once a night; once back in bed, she could usually be relied upon to stay there until morning.

Lisa was relieved she hadn't done it while she was in hospital. She'd come to the conclusion the alien nighttime environment of the ward with its dimmed lights and hushed voices had prevented her sleeping deeply enough to sleepwalk. She'd never slept the entire night through despite having her own room.

When she awoke the next morning, she was safely tucked up in the cavernous bed and starving. Her main concern was breakfast. She was blissfully unaware Dan had been woken around two in the morning by the soft *thud thud* of somebody moving along the hallway outside his bedroom in the direction of the living room.

He checked the clock and lay still, listening.

Thud! Pause. *Thud!* Pause.

Like somebody hopping on carpet.

Why would Lisa be wandering around in the middle of the night? Perhaps she'd forgotten where the bathroom was or maybe she wanted a drink of water. Dan climbed out of his cramped bed and let himself out into the hallway. It was empty. Picking up his pace, he walked along the corridor and nearly had a heart attack when he saw a pale figure hovering just above the steps leading down to the living room.

'Lisa?' He hurried towards her, his bare feet slapping on the polished wood. 'Lisa! Why don't you put the lights on? You'll fall—'

He reached her just as she lifted her broken leg to step out into nothing. Wrapping his arms around her, he dragged her back against his chest. 'Lisa!'

Her head lolled against his shoulder. She let out a gentle snore. Dan blinked in disbelief.

She was sleepwalking.

As she continued to snuffle against him, blissfully at peace, he couldn't help but shake with silent laughter. What would this woman do next?

He carried her back to her bed by hooking his arms beneath hers and tucking her against his chest. With a start he realized that he'd jumped out of bed stark-naked, and the gentle sway of her buttocks covered only by one of his T-shirts rubbing against his groin was giving him an erection he could have cut diamonds with.

Holding Lisa as far away from his pelvis as he could, Dan ferried her back to bed, acutely relieved that he didn't have time to turn on any lights, because *if* she woke up, she was in for one hell of a shock. It amused him that even in her sleep she still tried to hop on her good foot. As soon as he'd tucked her back into bed, she sighed and curled up like a little kid, looking lost in the big bed.

Dan gazed at her and the bed regretfully. Lisa made a sound, turning back towards him. He made a swift exit in case she opened her eyes and discovered him standing stark-naked beside her bed with a hard-on pointing to midnight, but as a precaution he left both bedroom doors open for the remainder of the night.

So when Lisa hopped into the kitchen on her crutches the following morning and Dan asked her if she'd slept well, he wasn't too surprised when she nodded.

'Yes, fine. Why? Did you have an uncomfortable night in your kiddy bed?'

'You could say that,' he replied cryptically, spooning cereal into his mouth.

Lisa felt vaguely discomforted by the sight of Dan fresh out of bed. In the past, she'd always seen him at the end of the day, dressed casually and once or twice in a suit. He was wearing a navy-blue towelling robe and, from the look of his bare feet and legs, not much else. His jaw was shadowed with stubble, his hair was mussed and sticking up on one side, and his eyes still looked sleepy. He looked good. *Better* than good. Lisa feared she was becoming another Mary.

He was sitting at the breakfast bar in the large, sunny kitchen with the morning paper spread out in front of him and a cup of coffee steaming gently by his elbow.

Lisa sniffed at the coffee hopefully.

Taking the hint, Dan went to get a mug from a collection hanging in the nook above a brick fireplace in the middle of the room. It separated the kitchen from a large, airy dining room with a long formal table flanked by chairs covered in a rich, raspberry fabric.

Lisa noticed him hesitate as he poured the coffee. 'How d'you like it?'

She appreciated the significance of the question. He obviously knew how Linda had liked her coffee. 'Just milk, please.' She managed to climb up onto one of the wooden stools at the breakfast bar. 'I'm starving.'

Dan rewarded her with a faint smile, one corner of his

mouth curling. 'Cereal OK?'

'Yes, please.'

Lisa munched on her cereal after filching the sports section of the paper from him.

'I was going to read that,' he protested.

'Nobody's stopping you.' She nodded at the section that he had laid out in front of him. 'I might have wanted to read that, but do you hear me complaining?'

'You want to read the business section?'

'No.'

They pretended to ignore each other until the toaster popped and Dan ferried toast back to the breakfast bar.

Lisa finished her cereal and began to butter some toast.

Dan was eating his with butter and jam. 'Have you only got jam?' she asked.

He swallowed. 'Jam?'

She nodded at the pot on the counter. 'Jam.'

'That's jelly.'

'Not in this hemisphere. That's *jam*. Jelly is wobbly stuff kids have at parties.'

'No, that's *Jello*.'

They squared off across the butter and toast. Dan looked distinctly hostile at the continued reminders that this woman just wasn't acting the way she should.

Lisa refused to back down. 'Do you have any Vegemite?'

'What the fuck is *Vegemite?*'

'I *wish* that woman from last night could hear you now. She told me off for swearing. She wouldn't think you were so wonderful if she could hear what you'd just said about Vegemite!'

They glared at each other.

Dan began to smile.

Lisa tried hard to hang onto her temper, but it was a lost cause.

'Is Vegemite that black stuff Kiwis like to smear all over their sandwiches?' he asked.

'There's nothing wrong with Vegemite,' Lisa replied petulantly.

He shrugged and went back to his paper. 'Just don't expect me to join you.'

'You have some?'

'No. We'll go to the supermarket today and stock up on a few things.'

It wasn't until they'd finished eating and Lisa had helped him stack the dishwasher that he told her she'd been sleepwalking.

'I'm so sorry!' she cried. 'I was worried I might!'

He frowned. 'Nobody told me you'd started sleepwalking.'

'I didn't in the hospital; it's only if I get into a deep sleep and that was impossible there. I've done it ever since I was little. If I'm worried or overexcited I do it, but it's usually only once a night. As soon as I go back to bed, I stay put.'

Dan braced his hands on the kitchen counter, struggling to contain his irritation. Linda had *never* walked in her sleep. 'You were just about to step off the top of the living-room steps when I found you last night. You can't take risks like that with your leg or your head injury.'

Lisa chewed her lip. 'I know.'

He watched her in tight-lipped silence. She knew he thought she was lying.

'There's a lock on your bedroom door,' he said at last.

She shook her head. 'I undo locks in my sleep. I even walked out into the street once.'

When? he wanted to snarl, because it sure as hell wasn't any time in the last eight years. 'Jeez, this just gets better and better!'

Her eyes shot sparks at him. 'I don't do it on purpose! I only do it when I'm worried or upset!'

Clearly, she laid the blame for that at his door.

'At this rate, I'll probably be joining you,' Dan retorted. 'I'm *worried* you're going to walk off the cliff during the night. The thought of that *upsets* me.'

She hopped towards the kitchen doorway, anxious to get away from Dan and his disapproving looks and snarky remarks.

Dam sighed. 'Aw ... Lisa! Look ... I'm sorry.' He hated seeing her struggling to get away from him on her injured leg.

She paused with one hand on the doorframe, her back still towards him. 'What am I going to do, Dan?' she asked in a muffled voice.

'I don't know. We'll think of something.'

She looked reluctantly over her shoulder at him. Twin flags of pink painted her cheeks. 'Do you want to use the shower first?'

He cleared his throat awkwardly. 'No. You go ahead.'

'Are you sure? I'm not used to showering on my own.' She cringed. It sounded as if she was asking for help. 'What I mean is I've always had one of the nurses to help.' That sounded even worse. 'I *mean* . . .'

Dan held up a hand. 'It's OK, I get the picture. I'll go first.'

They took care not to touch each other as he went through the kitchen doorway.

Shoulders slumped, Lisa went to find something to wear

from amongst his wife's clothes.

☆

There was a walk-in wardrobe off the master bedroom. Linda Brogan's clothes filled it. Lisa had never seen so many outside of a department store; even Sherry didn't own this many.

'Bloody hell!' she whispered and hopped in for a closer look.

It was a model of organization, unlike Dan's wardrobe in the other room.

Lisa trawled the shelves, opening drawers and stroking the luxurious fabrics. Jackets, shirts, trousers, dresses, skirts, vests and coats were hung in separate groups. Each group was classified by colour and length of sleeve or hem. There was a shelf for hats, and three tiers of shoe racks

filled with the most gorgeous shoes Lisa had ever seen. Boots, evening sandals, stilettos, aerobics shoes— you name it, Linda Brogan owned it, usually in several colours and styles.

Lisa stared at the beautiful jewel-toned clothes and thought how much Sherry would adore owning a wardrobe like this.

There wasn't any room for Dan's clothes.

'Lisa!' he called from the bedroom. 'Bathroom's all yours.'

She hopped to the doorway between the wardrobe and bedroom and swallowed. Dan was waiting just inside the bedroom door. He was wearing jeans and a white T-shirt, and his dark hair was wet. Her libido wanted to growl with hunger.

'Everything ok?' he asked warily when Lisa continued to stare at him.

'Mmmm? No – I mean, yes! Those clothes!' She waved an arm in the direction of the wardrobe. 'Are they *all* hers?'

His lips thinned. 'No, they're all *yours*. And *where* are your crutches? You should be using them, not holding onto walls and furniture to get around.' He stomped out of the room.

Lisa stuck her tongue out at his retreating back and mouthed, '*Arsehole.*'

'Leave the bathroom door unlocked in case you need help.'

Not happening. She'd rather risk breaking the other leg.

Lisa hurried through her shower, ignoring most of the jars and bottles of perfume and lotion stacked on glass shelves in the bathroom. She knew all about cleansing, toning and moisturizing - any woman exposed to the harsh New Zealand sun did. But Linda Brogan had taken things to a whole new level. How on earth did she make it out the door each morning if she used all the gunk on the shelves? Most of the labels made no sense. What on earth was Scaling Solution or Post Extraction Fluid? They sounded as if they belonged in a mechanic shop or a taxidermist.

However, Lisa did like the pretty, lacy underwear in Linda's lingerie drawers. Her revulsion at wearing another woman's knickers was dispelled when she recalled this body had been wearing them before she took it over. Unfortunately, she still had major problems with G-strings and Linda Brogan didn't seem to own anything else.

Sherry, who was the queen of G-strings and frilly balcony bras, enjoyed making fun of Lisa's preference for bikini briefs by announcing loudly - usually in a supermarket or shopping mall, 'Oh my god! You've got VPL!'

'Shut up!' Lisa would hiss. 'I'd rather have Visible Panty

Line than put up with my bum being flossed by a bloody G-string.'

When Lisa finally presented herself in the lounge, she was wearing a pair of white, wide-legged trousers that concealed her cast and rode low on her hips and a soft blue tank-top with a loose- sleeved white shirt over the top. She'd brushed her hair into a ponytail and her only nod to makeup was some lip-gloss.

Dan merely nodded when he saw her. Putting his book aside, he got to his feet, his expression as readable as Sanskrit. 'Ready?'

Lisa nodded back, feeling deflated. It was the first time she would be going out since she'd left the hospital and she'd been feeling a childish excitement. It would have been nice if Dan had said something pleasant about her appearance.

The sun was shining. Autumn in Auckland was often one of the best seasons. The humidity and heat of summer had passed and although the evenings were growing cooler, the days were usually bright and sunny.

Once again, Lisa noticed that Dan took a route that avoided the scene of the accident. In the supermarket, he pushed the shopping trolley while she limped alongside on her crutches, noticing the looks he drew from women as they walked by. When they reached the aisle with the jams, he picked up a black plastic container with a red lid and held it up for Lisa to see. 'This stuff?'

She shook her head. 'That's Marmite. I want *Vegemite*.' She limped forward and selected another black container with a different lid and held it up. 'See?'

Dan looked between the containers. 'They both look like black stuff to me.'

'Not to me.'

Lisa was surprised to discover he had a sweet tooth. 'Who are all the lollies for?' she enquired as he loaded various chocolate bars and packets of sweets into the cart.

'They're called candy and they're for me.' Dan replied firmly.

'They're called lollies.'

'S'cuse me, love,' a small woman with two toddlers sitting in the front of her trolley smiled at Dan. She looked like a grandmother babysitting for the day. 'Would you mind getting me a bottle of that honey, please? I can't reach.'

Dan and Lisa turned to look at where she was pointing.

Lisa took great delight in beating him to the honey. 'Here you go.' She beamed at the woman as she passed it over.

'Thanks, love.'

She continued to smile as Grandma trundled off.

'You look like you're about to break into song. Would you like some honey, too?' Dan asked.

Her smile stretched. 'Don't you just love being tall?'

Once again, she'd managed to confound him.

'I guess. I've never known any different.'

'I have.'

She swung off along the aisle on her crutches, humming.

That was about the time that Dan decided *he* needed an appointment with Craig Fergusson.

After they'd finished the shopping, Lisa dragged her crutches heading back to the car. Dan could see the pleasure the sunshine and fresh air was giving her and impulsively asked if there was anything else she wanted to do.

Her cheeks went pink with pleasure. 'Can we go look at books and then the pet shop and then maybe we could get a coffee?'

For obvious reasons, Linda *never* wanted to visit a bookshop. Dan, who loved to read, made it a rule to do all his book buying when he was alone. Linda liked animals as much as the next person, but he couldn't recall her ever choosing a visit to the pet shop over a clothes shop, makeup bar or sports equipment store.

'Damn,' he murmured, shaking his head slowly.

Lisa's face fell. 'Sorry.'

'It's not that we can't do all those things, but that's quite a list. I don't want you overdoing things on your first day out.' He lied.

Her expression turned pleading. 'Please, *please* let me overdo it!' she wheedled. 'It's so nice to be outside, and I promise to lie down for an hour when we get back to your house.'

Her reference to *your house* didn't go unnoticed, but he refrained from commenting.

They visited two pet shops and *oohed* and *ahhed* over the puppies and kittens. Dan was bitten by Snowy the white cockatiel when he foolishly put his finger through the wires.

Lisa laughed her head off.

'He asked for a scratch!' Dan complained, shaking his finger.

'See the sign?' She pointed to the white cardboard notice attached to the side of the cage warning people that Snowy liked to bite.

How had she been able to read the black, hand-printed sign? 'You've been in here before?' he asked with forced casualness.

'Lots of times. I always visit the pet shops.'

Dan drew in a breath and released it slowly. 'Now you want to go to the bookshop?' '

'Yes, please.'

In the bookshop across the road, she was immediately drawn to a table advertising five books for twenty dollars. 'Look! Five for twenty bucks!'

Dan watched in silence as she sorted through the books and selected a few. She turned them over and frowned at the back. The pleasure slowly faded from her face as she realized she couldn't make sense of what she was seeing.

She looked up at him, her eyes clouded. 'I think I'll have to work my way up to this. It's a shame because they're such a bargain. Do you want to look for yourself?'

Linda didn't care about *bargains*. After years of buying her clothes in sales and being forced to make ends meet, she declared she'd never buy anything for half-price again. Dan understood her insecurity and was willing to indulge her to a point. He wasn't poor; he earned more than his father had as a construction worker and wouldn't have begrudged the money Linda spent on clothes and things if it made her happy, but her happiness never lasted.

His own needs were simple. He wasn't a huge fan of clothes. He didn't gamble or drink a lot. A happy marriage and home life, doing the work he loved and making good investments for their future would have been enough for him. He'd even been willing to swallow his disappointment about children not being a part of their lives, but it was never enough for Linda. *Nothing* was *ever* enough for her. The woman he was with today wasn't like that.

Dan watched Lisa study the books in her hands, watched as her face changed and she slid a hand inside her bag for a wallet that wasn't there. She dropped the books back onto the pile on the table. He felt a wave of something he couldn't identify. Tenderness? Sorrow? Both?

'You can have them if you want.'

She shook her head and joked, 'But don't let me stop you. I can tell by the mess in your bedroom that you love reading. I don't mind waiting.'

She went to look at the greeting cards.

Dan scooped up the books she'd been looking at and some for himself and went to find her. He was buying books for Linda. *He was buying books for Linda that she'd chosen because she wanted to read them.*

She was in the self-help section, frowning at the back of another book, her lips moving as she sounded out the words. She started when Dan ducked his head to get a look at the cover. She pushed it back onto the shelf.

It was a book he'd read in the past about dyslexia. *Smart But Feeling Dumb.*

Chapter 12

Lisa sensed a change in Dan as they left the bookshop. He looked at her as if he were seeing her for the first time.

'How about that coffee?' he asked. 'Are you hungry?'

'Yes.' She eyed him warily. 'Starving.'

They dawdled over their coffee. Dan ate two chocolate muffins while Lisa munched her way through chicken risotto cakes with salad.

'How do you not get fat?' she asked.

He shrugged. 'Just lucky, I guess. My brother's the same.'

'Tell me about your brother.'

'He's a couple years younger than I am. His name's Glenn.'

Folding her arms on the table, Lisa watched him curiously. 'Is he as tall as you?'

He swallowed some muffin. 'Taller.'

'You're joking!'

'Nope. He used to play pro basketball.'

'What happened?'

'Bummed his knee. Anterior cruciate and medial ligament damage.'

'In English, please.'

Dan smiled and wiped his mouth on a napkin. 'Bummed his knee,' he repeated. 'He's doing some coaching now.'

She leaned closer on her folded arms. 'Did you ever play?'

'At high school and college, but I was never as good as

Glenn.'

'Did you mind?'

He seemed amused by her bluntness. 'Maybe when I was younger, but I always wanted to be a doctor. Sport was — no, sport *is* a passion for Glenn. We're complete opposites. He's a real extrovert.' Dan dropped his napkin onto his plate and mirrored her by leaning on his folded arms. 'I think we're both proud of what the other one has achieved. Anyway, he's my kid brother and I love him.'

Lisa smiled so sweetly he felt his breath hitch in his chest.

'Yes,' she said. 'I know what you mean.'

They were silent for a few moments.

'How old are you, Dan?' she asked suddenly.

'Thirty-six. Why?'

'I just wondered.' She paused. 'I'm twenty-seven. Right?'

He shook his head, feeling uneasy when he recalled he'd heard that the girl who had died in the accident had been twenty-seven. 'Try again.'

'Twenty-six?'

'Other way.'

'Twenty-eight?'

He shook his head again.

Lisa gasped. 'You mean I'm *twenty-nine?*'

His eyes crinkled with amusement. 'Not for much longer.'

She looked appalled. 'When do I turn thirty?'

'June 6.'

Lisa slumped back in her chair. Her birthday wasn't until the end of next February when she would have turned twenty-eight. She'd lost two years as well as her real birthday. 'Bloody George!'

The laughter faded from Dan's eyes. 'Who's George?'

'You don't want to know,' she muttered.

She was probably right. If she told him something else that didn't make any sense, his head would explode, and if he stuck with what logic dictated and remembered this *was* Linda, the prospects weren't any better.

Dan shoved back his chair and got to his feet. 'Come on. We'd better be going.'

He felt like a heel watching her struggle to her feet, her happy smile gone.

As they made their way slowly across the supermarket car park, she made Dan feel even worse by thanking him for the coffee and morning out.

'It was nothing,' he replied brusquely. 'I had to come out anyway.'

She kept her gaze averted; her entire concentration apparently focused on managing her crutches.

A stunning young woman wearing bright-red hipster pants and a white crop-top stepped off the kerb in front of the supermarket. Dan judged her to be almost six feet tall. She carried herself like a queen, shoulders back, head held erect on her long neck. Her long, dark hair swung about her shoulders and lipstick-red toenails peeped from slim, red sandals. The low-slung pants and short, sleeveless top revealed a taut, flat abdomen and toned arms. She easily carried a bag of shopping in each hand. The lady definitely worked out.

She noticed Dan on the opposite side of the road and frowned as if she were trying to place him. Dan was used to the relatives of a child he had operated on recognising him even if he didn't always remember them - although he never forgot any of the kids. But this was different. The look of confusion on her face lasted a split second before she transferred her gaze to Lisa, her expression hardening into one of such loathing that Dan reflexively put his arm in front of her.

Next to him, Lisa gasped and ground to a halt. He was alarmed to see her staring across the road at the woman in the red pants. 'Sherry!' she cried.

Dan looked from Lisa's radiant face to the shocked expression of the other woman. 'Lisa?' he began. 'Who—?'

'How do you know my name?' the woman demanded hostilely. 'It was *you*, wasn't it? *You're* the one who called my parents!'

'Sherry, it's *me! Lisa!*' Lisa cried.

Dan was alarmed at how pale she had become. He managed to stop her rushing headlong into the line of cars entering the supermarket car park. What was going on? What was this woman to Linda?

Lisa fought to free herself. '*Let me go!*'

They were holding up the flow of traffic. Drivers were starting to honk their horns and shout.

Dan wrapped his hands around her upper arms and shook her when she raised her hands to fight him off. 'Lisa!' he snapped. 'We have to move.'

'*No!*'

The other woman watched Lisa, her eyes blazing. She seemed oblivious to the red car she was blocking. The driver, a middle-aged man, climbed out looking furious.

'Sherry, *please* believe me!' Lisa implored. 'I *know* it sounds crazy, but it's me!'

The bags fell from the woman's hands. Jars, and loaves of bread spilled onto the asphalt. The driver of the red car paused mid-stride to stare in astonishment at the food strewn across the road.

'You keep away from me and my family! Just keep away!' The woman shouted and fled.

Dan grabbed Lisa around the waist when she attempted to follow. 'Lisa! What are you doing?'

She strained against him and shouted desperately, 'Sherry! I *know* you! I know you hate spiders!'

The woman stumbled.

'*Lisa!*' Dan was furious. '*Stop it!*' He grunted when Lisa managed to kick him in the shin with her cast.

'Who are the only women who wear scarves?' Lisa yelled.

The woman stopped. She slowly turned her head and looked back at Lisa, a haunted expression on her lovely face.

Dan watched her grimly. Linda or Lisa or whatever she wanted to call herself had finally lost it. 'That's enough!' he growled.

'Bank clerks, checkout girls, air stewardesses and porn stars,' Lisa whispered brokenly across the black stretch of asphalt.

She couldn't have heard what Lisa said, but she seemed to have understood it because her face lost what little colour it had left. Convinced she was about to faint, Dan hauled Lisa against his hip and set off awkwardly towards the tall woman, dimly aware of Lisa's crutches clattering to the ground behind them and the noise of car horns and abuse.

Sherry pressed her fingers together in a pyramid over her nose, her eyes huge with shock. Dan was struck by the similarity in appearance between the woman and Lisa.

They could almost have been sisters.

The thought came and went again just as quickly. Dan's priority was getting to the woman called Sherry before she fainted.

She suddenly thrust out a hand, stopping him in his tracks. 'Go away!' Her eyes were glued to Lisa. She pointed a shaking finger at her. 'You leave me and my family alone!'

Long legs flying, she disappeared up the main street.

'Sherry!' Lisa screamed and clutched Dan. 'Don't let her go!'

He gave her a shake. '*Stop it!* What do you think you're going to do? Run after her?'

She collapsed against him, sobbing. Dan was surprised to realize his forearms were already wet from her tears.

A man approached them carrying Lisa's crutches. 'You OK, mate?'

'Yes,' He lifted an unresisting Lisa into his arms, feeling obliged to explain. 'She just got out of hospital yesterday. She had a bad car accident.'

The man noticed Lisa's bright-blue cast poking from the bottom of her trousers and nodded. 'Where's your car? I'll carry these for you.'

☆

Lisa said nothing in the car. She seemed to have shrunk in size, hunched over with misery. Her teeth were chattering.

Despite the sunshine, Dan switched on the heater. He felt drained. He was so anxious to get her home that, without thinking, he took the fastest route, through the roundabout where the accident had occurred.

Lisa sat bolt upright as they approached it. Dan started to apologize until he realized her attention was focused on a brown wooden house with beautiful gardens. Dan often admired the gardens as he drove past. She gave a howl of pain much like the one Sherry had made as she ran away and slapped her palms against the car window like a child, crying brokenly, 'I want to go home! I want to go home!' She would have opened the door if Dan hadn't quickly snapped the auto-locking device on his side.

Lisa turned on him like a virago. 'Let me out!' she shrieked. 'I want to get out!'

She bore a striking resemblance to the Linda of old.

Dan managed to steer the car around the roundabout and hold her against her seat. '*Stop it!*' he roared. '*Enough!*'

Lisa froze; shocked by the sound of his big, deep voice filling the car and the fury in his eyes. She slumped against the door and began to weep.

When they got home, Dan put her to bed and spent the rest of the afternoon watching television in the living room, so he'd hear her if she called out or walked in her sleep. He was heartsick and nearing the end of his tether. She desperately needed to see Craig Fergusson. This was far more than a case of amnesia. His mind shied away from what Lisa kept trying to tell him. It was just too fantastic.

Who was Sherry? Why was she so disturbed by the bizarre things Lisa shouted at her?

Dan was mystified by the significance of the scarf comments, until he recalled that several of the blue movies he'd seen in his med-student days had featured women wearing nothing but a scarf knotted around their necks. Under other circumstances, he probably would have laughed.

When darkness fell and Lisa still hadn't emerged, Dan tapped on the door to ask if she was hungry.

'No, I'm not hungry but thanks for asking,' She clutched the door, her eyes downcast. Behind her, the room was lit by the bedside lamp and the bed covers were tangled as if she'd slept poorly.

He rested his forearm on the doorframe above his head. 'You haven't had anything since lunchtime,' he chided gently.

She shook her head, still not meeting his gaze. 'Really, I'm fine. I was more tired than I realized.'

Dan watched her helplessly. Was this gentle, funny woman sicker than he had originally thought? He was still shaken by the glimpse he'd had of something like the old Linda in the car when she was fighting to get out. He held up a bag with the bookstore logo. 'I got you those books you liked.'

Lisa studied the bag in surprise. Dan saw that, as he'd suspected, she'd been crying.

'Aw, Lisa . . .' he said on a sigh.

She ignored him and reached for the bag. 'Thank you. That was really nice of you.'

Dan handed it over. 'Want to talk about it?'

Her mouth twisted. 'You'd never believe me.'

'Try me.'

She was silent for so long he thought she wasn't going to answer. Eventually she looked up at him and said simply, 'Sherry is my sister.'

Dan gripped the doorframe hard to keep from exploding in sheer frustration. 'Linda, you don't have any brothers or sisters.'

She looked as if she felt sorry for him. 'That might be true for Linda. But I have a sister *and* a brother.' Her voice broke. 'Their names are Sherry and Ben.'

They regarded one another helplessly.

Dan shook his head. 'This can't go on.'

'I know it can't.' Lisa agreed in a low voice. 'It's too

painful — for everybody concerned.' She hugged the bag of books against her chest. 'I think I'll go to bed and read. Or *try* to read.' Turning, she hopped across to the bed.

Dan continued to lean in the doorway watching her. 'Do me a favour, will you?

She looked over her shoulder at him questioningly.

'Leave the bedroom door open before you go to sleep so I can at least check you're still in bed during the night.'

She nodded. 'Alright.'

'Night.' Dan said quietly.

'Night,' Lisa replied softly and turned back to her books.

✯

On Monday morning, Dan was so anxious about leaving Lisa alone that she was forced to put on a show of cheerfulness just to get him out of the house.

'You're sure you'll be alright?' he asked again as he hung about the kitchen, postponing the moment he had to leave. He was wearing a dark navy-blue suit, a crisp white shirt with a fine blue stripe, and a Shrek tie. In one hand he held a battered, black briefcase. His other hand was tucked into his trouser pocket, pulling the material taut across a thigh that looked as if it belonged on an athlete.

'Yes, Dad.'

He wasn't buying her jokes. 'You have the mobile phone I gave you?'

'Yes.'

Lisa refrained from sharing that despite his patient explanation of how the little silver machine worked she'd never gotten along with anything technical and was one of the few people who didn't own a mobile phone.

'My mobile number is in Contacts.' Dan told her patiently.

'So you said.'

He might just as well have said my mobile number is in the Franz Josef Glacier for all the sense it made to Lisa, although on second thoughts at least she knew where the South Island was and how to read a map — or at least, she used to.

'If you go out, make sure you call a cab.'

She nodded obediently. 'I will.'

He insisted on leaving her a hundred dollars in cash when it became obvious that Lisa couldn't use Linda's bank or credit cards because she didn't know the PIN number.

'And I can't do her signature,' she added. 'I've tried to forge it, but I'm afraid my criminal tendencies would only ever lend themselves to driving the getaway car.'

'That isn't funny,' he said.

'You're telling me,' Lisa replied glumly. She'd given up trying to spare his feelings when it came to his insistence that she *was* Linda. After the fiasco in the car park the other day, Lisa didn't see much point. 'Linda was right-handed, wasn't she?' she asked.

Dan began searching for his car keys. He seemed to have a problem keeping track of them.

'Wasn't she?' Lisa persisted.

'Yes!' he began pulling the fruit bowl apart.

'I knew she was because her signature slopes to the right. I'm left-handed and mine slopes to the left.' An orange rolled off the counter. Lisa dangled the key ring from her finger and gave it a shake.

Dan gave up examining the bananas. He scowled at the keys in her hand and muttered something not fit for children's ears.

'That's a physical impossibility.'

He glowered at her. 'I'm a surgeon, I'll make it possible.'

She laughed and was relieved to see a smile tug at the side of his mouth.

Dan continued to loiter, a troubled expression on his face. 'Lisa?'

'Yes?'

'Promise me you won't go to sleep.'

She sighed. 'Dan, I only sleepwalk at night. I never do it during the day.'

The night before, Dan had heard a crash and found Lisa sprawled on the floor in the laundry after she'd fallen over the ironing board. Waking up disorientated and in some pain had terrified her and frightened the life out of him. Somehow, she'd made it past his open bedroom door without him hearing. He still had visions of her walking out into the garden, climbing the fence and falling off the cliff.

'What the hell am I going to do with you?' he muttered blearily as he helped her back to bed.

'I dunno,' she laughed shakily. 'Sew bells on my slippers?'

'I won't go to sleep,' Lisa promised. She wasn't sure if she could hold out all day from falling asleep. Dan said he wouldn't be home until around seven or eight that night and hopping about on crutches was tiring.

'I'll get home as soon as I can.

She glanced at the clock. 'Hadn't you better get going? You have to get over the Harbour Bridge.'

He picked up his briefcase but continued to hesitate.

'What are you doing this morning?' she asked curiously. She'd never lived with a surgeon before.

'I'm in theatre.'

'Really? Doing what?'

'*Hamlet.*'

She rolled her eyes. 'Ha ha!'

'I have three children to operate on.'

'Oh.' Lisa felt useless in comparison. 'Hope it all goes well.'

He nodded and headed towards the laundry and the garage beyond. As he passed by, Lisa reached out a hand impulsively and touched his sleeve, feeling suddenly bereft at the thought of him leaving. He immediately stopped and peered down at her. 'You'll be OK?'

She nodded firmly. 'I'll be fine.'

Dan thought she looked incredibly sweet, dressed in a pink silk robe decorated with pink flowers and with her black hair in braids on either side of her face. She startled him by reaching up and giving the knot of his tie a tweak to straighten it.

'Shrek,' she said. 'Is there a cartoon character you *don't* have on a tie?'

'Yeah,' he said huskily, watching her soft pink mouth. 'I don't have the donkey out of *Shrek*.'

Lisa's hand lingered. She could feel the warmth of his chest, smell soap from his shower and the subtle, spicy aftershave he wore. She wanted to lean up and kiss him but wasn't brave enough and he was too tall for her to reach his mouth unless he cooperated.

Something quivered between them. Something they were both leery of acknowledging.

'I have to go,' Dan said awkwardly.

Lisa dropped her hand. 'Have a good day.'

He stared at her, his expression tense and unreadable before heading towards the laundry door. 'Yeah. You, too.'

Chapter 13

Lisa spent the morning rearranging the bedrooms and exploring the house. There were two more bedrooms. One had been made into a study for Dan and held his computer, more books, a weight bench, and some hand weights lying on the floor beside it. His desk was untidy, but Lisa refrained from trying to straighten things up. She smiled at the crayon and felt-tip drawings pinned onto a big cork board on the wall above, most with messages from children to Dr Dan. *I bruk my leg. Duckta Dan made me a new 1*. They reminded Lisa of the pictures she used to draw for Mr Wrigley, the surgeon who operated on her club foot when she was little.

She was surprised to see a guitar propped in a corner and disappointed to find it was for a right-handed player. She had a guitar back at her old house. It used to belong to Ben; he'd given it to her when they were teenagers. At the time Lisa was going through a Janis Joplin phase and tried to carve a rose on the back of it, but everybody thought it looked like a turtle. Brian and Jill were musical, and their children had been raised playing instruments and singing. Before Ben met Brenda he used to play in a band and write his own songs, but Brenda put a stop to that.

Lisa wondered who owned the guitar. Linda's hobbies seemed to be making herself look good and shopping for clothes. She couldn't figure out what Dan and his wife had in common. Clearly clothes weren't at the top of his list. She thought his mismatched socks and cartoon ties were endearing and had a hunch Linda didn't share her opinion.

His stubborn refusal to change bedrooms wasn't so endearing. It seemed stupid for him to be sleeping in the smallest bed while she felt lost in the master bedroom. He'd probably be annoyed with her for changing rooms but decided she'd use the excuse that sleeping in the smaller bed would make her feel more secure and hopefully less likely to walk in her sleep. She might even convince herself it was true.

Lisa was touched at how kind and patient Dan had been. Without him, she'd have been completely alone. He was trying hard to make the best of a difficult situation. He had no idea he was a widower and Lisa had no idea how to explain that his wife was dead. *She* didn't understand it. So why would he?

She kept thinking about the confrontation with Sherry on the weekend. At least she'd seen her sister, and her mother and father were less than ten minutes away down the hill. Somehow she'd find a way to see them. Somehow she'd make them believe she was still alive.

Lisa fed the mountain of laundry in Dan's room into the washing machine and managed to get it outside to the line by using one of her crutches to push the basket along the path in the back garden. She was balancing on her crutches, her mouth full of pegs and struggling to throw wet clothes onto the line when she got the feeling she was being watch. She paused and looked around. There was nobody in sight, but the feeling persisted.

She nearly choked on the clothes pegs when a voice called tentatively, 'Do you need a hand, Mrs Brogan?'

Lisa spat out the pegs and slapped a hand against her galloping heart. A fair-headed boy in his teens was peering at her from the garden next door, partially obscured by a camellia bush.

'Don't *do* that!' she cried.

'Sorry,' he muttered and began to retreat from sight.

'No! Don't go! I'm sorry I yelled - you gave me a fright.'

His narrow, anxious face reappeared between the glossy dark- green leaves. He blinked at her owlishly from behind silver-framed glasses. 'Sorry,' he repeated.

'That's OK.' Lisa was delighted to have somebody to talk to. 'Who are you?'

'Um ... Slade. Slade Cruickshank,' he stepped cautiously through the gap in the fence. 'I'm one of your neighbours.'

Lisa tried not to stare at his shiny, black leather trousers and pointed black boots with silver buckles. A pale-pink paisley shirt was buttoned all the way to his neck and the tails hung over his trousers which made his skinny legs look like two sticks of licorice. His gorgeous silvery-blonde hair and tilted hazel eyes reminded Lisa of a pixie.

'I've said hello before, but I don't suppose you remember,' Slade mumbled.

'I'm sorry, I don't' Lisa agreed. 'I've lost my memory. Or at least *some* of my memory.'

His pixie eyes widened. 'Wow.'

She grimaced. 'Yes.'

Slade ventured further into the garden. 'Mr Brogan said you'd been a bad accident,' he studied Lisa's cast. 'But he didn't say you'd lost your memory.'

'No, well it's not the sort of thing you chat about over the fence, is it?'

He opened his mouth, closed it again and settled on shrugging a shoulder.

Lisa began to giggle.

Slade laughed self-consciously.

'You've lost your American accent,' he remarked when they managed to settle themselves down again.

Lisa raised her shoulders, let them fall. 'Lost the memory, lost the accent, I think it'd be safe to say I've lost it.'

He blinked. 'I meant it when I said I'd help you with the washing if you want.'

'That's nice of you, but I have to get the hang of doing things on my own. You could carry the basket back inside for me when I'm done if you wouldn't mind?'

'OK.'

Lisa finished hanging out the last of Dan's shirts which wasn't easy; they were the size of small sails.

Slade carried the basket inside and accepted her offer of tea.

Lisa learned he was nineteen and suffered with asthma. He was studying at Auckland University and lived next door with his grandparents. She got the impression that Slade was a loner. His passion was motorbikes, and he owned a small Honda. In Lisa's experience, there was a Slade in every class — the clever, weird kid always on the fringes, never quite one of the in-crowd. The more she listened to him, the more she liked him, and when they discovered they were both left-handed they indulged in a bitching session about the difficulties and irritations of living in a right-handed world before Slade returned to the subject of motorbikes.

'I'd like a Ducati, but they're really expensive,' he confessed. 'I work at the garden centre in town on the weekends sometimes. I'm saving up to buy one.'

Lisa went on full alert. Her father managed the garden centre. 'So you know Brian Jackson?' she asked carefully.

'Yeah, he's a nice old guy. Do you know him?'

Lisa nodded and tried not to smile when she imagined how her father would react to being called an old guy. He was only fifty-five.

'He's really good to me. Makes sure I work with the succulents and trees in case the pollen upsets me.' Slade frowned. 'Not everybody is that thoughtful.'

Lisa sniffed. 'You mean Ray Tanner?'

He looked surprised. 'Do you know him too?'

She nodded and changed the subject.

Ray Tanner was supposed to be the assistant manager. He was lazy and arrogant and a thorn in the side of her placid, gentle father. He had the gall to ask Sherry if she wanted to go out with him the same day Brian nearly fired him over his treatment of some of the junior staff. Sherry told Ray she'd rather run away and join the circus.

Lisa was alarmed when Ray turned his attentions to her. She wasn't sharp-tongued and tough like Sherry and stopped visiting the shop when she knew he was working. In the meantime, their father began the laborious process of verbal and written warnings, with the hope that eventually he could fire Ray without being landed with a personal grievance claim. Ray was canny enough to know just how far he could push before Brian could fire him.

Slade finished his chamomile tea and rose. 'I have to go down to Browns Bay and do some things for my grandmother.'

Lisa rinsed his mug. 'I'm going to call a taxi and go down there myself. I wanted to go for a walk on the beach or rather, a *hop* on the beach.'

Slade studied the blue skies and sunshine through the window. 'The tide's out, so you'll be OK. If it weren't for your leg, I'd offer you a lift. I'm a very safe driver.'

After the chamomile tea, Lisa didn't doubt it. She chewed her lip. She shouldn't even consider it. Dan would be furious.

But she was feeling lonely, and it would be hours before he came home. He didn't need to know and the thought of getting into a strange car without him at the wheel made her feel nauseous.

'Do you want to catch a ride with me in the taxi?' she asked hopefully.

Slade shook his head. 'It's nice of you to offer but I like getting out when the weather's so nice.'

He sounded like a ninety-year-old trapped in a nineteen-year-old body.

She sighed. 'I can't get on your motorbike, there's nowhere to put my crutches.'

'If you click them right down, they might fit in the panniers.'

Lisa brightened. 'Really?'

He nodded.

Just before they left, Lisa saw Linda Brogan's little silver phone vibrating across the tiled kitchen counter as if an unseen hand was guiding it.

'Slade?'

He had just returned with a spare helmet for her. 'Yes?'

She pointed at the phone which had stopped vibrating 'Can you check that for me?'

He gave her an odd look and picked up the phone. 'You've missed several calls and there's a message.' He looked across at her, thumb hovering over the buttons. 'Want me to check who they're from?'

Lisa grimaced. 'It'll be Dan checking I'm alright. *Why*

didn't the damned thing ring?'

His agile thumb darted across the buttons. 'Because it's been set to vibrate.'

'It's supposed to be a bloody mobile phone not a vibrator!' Lisa protested indignantly. She regretted her outburst when Slade blushed and remembered he was only nineteen and it seemed likely that the most intimate relationship he had was when he climbed aboard his motorbike.

'There is a message from Mr Brogan: *R U OK? Call me ASAP.*'

Dan must have been desperate if he'd resorted to leaving her a message it was doubtful she'd be able to read. Lisa peered over Slade's shoulder, struggling to read the text in the little window. She doubted Linda Brogan's dyslexia had anything to do with her inability to make sense of it.

Slade looked worried. 'He sounds a bit annoyed.' He showed Lisa how to find Dan's mobile number and send a text message. 'What do you want to say?'

'I'm OK but I'm going down to Browns Bay with you and I don't feel sleepy.'

'OK.' He began to text.

'On second thoughts, just tell him I'm OK. There's no need to mention I'm going for a ride on your motorbike.'

Slade eyed her uneasily. 'I don't want to do anything to upset Mr Brogan. He's always been nice to me. Perhaps it isn't a good—'

'No! You *have* to take me with you! *Please!*' She was an octave off whining.

He gazed at her in astonishment. 'Wow. You sure are different,'

If only he knew.

'What was I like before?'

He hesitated.

'You can be honest.'

'Well ... sometimes you'd talk and sometimes you'd ignore me or look right through me like I wasn't there.'

Lisa hoped George was helping Linda work on her manners.

'I apologise for being so rude, Slade.'

Having opened the can, he decided to dig out a few more worms. 'One time Nan and I heard you out in the garden telling Mr Brogan that we weren't the sort of people you wanted to have as friends.'

Lisa squirmed. 'What did he say?'

'I couldn't hear him properly, but he sounded angry and you both went inside.'

'I am *so* sorry, Slade!'

Lisa doubted there was a hole big enough that she could hide in. The Grand Canyon would fit the bill. Was she going to spend the rest of her – *this* – life bumping into people Linda Brogan had treated badly? It wouldn't surprise her if there was a hitman creeping about Auckland with a contract to knock her off.

'Why on earth did you bother to help me in the garden? Most people would have ignored me if there'd been in your shoes.'

'I like Mr Brogan. He's a nice guy and he's not here.'

He was helping her out of loyalty to Dan. Lisa could understand that.

'You seem really different, Mrs Brogan.' Slade repeated.

Lisa sighed. 'You have no idea.' She paused. 'Would you mind not calling me Mrs Brogan?'

'What do you want me to call you? Linda?'

'No!'

Slade blinked.

Lisa forced a smile. 'Er ... no, not Linda. I'd prefer it if you called me Lisa.'

Slade shrugged his pink paisley shoulders as if to say *whatever*. Lisa suspected he didn't think she had both oars in the water but was too kind to say so. There wasn't much she could do about that apart from be on her best and *sanest* behaviour from now on.

She almost changed her mind when she saw the gold-coloured Honda parked in the driveway. 'You will be careful, won't you?'

Slade placed the spare helmet carefully on her head and replied solemnly, 'I promise.'

☆

Lisa *loved* the motorbike. She felt more comfortable riding it than getting in a car. Cars brought back the memory of the accident.

True to his word, Slade drove carefully. They'd solved the problem of her crutches by placing them along the vinyl seat and sitting on top of them. Wearing the bright-red helmet and Linda Brogan's sleek, black Ray Bans, Lisa buzzed off down the hill behind him wearing a big smile.

Slade managed to park in the main street. Lisa was touched at the way he carefully helped her off the back of the bike and clicked her crutches back to exactly the right setting.

'I have to go to the drycleaners and the bank for my nan,' he said.

Lisa nodded back happily. 'I have to buy some new knickers.'

Slade reddened. 'I'll see you back here in about half an

hour,' he said and beat a hasty retreat.

Lisa spent twenty minutes buying some underwear and visited the butcher to buy a leg of lamb for dinner. She was back waiting for Slade on one of the metal benches edging the pavement, well before their appointed time to meet.

As she watched the traffic and people going by, she spied Ben's girlfriend, Brenda, disappearing into the two-dollar shop with her younger sister in tow. Lisa's breath caught at the sight of somebody from her old life. She stared wide-eyed at the shop, her heart hammering.

And frowned.

The two-dollar shop.

Slade appeared at her side carrying a red, white, and black plaid kilt, draped in plastic.

'Sorry, I took so—' he began.

'Slade, what's the date today?' Lisa's eyes were glued to the shop across the road.

'April 29.'

She scowled and grabbed her crutches. 'The slapper!'

Slade squinted across the road and back at Lisa. 'Who?' he asked in bewilderment.

'My brother's girlfriend, that's who! I'm going to kill her!'

☆

Brenda was shopping for Ben's birthday on May the first. Her teenaged sister, Christine, had decided to keep her company and was dawdling along behind Brenda making smart remarks about everything she picked up. They weren't close. Christine thought Brenda was a tightwad and Brenda thought Christine was a tart.

'You're not buying a present for Ben's birthday, are you?' Christine asked suspiciously.

Brenda ignored her.

She had an unpleasant memory from this time last year when Ben's sister Lisa had discovered her in this very same shop buying his presents. Brenda still shuddered when she remembered how Lisa had escorted her outside and told her that if she bought Ben so much as a keyring from the shop, Lisa was going to tell him.

Brenda was humiliated at being caught and tried to deny she was buying for Ben and then she tried to trot out the old favourite about it being the thought that counts, but it had fallen on deaf ears; *everybody* knew Brenda was tight as arseholes when it came to money. Brenda once overheard Sherry Jackson say Ben's girlfriend was so mean that if she saw a fly land in the sugar bowl, she'd shake it before she killed it.

It was all very well for Sherry and Lisa. They were single and commitment-free, whereas she and Ben were saving for a deposit on a house *and* a wedding and had to be careful with their money. Brenda conveniently forgot that Sherry was already saddled with a mortgage she was paying on her own and that Lisa's income was unreliable due to her health. Anyway, Ben wasn't the slightest bit interested in expensive presents, she thought defensively. He would have been happy with a card.

'Well, *are you?*' Christine insisted.

Brenda continued to feign deafness. She'd just picked up a keyring to go with the plastic phone holder and adhesive ballpoint for the car when she felt a tap on her shoulder. Turning, she found herself looking up into the fierce blue eyes of a beautiful, black-haired woman on crutches. Behind her a thin, fair-haired youth wearing skinny leather trousers looked on anxiously.

'Yes?' Brenda quavered.

'Brenda, that had better not be a present for Ben's birthday,' the woman hissed.

'Wha ... what?' Brenda squeaked while Christine goggled at the stranger over her shoulder.

'You heard me! What did I tell you last year?'

'What ... Who *are* you?' Brenda backed away from the intensity in the woman's gaze, straight into Christine, who shouted, '*Ow!*' and shoved her in the back.

'Never mind who I am! Stop being such a miserly cow and put that lot back!' the beauty queen snapped. 'I *told* you last year this wasn't on. *Didn't I, Brenda?*'

The skinny boy spoke up tentatively. 'Um ... Lisa?'

Brenda's eyes almost popped out of her head. The hairs stood up on the back of her neck.

'Lisa?' she whispered. '*Lisa?*'

She dropped the basket and ran from the shop, almost knocking over a display stand in her haste.

Christine followed more slowly, fascinated by the beautiful nutcase who had upset sister and who that geek Simon Cruickshank who used to go to her school had called Lisa. It was radical. 'Is your name really Lisa?' she demanded.

'Go away, Christine,' the woman snarled.

Christine felt goosebumps break out all over her body. The way the stranger spoke and screwed up her nose reminded her spookily of Lisa Jackson. But Lisa was dead. Christine had gone to the funeral and seen them put the coffin in the grave.

She fled in the same direction as her sister.

Lisa was suddenly aware she had the attention of the entire shop, including the owner, who was glowering at her from behind the counter. 'I ... let's get out of here.'

There was no sign of Brenda or her sister in the main street. Slade helped Lisa to the metal seat next to where he'd parked his bike. He downsized the crutches and silently handed her the red helmet.

Lisa stared at the helmet but made no attempt to put it on. 'Aren't you going to ask me who that was?'

Slade shook his head and strapped on his shiny black helmet. 'No.'

Lisa stared. 'You're not?'

'I know who the younger one is. Her name's Christine Buckner. I used to go to the same high school.'

'Oh.' He must think she was completely off her rocker. 'Aren't you the slightest bit curious? I mean I would be if a person I had just met harassed somebody while they were out shopping - which isn't something I usually do.' Lisa added hastily.

Slade shrugged. 'Most families have weird people in them.' He slipped on his black wraparound sunglasses and muttered, 'I should know.'

Lisa decided he had a remarkably mature attitude for such a nerdy-looking nineteen-year-old.

'Is it OK if we go?' he asked politely, climbing onto the bike. 'I have to get my grandad's kilt back. Nan and him have their Scottish-dancing class tonight.'

He held Lisa's hand to steady her as she climbed on behind him, clutching the bags containing her underwear and Dan's dinner.

'Slade?'

He looked over his shoulder. 'Yes?'

'Is there somewhere I can put my knickers?'

He blushed from his neck to his sunglasses.

When they got home Slade introduced Lisa to his

grandparents, Edie and Norm. Edie's lukewarm greeting confirmed Linda Brogan hadn't been one of her favourite people but her face lit up at the mention of Dan.

Norm was a big, lanky man in his seventies, with false teeth that clacked when he spoke. He bred budgies in his spare time. Edie was just as big with salt-and-pepper hair and filled her spare time with gardening, something she was spectacularly bad at. They were both passionate about Scottish dancing, especially Norm as his knee replacement earlier in the year had given him a second lease of life on the dance floor.

'They nearly lost me in the hospital when I had it done, you know,' he told Lisa when she followed Slade into the untidy dining area at the back of the house.

Lisa thought she heard Slade groan, but his face remained expressionless as he handed his grandfather the tartan kilt.

Edie spoke up from the dining table where she was perusing the daily paper. 'Well, hospitals are big places,' Licking a forefinger, she turned the page.

'That's not what I meant, Edie, and you know it!' Norm cried indignantly.

She ignored him and began to do the crossword.

A budgie flew past and landed on the plastic bag covering Norm's kilt, where he'd hung it on the back of a chair. He flapped a hand. 'Get off, you cheeky bugger!'

As he was chasing the budgie into the conservatory Lisa noticed row upon row of sickly-looking pot plants.

Slade regarded the plants with pity. 'That's Nan's garden,'

'Just need a bit of water,' Edie said defensively.

Lisa looked at the water-logged saucers and saw an

opportunity. She offered to take the worst of them home and try to save them, saying she had too much time on her hands and nothing to do.

'I s'pose so,' Edie looked down her hooked nose. 'I could sort them out myself but seeing as you need something to do.'

Slade carried the plants into Dan's garage. 'Whatever you do, don't send them back to Nan.' He nudged a pot with his boot. 'They're the lucky ones that got away.'

Lisa beamed at the ugly, yellowing plants fainting over the sides of their plastic pots. They were her passport to her father.

Chapter 14

Dan had been eaten up with guilt all day about leaving Lisa alone. Her failure to reply when he called made him feel even worse and her message about going to Browns Bay nearly gave him a heart attack. In the few days since she'd come home Dan had discovered that things *happened* when Lisa was around, bizarre things that couldn't be explained or anticipated. The thought of her out alone on her crutches was alarming. However, the phone call from Edie Cruickshank, his warning him that his wife had just ridden off on the back of her grandson's motorbike that escalated his alarm into outright fury.

'I didn't like to call you at the hospital but do you think it's a good idea for her to be riding around on the back of that bike with a broken leg?' Edie asked.

Dan swallowed his anger long enough to thank her and agree that it wasn't a good idea at all. He refrained from adding it was *fucking insane!* If the ride on the bike didn't do some damage to Lisa, then he would. Knowing how Edie felt about her, he appreciated her call. 'At least someone has got some fucking common sense!' he snarled to himself as he fought his way through the traffic across the Harbour Bridge.

He understood that she wanted to go out. He couldn't expect her to sit at home twiddling her thumbs waiting for him to come home each night. But he'd left her more than enough money to get a cab to Browns Bay and back, so why the hell hadn't she taken one?

The memory of her frightened face when she'd climbed

into the car the night he brought her home from the hospital, tugged at him. How had a nineteen-year-old boy with a motorbike managed to inspire her confidence? Admittedly, Simon Cruickshank was the least threatening, most uncool teenager that ever existed. His biggest display of rebellion was calling himself Slade and Dan had the bad luck to get stuck behind him on the road and knew he adhered to the speed limit. Still, the thought of Lisa perched on the back of the motorbike with her broken leg and her still-healing brain at risk of being smashed against the asphalt made him feel sick.

Did she care so little for herself? Did she care so little for him?

He was being ridiculous; she didn't even remember him. He'd foolishly begun to believe that something had begun to build between them, something tenuous but honest. Losing his temper wouldn't solve anything. On the rare occasion it happened, he always, *always* regretted it later.

When he arrived home and parked in the garage, Dan thought he'd gone to the wrong house. A row of straggly, sickly-looking pot plants were lined up along the garage wall and the delicious smell of roasting meat was coming from the house.

Linda's vegetarian beliefs meant she had strong ideas about cooking meat. When she finally accepted that Dan was never going to become a vegetarian, she prepared some sort of a meat dish for him most nights but when he stepped into the kitchen it looked as if Lisa had roasted an entire sheep.

'She sent him a big smile when she saw him hovering in the doorway. 'Hi!'

She was leaning against the kitchen counter, balanced on

her good leg and attempting to carve a leg of lamb. As Dan watched, she blithely swiped the carving knife only inches from her abdomen, slicing into the fragrant meat on the board in front of her, steam rising gently about her head.

He dropped his briefcase and rushed across the kitchen to take the knife from her. 'I'll do that!'

Lisa seemed happy to relinquish the knife and hopped across to the wall oven, balancing on the backs of chairs and the kitchen counter as she went. 'Hope you're hungry. There's heaps to eat.'

Dan opened his mouth to say he was starving but stopped when he saw that she was pulling a roasting tin full of potatoes from the oven with one oven-mitted hand whilst clutching the oven door for balance. It was worse than trying to keep track of a toddler.

'Give me that!' He snatched up a dishcloth and took the spitting pan from her.

Lisa frowned. 'Did you have a bad day or something?'

Dumping the hot tin on the kitchen counter, he turned to glare at her. 'I had a great day, right up until I got a phone call that you'd been riding around Browns Bay on the back of a motorbike!'

'What? Who told you that?'

'Never you mind!' Dan fired the dishcloth into the kitchen sink and gripped the edge of the counter-top to stop himself throttling her. 'Just as well somebody did. Or were you planning on telling me?' he demanded grimly.

She opened her mouth, closed it, tried to look defiant and failed.

'Did you lose your common sense *as well* as your memory, Lin -'

Her brows slammed together.

'Lisa!'

'That's not fair!'

'None of this is fair! Do you think it's smart to be riding around on the back of a motorbike with your leg in plaster and still recovering from a subdural haemorrhage?'

That seemed to set her back on her heels. 'I was wearing a helmet.'

It was the second time in two days Lisa had seen Dan lose his temper. He'd been irritated with her at times in the hospital, but he'd never lost his temper.

'All it would take is one crack—' He banged the heel of his hand against the side of his skull, making her jump '—to your head to put you right back where you were a few weeks ago. Your brain was *bleeding*, Lisa, it's still healing. Don't you understand that?'

She dropped her gaze. 'No — I — I didn't know.'

'What you *mean* is you didn't *think*.'

Dan turned to the kitchen sink and stared out the window above it, his shoulders hunched.

There was a long silence.

He felt the touch of her hand between his shoulder blades, tentatively stroking his bunched muscles.

'I'm sorry,' she said in a small voice.

Dan closed his eyes. Linda had never been able to apologise because it would have been an admission that she was in the wrong in the first place.

When he turned, Lisa dropped her hand and retreated. He tucked his hands into his armpits, crossed his ankles and studied her. With those ridiculous pigtails she'd taken to wearing and her face scrubbed clean of makeup, she was downright adorable. And desirable. He was amazed he had any sexual feelings for her at all. The shock and disgust he'd felt at the sight of her half-naked in Millar's arms had killed any sexual attraction he'd once felt. It had been a big part of their relationship and was how he knew things were over.

It was the loss of Linda's physical hold over him that had made her become increasingly reckless in the days leading up to the accident. She'd tried to seduce him one last time by wearing the lingerie he most loved to see her in and waiting on the bed where he had taken to sleeping alone. Dan remembered stepping out of the bathroom, naked apart from a towel wrapped about his waist. Linda had climbed from the bed, smiling, and tried to cup him through the towel. He'd been so disgusted that the shove he'd given her sent her tumbling backwards onto the bed.

The ensuing argument was ugly. Linda promised she'd change if he would take her home to the States. Dan knew things had gone beyond that. He told her he didn't love her anymore and watched the colour drain from her face.

'No! That isn't true! I don't believe you!'

Later, when he found out she'd been pregnant, Dan wondered if she'd tried to sleep with him so she could claim the baby was his.

'It's ruined,' Lisa said forlornly.

Dan blinked and refocused his attention.

She was looking at the roast lamb and potatoes going cold on the counter beside him. It was eerie looking at her. He saw Linda's beautiful, perfect face but the forlorn expression wasn't Linda's. They belonged to the Linda who had woken up in the hospital. They belonged to Lisa.

He reached out and stroked the back of his index finger across her cheek.

Lisa tensed. She looked up at him questioningly for a few beats and then her lashes dipped, and she slowly began to stroke her cheek back and forth against his finger like a cat.

Dan froze. His mouth went dry. His cock went hard. Snatching his hand away, he stepped around her and made for his bedroom, running like an adolescent virgin. Except when he got there, it didn't look like his bedroom anymore. For a start it was tidy and the duvet cover on the bed had been changed, replaced by a lacy white one with frilled pillowcases. His books were gone too. When he checked the bedroom next door, he saw his black and white duvet cover with the Japanese symbols was on the king-sized bed and his books were stacked neatly on the bedside tables.

He removed his suit jacket and tie and once he was sure he could trust his dick not to stand up and beg, made his way back to the kitchen.

Lisa was putting a plate of food into the microwave. She avoided his gaze. 'It's gone cold. I'll heat it up.'

He sensed her hurt and confusion and told himself it was for the best. The last thing she *or* he needed was to give in to the spiraling sexual tension that seemed to roar to life whenever they touched. In some ways it reminded him of when he had first met her. And yet it was also nothing like it at all. It was sweeter. Stronger. Lisa wasn't an immature kid. And Dan was a lot more wary and battle-hardened.

The smart thing to do was ignore what had just happened.

He asked briskly, 'Why did you change bedrooms?'

She concentrated on pushing the buttons on the microwave. 'I hope you don't think it's a cheek. It seemed stupid for you to be sleeping in the small bed while I had the big one.'

He fought off a smile at her quaint turn of phrase and managed to frown instead. 'I was fine in there.'

She stared at the plate rotating inside the microwave as if it held the secrets of the universe. 'But I wasn't fine in the other one. I kept getting lost in that bed. It was like sleeping in the middle of the Bermuda Triangle. It's too big.'

The microwave beeped. She opened the door to remove the plate and held it out without meeting his eyes. 'This one's yours.'

Dan took the plate, trying hard not to give in to laughter. Placing it on the breakfast counter he went to pull a bottle of red wine from the rack mounted on the wall. 'Would you like a glass of wine?'

'Am I allowed one after misbehaving so badly?'

'Considering it's a first offence, I'm prepared to give you another chance.'

She shot him a poisonous look.

He poured the wine. 'Why do we suddenly have a lot of sick-looking plants in the garage?'

'Oh, those,' Lisa studied the plate of food in her hand. 'They belong to Edie Cruickshank. I offered to rescue them for her.'

She didn't share that the sight of the dying plants had given her an idea about how to see her father. From now on she would be on the lookout for every dying, diseased or distressed plant she could get her hands on so she could take them to the garden centre and ask his advice.

'I see,' Dan lied.

They sat at the breakfast bar and ate in silence for several long moments.

Dan wolfed down the meal. He was starving and everything was delicious. He was relieved to see Lisa was eating and not indulging in a sulk. He took a sip of wine. 'Promise me you won't do anything foolish like riding on

Slade's motorbike again.'

She considered his request. 'Why? Will you ground me if I say no?'

'No,' he sliced a roast potato neatly in half. 'I'll just take your crutches away.'

'You can't do that!'

Dan merely raised his brows and watched her over the rim of his wineglass.

Lisa was so annoyed her pigtails quivered. She shoved her plate away. 'Are the neighbours going to be spying on me every time I step outside the door?'

'They're not spying on you, Lisa. Edie was concerned.'

She snorted. 'Slade introduced me to his grandparents when we came home. His grandfather showed me the scars from his knee replacement and told me the entire story of the surgery right from the first suppository to the last stitch removal.'

'I've heard it too. Several times in fact.'

She flipped a pigtail over her shoulder and began running her fingertips up and down the stem of her wineglass. 'Edie seems to be a bit of a hard case.'

Dan watched her fondle the wineglass.

'Norm said they almost lost him in the hospital,' Lisa continued. 'I assumed he must have had some sort of crisis, but Edie, who was sitting at the kitchen table reading the newspaper, suddenly piped up and said, "Yeah, well they're big places, hospitals." I had a hard time keeping a straight face.'

He laughed.

Lisa was glad he wasn't angry with her anymore. His grey eyes were smiling, and the deep grooves that bracketed his mouth were less pronounced. Her eyes lingered on his lips.

She wondered what he'd do if she leaned over and kissed him. Probably confiscate her crutches and send her to bed.

'Why did you get on that motorbike with Simon? I left you money to get a cab.'

Lisa blinked. 'Huh?'

'Why did you get on Simon's motorbike?'

She was disappointed to see that happy, playful Dan had been replaced by serious Dan. 'Who's Simon?'

'Slade. His real name's Simon.'

'Oh.' She took a big sip of wine. 'He's very sweet.'

Dan topped up her glass. 'Some of the neighbours act as if he's a fully paid-up member of a biker gang.'

She choked on her wine and slapped her chest. 'Wingnuts! He hardly ever gets that bike out of third gear!'

Correctly surmising the definition of a wingnut, Dan silently wondered yet again how his American wife had become so fluent in the local vernacular. 'So why didn't you get a taxi?'

She went back to toying with the stem of her wineglass.

Dan gritted his teeth against the surge of lust her busy little fingers were provoking and hoped his expression conveyed that he wasn't going anywhere until he got an answer.

'Did anybody ever tell you you're a pain in the arse?'

He shook his head. 'No. Never.'

Lisa huffed.

Dan sipped his wine and waited.

'Being in a car frightens me,' she said at last. 'It reminds me of the accident.'

He felt as if he'd been punched in the chest. 'I know you had trouble getting in the car the night you left the hospital, but you seemed to cope OK when we were out on the weekend.'

'I'm a good actress.'

His sympathy withered and died. When it came to acting, Linda could have won a raft of Oscars. 'If you'd told me, I might have been able to help.'

Lisa shook her head wearily. 'Nobody can help, Dan. Believe me when I say my situation is unique.'

'I wish you wouldn't keep saying that. I know you don't believe me, but this *has* happened to other people and they *have* got their memories back.'

'I keep telling you, I *haven't* lost my memory.'

Lisa sensed Dan's withdrawal and the familiar feeling of hopelessness wash over her. 'Leave this,' she said abruptly, indicating their plates and cutlery. Grasping the breakfast bar, she turned towards him and began to slide from the tall chair. 'I'll clear it away in the morning.'

Dan reached out to help her. Their knees bumped. Lisa slipped and grabbed at him to stop herself falling. He caught her around the ribs, his thumbs framing the swell of her breasts.

They froze and stared at each other, their faces inches apart.

Lisa had landed astride one of his thighs. She felt heat explode in her groin at the hard muscle pressed so intimately against her. She hadn't been touched by a man there in over three years and instinctively deepened the contact. Her breath hitched and her breasts rose.

Dan's gaze dropped. His thumbs stroked slowly upwards, pausing just short of their target.

Lisa wanted to mewl with frustration. Instead, she remained motionless, her breathing unsteady, willing him to slide his thumbs higher.

Dan told himself to ignore the warmth and softness beneath his hands and set her on her feet, to remember that this was Linda, and she was poison.

But she didn't smell like Linda. She smelled like Lisa. She *sounded* like Lisa.

He dipped his head, set lips against the soft skin at the side of her neck and tasted her with his tongue. At the same time, he braced his foot on the rung of her abandoned chair and increased the pressure of his leg. The heat of her scalded him through his trousers.

Lisa slid her arms around his neck and her palm between his shoulder blades. His back felt warm and solid. Her head fell sideways to give him better access to her throat as she tunneled her free hand into the dark hair at the nape of his neck. She pressed down against his thigh and moaned.

Dan made a hoarse sound deep in his throat, the stubble of his five o'clock shadow scraping the tender skin of her chin as he found her lips in a hot, open-mouthed kiss.

They went from zero to ninety in the space of a few seconds.

She tasted of lamb and wine and *her*.

He tasted of wine and lamb and *him*.

Dan was unaware that she'd tugged his shirt from his trousers until he felt her fingers slid up his chest and touch his nipples. He sucked in a breath. A lot of women were unaware how sensitive that part of a man's body was. He was surprised at how clumsy and untutored her caresses seemed. He muttered her name, tugged at the buttons between her breast to reveal a lacy shell-pink bra. Lowering his head, he closed his lips around one peaked nipple and sucked her deep inside his mouth.

Lisa closed her eyes and her head fell back.

Dan reclaimed her mouth and caught her full lower lip in his teeth before sliding his tongue inside her mouth. Lisa rocked against him, pressing the hot, aching flesh between her legs against his thigh. He slipped his fingers inside her panties and almost disgraced himself in his underwear when he touched the hot, wet flesh hidden there.

'Jeezuss...'

He needed to find a place to lay her down and slide inside her.

Lisa gasped, thrusting herself urgently against his hand. While his fingers slipped back and forth, Dan held her right breast with his free hand and feasted on it like it was a banquet laid out just for him. He felt her flesh heat and raised his face to watch her as she began the climb, stunned at how potently female and beautiful she looked with her head tilted back, her skin flushed, her eyes closed, and her lips parted as she rocked against his fingers.

Lisa moaned and dug her fingers into his shoulders.

He was clinging to his self-control by a thread. 'Just let it go, Linda.'

She stiffened and began to convulse.

Once. Twice. And again.

Lisa collapsed against him, her face buried in his shoulder, her arms scissored around his neck. Dan reached behind his neck to gently remove her arms; the headlock she had him in would have done a pro-wrestler proud. He continued to support her while they both got their breath back, shuddering when she slid a hand across his chest, letting it come to rest against his thudding heart.

'You OK?' he asked huskily.

She nodded against his shoulder. 'But you didn't . . .' She slid her hand down his abdomen towards the hard ridge of flesh beneath his zipper.

Dan caught her hand before she reached her destination. 'Don't! If you touch me I'll probably embarrass myself.'

The ragged edge to his voice helped Lisa feel a little less self-conscious. She risked a look at him. 'Like I didn't?'

He smiled at the telltale pink flush on her cheeks. 'I enjoyed watching you.'

She made a strangled noise and buried her face in his shoulder again.

He laughed. And then he frowned. He had called her Linda as she came. She *was* Linda. How had he let himself forget?

Lisa felt the change in him. When she looked up, she saw that his face had become unreadable. He'd left her again. 'Dan?' she murmured, bewildered. What had she done wrong?

He lifted her off his leg, averting his eyes from her breasts in the fine cobweb lace of the pink bra. 'Where are your crutches?' he asked curtly.

She gestured vaguely to the opposite end of the breakfast bar.

Dan handed them over. 'It's late. You've had a long day; you should go to bed. I'll finish cleaning up out here.'

Stunned, Lisa tried to figure out what had caused Dan to distance himself from her as if the intimacy of the last few minutes had never taken place. She suddenly remembered he'd called her Linda. He'd been making love to his wife, not *her*. She wanted to crawl into a hole and hide. She pulled the front of her shirt together, fumbling to get the buttons through the holes and threaded her arms through the plastic cups of the crutches.

How could she have been so *stupid?* It had taken just one

kiss to fan the sexual tension between them into a bonfire. Clearly, Dan regretted it and didn't want to take it through to its natural conclusion. She fled from the kitchen as fast as she could.

That night, Lisa lay in Dan's old bed reliving the touch of his hands and mouth and tongue against her, knowing that although he was sleeping just two rooms away, he might as well have been on the moon. How was she going to face him in the morning?

Staring into the darkness, Lisa was forced to admit that the truth of the matter was, she couldn't bear not to.

Chapter 15

Sherry heard all about Brenda's run-in with Linda Brogan from her sister, Christine.

The high school Christine spasmodically attended ran an education programme for problem kids that was facilitated by the police. Christine Buckner definitely fell into the category of problem kid. Sherry thought Brenda's sister was a pain. The only thing they agreed on was that Brenda was a pain as well.

'Did you hear some woman had a go at Bren in the two-dollar shop on Monday?' Christine demanded the moment she set eyes on Sherry in the school car park.

'No,' Sherry locked the door of the squad car. She was in a foul mood because she hated doing these community projects and pulled it today because Dillon Taylor had to testify in court. Sherry wasn't keen on kids. As far as she was concerned, they should be separated from the public until they were at least eighteen. Preferably in a zoo. Although she knew better than to share her thoughts on children and how to raise them with her superior officers, it was generally recognized that Sherry Jackson was not the first port of call when it came to community-policing projects. She much preferred the dirty work.

She started walking towards the administrative block, nodding at a couple of kids on the way. They flinched when they saw her; she'd arrested them both in the past.

Christine thought Sherry Jackson was cool for a cop. She tried to stroll along nonchalantly along beside her, but her legs were too short to keep up with Sherry's so was forced to trot instead, which she hated because it made her look stupid.

'She tried to pretend she wasn't, but I think she was buying Ben's birthday present,' Christine panted and was relieved when Sherry stopped.

'What?'

'I think Bren was buying Ben's birthday present in the two-dollar shop.'

Sherry's eyes narrowed. 'The slapper!'

Christine nodded delightedly. 'Yeah. Well, this woman bailed Brenda up in the middle of the shop and tore a strip off her as if she knew *exactly* what Bren was up to. It was *so* cool.'

Sherry's scowl faded. She stared at Christine for several moments. 'What did she look like?'

'Who?'

'The woman who shouted at Brenda, you gormless article!'

Several boys passing by gave them a wide berth.

It was Christine's turn to scowl. 'I dunno. Old.' She eyed Sherry viciously. 'About *your* age, I guess.'

The insult bounced right off her. 'What colour was her hair? What colour eyes did she have? Describe her to me.'

'I dunno!' Christine was beginning to regret she'd brought it up. When Sherry went all slit-eyed again, she added hastily, 'A bit like you. Black hair and blue eyes — big, blue eyes. Oh, and she had a broken leg.'

Sherry swallowed audibly. Despite the warmth of the sunshine on her blue uniform shirt, she felt suddenly cold. 'What ... what else did she say?'

'Something about telling Brenda last year that it wasn't on buying Ben's presents at the two-dollar shop.' Christine frowned. 'But Bren didn't seem to know her, which was weird.'

Sherry felt sick. Lisa had caught Brenda in the shop last year and told her off about it.

'Are you OK?' Christine peered at her pale face. 'You're not going to faint or something, are you?'

Sherry glared at her. 'You wish!'

Christine felt offended. Sherry was her hero. Her role model. It was just a shame she was a cop because Christine's inclinations leaned more towards the dark side of the force.

★

Sherry made it through the morning. Just. She almost made one of the boys cry when the little arsehole persistently heckled her with smartarse comments from the back of the room. Eventually she lost her patience and snarled back. When they were putting the chairs away at the end of the session, the teacher who helped run things asked, 'When's Dillon coming back?'

Sherry regarded the teacher stonily. 'Soon,' she replied tersely. '*Very* soon.'

For the remainder of the day her mind was on what Christine had told her. She kept remembering the things Linda Brogan had shouted at her in the supermarket car park. The experience had shaken Sherry so badly she went home and cried for only the third time since Lisa died. The Brogan woman had freaked her out. She looked nothing like Lisa. She was tall and dark-haired and beautiful, whereas Lisa had been small, fair-haired, and cute.

And Lisa was dead.

So how did Linda Brogan know things only Lisa could have known? How did she know about Sherry's fear of spiders, and their joke about the scarves?

Sherry had been sleeping badly ever since. She kept dreaming of Linda Brogan's desperate face as she struggled against the big American guy Sherry remembered seeing in the Emergency Department on the day Lisa died. She kept hearing Lisa's voice coming out of Linda Brogan's mouth — maybe not exactly the same, but with a rhythm and inflection that *sounded* like Lisa. She kept hearing her frantic cries of, 'Sherry, it's me! *It's Lisa!*'

Dillon was going to interview Linda Brogan this week to get her statement about the accident. Because there had been a fatality, it would be going to the coroner's court. Linda Brogan would probably get community service and a hefty fine. Sherry burned with the injustice of it: Lisa's life paid for by a few measly hours at some community project and a tiny dent in the Brogans' bank balance. She hadn't told anybody what had happened in the car park, not even Ben. *Especially* not Ben. He kept on warning her to stay away from Linda Brogan.

'Mum and Dad have had enough grief. They don't need you to give them any more.'

He'd shocked the whole family by suddenly setting a date for his wedding to Brenda. It was only a couple of months away. Sherry and Lisa had stopped worrying about Brenda ever getting Ben to the altar. They'd been engaged for three years, and Brenda seemed to have accepted her role as fiancée in waiting and put her efforts into saving for the deposit to build a house instead. But every now and then, she got hold of an old bridal magazine and started making noises about wanting to get married sooner.

'I pray every night that the price of land keeps on going up on the North Shore,' Lisa had confessed.

Sherry nodded. 'And that Brenda can't find enough of

that avocado satin material to make the bridesmaids' dresses.'

Sherry, Lisa ,and Christine had been given the dubious honour of following Brenda if she ever made it up the aisle.

Lisa had always been the kinder of the two. 'We're being cows.'

Sherry knew she was a cow and proud of it. 'Long live the cows, I say, and down with the herbos.'

Ben didn't have any cow tendencies at all; he was the diplomat of the family. She had a hunch that he'd decided to get married to give their parents something to take their minds off losing Lisa but he denied it when Sherry confronted him.

'Brenda and I have been planning to get married for ages.' he insisted.

'That's right. So why don't you just keep on planning?'

'I know Brenda's not your favourite person—'

'She's *nobody's* favourite person, Ben.' Sherry glared at her baby brother 'If you were honest you'd admit she's not even yours.'

He flushed. 'Butt out, Sherry. You're out of line.'

'Better than being *out of my mind!*' she yelled.

They hadn't spoken to each other in over a week.

And now it seemed that Brenda was up to her old tricks, shopping for Ben's birthday present in bargain shops. At the end of her shift, Sherry was still so rattled by her conversation with Christine, she dropped in at the plant shop to see her father.

Brian was unloading a delivery of lemon trees at the back of the outdoor display area when she found him. He smiled when he saw. 'Hello, love. Just finished work?'

Sherry kissed his cheek, feeling saddened by the new

lines that seemed to accumulate on his weather-beaten face every time she saw him. He carried his sadness about him like a cloak. She looked about. 'Where's Rambo Ray? Why isn't he helping you?'

Brian shook his head. 'Leave it, Sherry.'

She pulled a face and began to help shift the trees.

'You don't have to do that.'

Her father was the only man she knew who treated her like she was made of spun glass. He didn't seem to notice that she towered over most women – and a few men too – or that she was striking rather than pretty and her sharp tongue scared people.

She'd lost count of the number of times people had asked her if she'd ever considered becoming a model. *As if.* The thought of so many eyes focused on her made Sherry's skin crawl.

She never wore makeup on duty, and with her bone structure and vivid colouring, didn't need it anyway. But off-duty Sherry indulged her love of beautiful, feminine clothes and makeup to the max. She had two distinct personas: her cop one and her private one. Her colleagues were surprised when they saw how she looked out of uniform and outside of work people were shocked when they found out she was a cop.

It was as she was shifting the last of the trees that she noticed Linda Brogan standing on the far side of the concreted area that housed the outdoor plant display. She was staring at Sherry and Brian intently, her plaster cast propped on the ground before her and a plastic bag with a plant inside it dangling from one hand. Sherry recognized the black, draped skirt she was wearing as a Lisa Ho design. A fine white, scoop-neck T- shirt and a blue denim jacket completed the outfit but it looked as if Linda ran out of time or interest when it came to doing her hair because it was piled haphazardly on top of her head and secured with a black slide.

Sherry's hands curled into fists. She wished she wasn't wearing her uniform. Maybe she'd get lucky and the Brogan woman would shoplift a pansy or something. She watched Ray Tanner stroll into view, his gaze riveted on the American woman. Sherry's upper lip curled. Ray seemed to have an in-built radar system capable of detecting an attractive woman through the walls of buildings. He reminded her of a shark circling for the kill but instead of a great white, he was more like a hammerhead.

She nudged her father. 'Hey, Dad.'

Brian lifted his head. 'What?'

She inclined her head towards the display area on the other side and began to hum the theme from *Jaws*. '*Dah dum! Dah dum!*'

Ray cut around a tub of tulip bulbs and sauntered closer to Linda Brogan, who remained oblivious to his approach, her gaze still fixed on Sherry and Brian.

'*Dah dah! Dah dah! Dah dah! Dah dah!*'

Brian began to smile.

'*Do-do! Do-do! Do-do! Do-do!*'

Suddenly sensing danger, Linda Brogan lifted her head and spotted Ray. A look of horror unfurled across her face. Pivoting on her crutches, she looked at Sherry and pulled a face that plainly said *Yuck!* A face Sherry had seen Lisa pull countless times in the past. Frozen, she watched Ray smile unctuously and try to strike up a conversation.

Brian lost interest and returned to arranging trees.

Linda Brogan looked as if she wanted to hit Ray with one

of her crutches. She gazed pleadingly across at Sherry before turning back to Ray and crying loudly, 'I'm married!'

Brian looked up again and frowned.

'To a woman!' Linda shouted triumphantly, which drew the attention of the other customers wandering about the outdoor display.

Ray's smile slipped. He scowled when he saw everybody was watching him make a fool of himself and, even worse, one of them was the boss's smartarse daughter.

Sherry choked back laughter.

Ray backed away from Linda Brogan, his scowl deepening when he saw Sherry strolling towards him.

'Wow, Ray. Which charm school did you go to again?' she asked admiringly. 'Because I know a guy I'd like to send there. He's a slug too.'

'Piss off!' Ray snarled.

'*Oh Ray!*' Sherry and Linda Brogan cooed in unison. '*You're so butch!*'

Sherry's voice faded away. She stared into Linda Brogan's blue eyes.

'Here, Butch ... here, Butch,' the other woman said softly, and her eyes began to fill with tears.

Brian came up behind Sherry. He'd heard what Ray had said to Sherry. Anger vibrated from his wiry frame. Ray's fate was sealed when Linda Brogan looked at Brian and tears began to slide down her cheeks.

'I'm so sorry about this!' Brian exclaimed. 'Ray! In my office!' He turned to Sherry. 'Sherry? Can you—?'

She nodded absently, unable to her eyes from Linda Brogan.

'Hang on a minute!' Ray began to protest. 'I never—'

'Ray,' Brian said through his teeth, 'Come with me!

Now!'

Ray was shaken at seeing his easy-going boss look so angry and followed Brian into the shop.

Sherry gave Linda Brogan her most intimidating stare. 'What are you doing here?'

She stared right back. 'I came to see Dad.'

Sherry recoiled. '*He's not your father!*'

'Yes, he is,' Linda replied stubbornly. 'I wanted him to look at this plant for me. It's sick.'

'It's not the only thing that's sick!'

'And you're my big sister, Sherry.'

Sherry stepped closer, making the most of her extra inches in an attempt to intimidate Linda Brogan.

She refused to budge. 'Don't try and intimidate me with your height! I'm not much shorter than you now, and besides, living with a man who's six feet five inches tall makes you look small.'

'Shut up! I'm not your sister! *My* sister is dead. *You* killed her.'

Linda's face was chalk-white and she was trembling, but she refused to back down. 'I saw you, Sher. I saw you at the hospital when they sent me back. You were in a corridor outside a room with Dillon Taylor. He was stopping you from going into the room. As I went by I said your name and touched you, and for a moment you looked right at me.'

Sherry recalled the odd, eerie feeling she'd experienced out the Resus Room when she felt that light as feather touch on her arm and heard Lisa calling her name. She felt like somebody was trickling ice into her bone marrow. *How? How did this woman know about that?* She swayed, made a grab for a green wooden display table, and heard Linda Brogan cry, 'Sher!'

They landed together on the concrete with a thump, Sherry's body cushioned by Linda Brogan's.

'For God's sake, Sherry! Don't faint on me! *I'm* the one who faints, not you! I won't be able to pick you up, you silly cow!'

Sherry raised her chin off her chest and looked dazedly at the woman sitting on the ground beside her. 'Who the hell *are* you?'

☆

They went to a nearby café.

Sherry collected a white, hooded Esprit sweater from her car and wore it to conceal her telltale blue uniform shirt. Once they were inside, she sat down at one of the tables and looked at Lisa expressionlessly, making no offer to help her with her chair or crutches.

Lisa knew better than to think Sherry would be easily convinced, particularly when she'd had time to regroup since they'd left the garden centre. She checked how much money she had in her purse. She hated asking Dan for money; she felt guilty enough about living in his house and eating his food when she didn't have any right to be there.

Since the unforgettable scene in the kitchen, they'd pretty much avoided each other. Lisa had always been an early-to-bed-early-to-rise person, but now she disappeared into her bedroom as soon as they finished eating the meal she cooked each night and tried to practice her reading and writing.

She'd contacted SPELD, the learning disabilities centre in the city, and planned to start taking classes there as soon as she could figure out a way to pay for them. Lisa knew Dan would have agreed to cover the cost, but she didn't want to take any more from him than she had to, so she kept her plans to herself. Slade spent his spare time helping her on sentence construction with flash cards they'd made after getting books from the library on dyslexia. Lisa didn't know what she would have done without him. He was sweet and kind and wise beyond his years.

Dan gave up asking her if she needed anything because she always said no. Instead, he left her a generous amount of cash on the kitchen counter each morning. So far Lisa had only taken some of it twice. By catching buses instead of cabs into Browns Bay and the shopping mall at Takapuna, she made the money last. Slade offered to take her on the bike, but out of respect for Dan's feelings, Lisa declined his offer.

Slade surprised her by sometimes tagging along on her lonely bus rides around the North Shore and helping her with the more difficult household tasks like grocery shopping at the supermarket. Dan took care of the rest on the weekends from the list Lisa gave him. She always found an excuse not to go with him. She couldn't bear being in his company when she recalled how he'd pushed her away. Her sense of humiliation and rejection was deep, and the hurt too painful to examine. Lisa felt like a leper. She needed her family more now than ever.

Dan got up early most mornings to run or take a bike ride before work. On the weekends, he took his windsurfer down to the beach and spent hours criss-crossing the water, unaware that Lisa sat in the garden on top of the cliff nursing a cup of coffee and watching him. She almost dropped a basket load of cutlery she was unloading from the dishwasher the first time Dan arrived home to clean his board and wetsuit. He came strolling through the kitchen from the garage with his wetsuit slung over one shoulder and a pair of wet, black Speedos riding low on his hips.

Lisa nearly swallowed her tongue. The sight of him semi-naked and looking a hundred times better without his clothes on than she'd imagined sent the cutlery basket crashing to the floor He was beautiful. Wide shoulders, broad chest, washboard abs and the one of the most gorgeous male bums she set eyes. The bulge at the front of his Speedos indicated everything was in proportion to the rest of him. She realized Dan felt comfortable walking about in front of her like this because he still thought of her as Linda.

Lisa studied Sherry's expression and felt even more lonely. She belonged nowhere and to nobody. But Sherry wasn't the only stubborn one in the family. 'I'll get the drinks.'

Sherry shrugged ungraciously. 'I'll have an—'

'Earl Grey tea,' Lisa interrupted. 'Yes, I know.'

She was gratified to see this disturbed Sherry, and that she seemed even more perturbed when she heard Lisa order a trim mochaccino *without* the marshmallows for herself. Lisa hated marshmallows. She hopped back to the table and sat down, wishing she could give in to the impulse to throw her arms around Sherry in a bear hug and then go across the road and do the same to her father. Instead, she said, 'Dad doesn't look very well.'

Sherry folded her arms and leaned back in her chair. 'He just buried his daughter.'

Lisa gasped. 'You *buried* me?'

A man and woman sitting at a nearby table looked across at them with raised brows.

Sherry shifted uncomfortably. 'Mum and Dad couldn't face the thought of a cremation. *For Lisa,*' she added pointedly.

Lisa shuddered. 'How's Mum?'

'Smoking.' Sherry retorted, watching her intently.

'She's *what?* After I nearly gave myself lung cancer getting her to stop?'

The couple got up and shifted to another table.

Sherry regarded Lisa her with a wondering expression on her face. 'I don't know who the hell has filled you in on us, but I have to admit I'm impressed.' She narrowed her eyes. 'What's your game?'

The waitress arrived carrying the drinks. The braces on her perfect white teeth matched the bolt in her eyebrows. 'Mochaccino and Earl Grey,' she announced brightly.

Lisa gestured at Sherry. 'Earl Grey.' She noticed with satisfaction that Sherry had to stop herself from pointing back and saying, 'Mochaccino.' It was a repetition of a scene they'd played out countless times before.

After the waitress had gone, Lisa began to talk, hesitantly at first, but eventually the words were rushing out in a torrent as she told the whole story for the first time, editing some of the more recent events. For instance, she omitted almost having sex on the kitchen counter with Dan Brogan or that she'd been imagining having sex with him ever since.

Sherry listened in stunned silence, her tea going cold on the table. 'So you're saying some renegade angel sent you back, but in the wrong body?' she said at last.

Lisa checked to see if anybody had heard her. 'Well, *not* an angel exactly, he said they don't have angels — or at least not the way we imagine them.'

Sherry studied her incredulously. 'I don't believe I'm having this conversation. 'Are you sure you didn't go the other way?' She jabbed a finger at the ground.

'No, I did not!' Lisa cried indignantly. 'If anybody was likely to go south, it'd be you!'

'I'll ignore that,' Sherry said in a strange voice.

Lisa saw that her bottom lip was trembling, and her eyes were glassy. 'Sher?'

'*What*?' she snapped.

'Do you believe me?'

Sherry took her time answering. She couldn't trust herself to speak. People didn't *die* and return in somebody else's body. But the woman sitting opposite sat just the way Lisa sat and shrugged and pulled faces just the way Lisa did. She *knew* things only *Lisa* could know.

'I don't know what to think,' she muttered. 'But it's just the sort of mess Lisa would get herself into.'

Lisa's lip trembled. She felt a thrill of hope but knew better than to rush things. Sherry would fight her all the way. She sighed when her sister leaned back in her chair, her eyes narrowed and feline. Typical Sher. She'd spotted Lisa's quivering lip, and the sign of weakness in her opponent had shored up her own wavering confidence.

'You could have found out about what Lisa did to stop Mum smoking from family friends,' Sherry pointed out coldly.

'What about back at the plant shop with Ray?'

'What about it?'

'Here Butch! Here Butch!' Lisa sing-songed.

'I've heard other people make the same joke.'

'What about the scarf joke? Have you ever heard anybody else say that besides you and me?'

'Besides *me* and *Lisa*. No.' Sherry agreed grudgingly.

'Tia Maria. Cointreau. Jack Daniels. Remy Martin.' Lisa leaned across the table and hissed, '*Harvey's Bristol*

Cream.'

Sherry's eyes widened. She swallowed.

'Have you still got the ashtray, Sher?' she demanded.

Sherry regarded her with a kind of horrified fascination. 'What ashtray?'

Lisa scooted closer. 'The awful old orange thing Mum's Auntie Violet sent her for Christmas one year and we've been trying to get rid ever since. The one we send to each other for birthdays and any excuse we can find to get rid of it. The one I broke and glued back together and gave to Ben and Brenda as part of their engagement present. The one I sent to you in England when you were on your OE. The one—'

'Shut up!'

'Do you believe me?'

'I ... don't know ... what to believe.' Sherry looked away. 'Anybody could have told you about the ashtray.'

Lisa attempted to leap to her feet and managed to bang the toes of her injured leg on the table leg. 'Ow! Fuck!' she gripped the edge of the table as pain ricocheted up her foot.

'Now I know you're not Lisa. I can count the times she said fuck on one hand.'

'Yeah?' Lisa snarled. 'Well that was before I died, went to heaven and got booted out again! I think that entitles me to say *fuck* as much I like!'

The elderly couple sitting at the other table were slack-jawed with shock, while the girl operating the espresso machine looked as if she was about to throw them out.

'Sit down before you get us thrown out!' Sherry hissed.

Mortified to find herself in danger of being asked to leave a shop for the second time in weeks, Lisa sat back down. However, if Sherry thought she'd taken the wind out of her sails, she was sadly mistaken. 'You are such a pain in the arse, Sherry Jackson! There's nothing between your ears but bone. I don't know why I love you.'

Sherry bit her lip and sighed. 'We can't talk about this here. Come on.'

☆

They went back to Sherry's house in Torbay.

Sherry refused to believe Linda Brogan was Lisa, but they couldn't continue their heated discussion in public without Sherry having to arrest her for disorderly conduct.

For Lisa, going to Sherry's house was the next best thing to going home to her parents. Ben had built the house for Sherry a couple of years earlier and their father had landscaped the gardens. Lisa was shocked at the signs of neglect outside.

'Dad's not really been in the mood lately,' Sherry said tightly.

Lisa was appalled. Gardens and plants were a passion for their father — he couldn't bear to see living things neglected. 'They're bad then?'

Sherry was sitting on a stool in the kitchen, her hands clasped between her knees. 'It's knocked the stuffing right out of them both. They miss Lisa ... so much.' She cleared her throat. 'We all miss her so much.'

Lisa limped closer and tentatively reached out to touch her sister's hair, but Sherry deflected her with the back of her hand.

Lisa curled her fingers into a fist, fighting the pain of rejection. 'I know. I miss all of you.' A tear plopped down her cheek.

'So you keep saying.' Sherry replied tightly. 'I suppose I should offer you a tissue.'

She watched in astonishment as Lisa hopped over to the tall pantry cupboard in the corner of the kitchen and applied just the right amount of pressure to lift the bottom right-hand corner of the door that always stuck on the linoleum so she could open it. Reaching inside, she unerringly located a fresh box of tissues on the bottom shelf next to the kitchen towels, before hopping back to the kitchen counter where she opened the box, pulled out a tissue and blew her nose.

Sherry watched her mutely, shaken by the ease with which this strange woman navigated her way around her kitchen. 'I refuse to believe this.' She said brusquely. 'You're the woman who drove the car that killed my sister.'

'*Who* do I sound like? *Who* do I act like?'

Sherry looked away. She wanted to give in and hug her, but whenever she looked at her, she saw a stranger. She wasn't like Lisa and Ben, she was ruled by her head, not her heart. When they were kids, she'd always been the voice of reason; the older, sensible sister. That didn't change when they grew up.

'I know how hard this is for you, Sherry,' Lisa said softly. 'Believe me, it was hard enough for me when I woke up in hospital and looked in the mirror. I needed you all so much.'

Sherry tried to find a line of questioning that would lead her to some sensible answers. 'So what does Dan Brogan think?'

'That I've got a screw loose.'

'But he thinks you're his wife?'

Lisa laughed hollowly. 'I think he's beginning to have some doubts.' She moved away to look at some photos of Ben and Brenda on the fridge. 'I don't think he knows what to think. He had an American wife who had a car accident and now he's got a New Zealand ... something.'

Sherry busied herself with making tea and coffee. 'What's he like?'

She'd noticed that Linda or Lisa or whoever she really was wouldn't meet her eye when the subject of Dan Brogan came up. She watched curiously as Linda, as she insisted on thinking of her, poked amongst the CDs neatly stacked on Sherry's computer desk in the niche by the kitchen table and fiddled with the mail spread on the kitchen counter before returning to the photos of Ben and Brenda.

'Very nice, kind, a gentleman, I guess. When were these taken?'

'A couple of weeks ago,' Sherry paused. 'They've set a date for the wedding. It's the second week of July.'

'*What!!*'

It was exactly the way Lisa would respond.

'Why did he do that?' her visitor yelled. 'Has he lost his mind?' She sucked in a breath. 'Brenda's not pregnant, is she?'

Sherry gave her a disgusted look. '*Pelease!* Do you honestly think Brenda would allow Ben to knock her up? She'd have to give up work and that would mean less money coming into the house.'

'But think of the savings in condoms or the Pill or whatever . . .'

They snorted.

Sherry's heart was thumping hard against her breastbone. She had her sister back. Crazy as it seemed, Lisa was here talking to her.

Lisa was so busy ranting about Ben marrying Brenda that she didn't see the tears slipping down Sherry's face. 'You know I caught that slapper buying his presents in the two-dollar shop after I'd warned her about it last year?'

'I heard.'

She stopped mid-rant. 'You did?'

'The wild child gave me all the details.'

'Christine?' Lisa blinked. 'You're ... crying.'

'Looks like it.'

Lisa longed to hug Sherry but knew better than to try. She'd made a lot of progress today but knew better than to try to push too hard with somebody as stubborn as Sherry. She moved away when Sherry stepped to the fridge to take out milk for their drinks.

'You were the one who made the phone call, weren't you?'

'Yes.' Lisa admitted softly.

Sherry carried the milk to the kitchen counter. She had her sister back. Crazy as it seemed, Lisa was here talking to her.

'Do you think Mum and Dad will be able to cope...if we tell them?' Lisa asked.

'We're not going to tell them.'

'What? Why not?'

'Because you can't! I won't let you!' Sherry snapped.

'You can't stop me! I want to come home!'

'You think they're going to believe your crazy story?'

'You did.'

'I don't know what to make of it.'

Lisa sank into a chair and whispered, 'You're lying. You know it's me.'

Sherry was torn between putting her arms around her and shoring up her walls of defense. 'What's the husband like?'

'Okay.'

'He thinks you're his wife, doesn't he?'

Lisa avoided her gaze.

'Are you sleeping with him?'

'Of course not!'

'Is he gay?'

'No!'

'How do you know?'

Lisa reddened.

So, her little sister had been getting down and dirty with the handsome Yank doctor — or close to it. Lisa refused to discuss him, which surprised Sherry because Lisa had always confided in her in the past. Sherry was the one who played things close to her chest. If anybody knew the best way to handle the situation it would be her, she was always in control when it came to the men in her life.

'He's a good-looking guy,' Sherry's eyes were bright with curiosity. Just what had her baby sister been up to with the good doctor?

Lisa shrugged. 'I suppose so.'

'Have you still got endometriosis?'

She smiled for the first time. 'No. I finished a period a few days ago. It was a breeze.'

'Oh Lees, I'm so pleased for you!'

Sherry remembered all the times she'd seen Lisa curled up in a ball on her bed clutching hot-water bottles and wheat bags to her stomach, and all the blood tests and medications to stop her getting anaemic.

'But I have dyslexia instead.'

Sherry spilled milk on the counter. 'What?'

'Linda Brogan was dyslexic. So now *I'm* dyslexic.'

She stared at the puddle of milk. 'I can't believe I'm having this conversation! *You are Linda Brogan, for God's sake!*'

There was a pregnant silence finally broken by the sound of Lisa hopping across the linoleum to Sherry's side. 'Believe me, Sher, it isn't something I'd joke about.' She wiped up the spilt milk when Sherry showed no sign of doing it. 'Look, I'll go. I know how you feel. I've had a lot longer to get used to it, and I still feel as if somebody has tipped me upside-down and shaken me by the ankles. I'll call a cab if that's OK—'

Sherry came out of her trance. 'You think I'm going to just let you walk away? Are you mad?'

'That seems to be the general opinion.'

'I don't know for certain who you are, but there's something very weird going on here—'

'Uh-huh—'

'—and I intend to find out what the hell it is.'

'Right.'

'But until then . . .'

'Yes?'

'Until then ... I'll reserve judgement — it's the best I can do.'

'Fair enough.' Lisa cleared her throat, fighting a fresh flood of tears. 'I can't ask for more than that.'

Sherry stared at the two mugs on the kitchen counter. 'So what are you doing about the dyslexia?'

'I'm going to start SPELD classes soon.'

'What are they and . . .' Sherry peered at Lisa's face. 'What's wrong?'

'Nothing.'

'*What's wrong?*'

Lisa told her about the cost of the classes and her reluctance to ask Dan for the money. 'I know he'd pay for them, but I can't take it from him. He thinks he's paying for his wife and he isn't. Sometime soon I will have to move out and find a job.'

Sherry took her time answering. 'I don't know how to say this.'

Lisa eyed her warily. 'What? Say it! I'm getting used to hearing bad news.'

'Linda Brogan is — *was* — American, right?'

She nodded.

'So she would have had an American passport?'

'I guess so.' Lisa gasped. '*Oh no!*'

'Lisa Louise Jackson is dead. She no longer exists. You're an American citizen now. You *can't* leave Dan Brogan. His work is all that allows you to stay in New Zealand.'

Chapter 16

Lisa watched Sherry's car disappear into the darkness and tried not to feel like she'd been abandoned. She was late getting home because she'd spent so much time talking to Sherry. They'd examined her citizenship problem from every angle and come up with zilch.

Dan opened the door before she could even get her keys out of her handbag. 'You're late. I was worried.'

He didn't look or sound very friendly. His hair was mussed, a sure sign something was bothering him. It had been mussed *a lot* lately. His Yosemite Sam tie was loosened, and the top buttons of his shirt were undone.

Lisa trailed dispiritedly past him. 'Sorry.'

Dan frowned at her drooping figure. 'I wasn't sure if you'd run out of money for the bus fare home,' he paused and said heavily, 'But I see you got a ride.'

His temper sparked further when Lisa failed to answer his unspoken question. He'd been waiting anxiously for the past hour for her to come home, all the time imagining the worst. Twice there'd been a knock at the front door, and each time Dan answered a neighbour had been standing there with a dead-looking plant in their hands asking if Lisa was home. He'd taken the plants and put them with the rest of the dead and dying vegetation beginning to fill one side of the garage, thinking that at this rate he'd have to start parking his car on the road.

When he heard a car door slam outside the house, he was just had time to see the vehicle pull away. It was a black SUV. Jack Millar owned one just like it. Dan stared grimly at Lisa's slumped shoulders as she hopped away from him; whatever she had been doing that afternoon seemed to have drained her.

The police had finally made contact about interviewing her, or rather, Linda. Apparently, they'd called several times this week to arrange a time to take her statement and hadn't been able to get hold of her because she hadn't replied to any of the messages they left. It drove Dan nuts that she treated his home, *her home,* like she was a boarder, which made listening to Dan's messages off-limits and meant she didn't listen to her own either. Something he'd been unable to explain the police.

'Lisa, did you get any calls from the police? They said they've been trying to contact you to take your statement.' he asked curtly.

She stopped in the hallway and looked at him with wide eyes. 'No. I've hardly been in.'

He wanted to snarl, where the hell *have* you been? But refused to ask.

She behaved more like his housekeeper than his wife. Ever since that night in the kitchen, she'd hidden away from him. She cooked his evening meal, his dirty laundry was returned clean to his wardrobe, the house was spotless, but the essence of her — the laughter and quirkiness — had disappeared. She stayed in her room and took herself God knew where during the day when he was out. She asked him for nothing.

Recognising the fear on her face, he chose his words carefully. 'Did you check to see if there were any messages?'

She shook her head.

'Lisa, you have to remember to check; there's at least three messages from the police asking you to contact them.'

'I didn't do it deliberately,' she mumbled miserably. 'I just didn't expect there to be any messages for me and I don't like to listen to yours.'

He thrust his hands in trouser pockets and clenched them in frustration. 'You're my wife. You're *allowed* to listen to my messages.'

Lisa shrugged wearily and hopped away to her room.

Dan followed her to the bedroom door. She was sitting on the bed counting out the change in her purse. That was another thing that infuriated him, her refusal to accept his money. She rode around the countryside on buses — she'd got caught in the rain and come home looking like a drowned rat twice in the past week — rather than take *anything* from him.

Or at least nothing you're willing to give, a voice inside his head whispered.

'Can you tell me the point of this Orphan Annie act of yours?' Dan snapped.

Lisa's meeting with Sherry had left her feeling wrung out like a dishcloth. The realization that she'd even lost the right to remain in her own country and having to leave the familiar surroundings of her sister's house and return to Linda Brogan's home and her husband made her want to cry and scream at the same time. She felt a deep sense of injustice at Dan and the world in general. How dare *he* snap at *her?* All the pain and confusion of the past two months boiled up inside her.

'What Orphan Annie act?' she yelled, gratified to have an outlet for all her fury and sense of unfairness at her life. If it wasn't for *his* stupid wife, *she* wouldn't be here now. She shook the coins from her purse onto the bed, knowing it made Dan furious because she wouldn't take his money and because she wanted him to feel every bit as bad as she did. 'How *dare* you call me Orphan Annie! I've got a dollar thirty!' She scooped the coins off the bed and threw them at him.

Dan ducked but some of the money bounced off his chest. He regarded her incredulously. 'What the *fuck* did you do that for?'

Under normal circumstances, Lisa would have been ashamed of herself, but instead she felt a heady rush of freedom. She wanted to break free of all this bullshit, to stop pretending and be herself. She got to her feet and held out her arms. 'Because I felt like it!' She stopped short of adding *nah, nah, nah, nah, nah!*

She didn't expect Dan to come in. He treated the threshold to her bedroom like his own personal Berlin Wall, only venturing across it to return her back to bed when she'd been sleepwalking. She was astonished when he crossed Checkpoint Charlie and stalked across the carpet towards her.

'Hang on a minute!' She held up her hands like a police officer stopping traffic. 'You're not allowed to come past the doorway! You *never* come past the doorway!'

He loomed over her. 'I just changed the rule.'

Lisa was so surprised she plopped onto the bed. She stared up at him in confusion. Where had calm, pleasant, sensible Dan Brogan gone? She didn't recognize this narrow-eyed, granite-faced individual snarling down at her and felt a frisson of sexual excitement uncurl in her belly.

'This is *my* room!' she pointed at the door. 'Get out!'

'This is *my* house. If you want to get rid of me, you'll have to throw me out.'

Lisa opened her mouth and closed it again. She didn't

have an answer for that.

'Where the hell have you been all day?'

A perverse sense of mischievousness stole over her. 'All day?'

He growled something unrepeatable in the back of his throat.

'OK! Keep your hair on.'

He blinked and frowned. Clearly it was a turn of phrase he wasn't used to.

Lisa was beginning to enjoy herself. The blood was rushing through her veins and for once she wasn't feeling like a victim in some grotesque experiment.

Dan thrust his hands into his trouser pockets. 'I'm waiting.'

Lisa noticed he way the material pulled across his thighs and murmured, 'So you are.' She leaned back on her elbows, crossed her cast over the opposite knee and gently bounced her foot. 'I actually set out today to rob a bank.'

Dan appeared momentarily speechless. He looked like he wanted to kill her. He opened his mouth to say something Lisa was sure he'd later regret. She held up her hand and was pleasantly surprised when he stopped, his lips parted in shock.

'But I realized I hadn't brought any pantyhose along with me, so that was the end of that, my disguise had gone up in smoke.'

She was blithely unaware that her skirt was sliding up her thigh with each bounce of her cast.

Dan ground his teeth. She thought this was *funny?* He noticed what was happening with her skirt and felt his anger abate. His gaze fastened to her rising hemline. 'How did you plan to make your getaway?'

'By bus. I have the schedule committed to memory and nobody would suspect a woman with a broken leg catching a bus to be a robber.'

'Guess not,' Dan willed the skirt to slide into home base. 'The pantyhose might have been a giveaway — if you'd had them with you.'

Lisa rolled her eyes. 'I wouldn't have worn them on the bus. I'm not stupid, you know.'

'The thought never crossed my mind.'

'And I had a cunning plan to hide them in my cast instead of chucking them in a rubbish bin.'

Dan inclined his head. 'Brilliant. Although I feel duty bound to point out that as an orthopaedic surgeon I wouldn't have advised it.'

'I can respect that.'

'Thank you.' He paused. 'Lisa?'

'Yes?'

'Can you please stop kicking me in the leg?'

'Oh! Sorry!' She sat up and frowned down at his trouser-clad leg which was at least a foot away from her cast. 'Hang on! I never touched you!'

'No,' he drawled. 'But every time you swing your leg I get a view straight up your skirt to your tonsils.'

She squawked and trapped her skirt between her knees with her hands. 'You could have said something sooner!'

'And spoil the show? I don't think so.'

Lisa was confused. Was she meant to feel encouraged or rebuffed?

Dan sat on the chair in front of the dressing table. He looked a lot more like his usual self, in control, calm. Leaning forward, he braced his arms along his thighs and pressed the tips of his long fingers together. Lisa loved his hands. Although they were big like the rest of him, she loved the way he handled things, never clumsily and always with great sensitivity.

'I think we need to talk about a few things that have been getting between us,' Dan said.

She dragged her eyes away from his hands. She didn't like the sound of that. But she did like the way his shirt pulled across his shoulders and tapered to his waist. Beyond that waist was a hard, muscular bum. She did love Dan's bum. If he was about to explain to her why she turned him off, she'd rather he just kept it to himself.

What he said next almost made her fall off the bed.

'Lisa, did you know you were pregnant when you had the accident?'

Her mouth fell open. 'No!'

Dan nodded. 'You had a miscarriage in the Emergency Room.'

'*Ohhh...*' she gasped softly. 'I'm so sorry, Dan!'

He gave her a long, contemplative look. 'Losing a baby is always a tragedy, Lisa.' He paused. 'But I wasn't the father.'

At first, she didn't hear him. She was remembering the little boy in the waiting room, the child that had made Linda Brogan so agitated. 'It was a boy!' she cried. 'I *saw* him!'

Dan frowned and sat back in the chair. 'What do you mean, you *saw* him?'

Her brow furrowed. 'What do you mean you *weren't* the father?' '

Work it out ... *Li-sa*,' he replied sarcastically, drawing out the two syllables of her name.

She hugged her arms tightly around her waist as several pieces of the puzzle fell into place. The picture wasn't a pretty one. Linda Brogan had been having an affair. No wonder Dan seemed so distant. No wonder he kept her at arm's length.

But I'm *not* Linda! she wanted to shout. I'm not your wife!

Her shoulders slumped. It was hopeless. Dan wouldn't kick her out on the street, but he wouldn't allow himself to care for her either. And, silly cow that she was, she'd begun to get emotionally involved with him, to imagine a relationship where none could ever exist.

The episode in the kitchen made horrible sense now. Lisa was amazed he could even bear to touch her, to have her living in the same house with him. She looked at him sadly, struggling to contain the anguish building inside her. It would be so easy to fall in love with this man. She was halfway there already.

'Well that explains a lot of things,' She murmured at last.

'Does it? Like what?' Dan replied tersely.

'Like it was fairly obvious there was something very wrong with your marriage to Linda.'

'Is that so, *Lisa?*' he replied coolly. 'And just what gave you that idea?'

Lisa flinched at his tone, but she'd gone too far to back down now. She forced herself to meet his gaze. 'You never touch me the way a husband touches his wife.'

Dan grew very still, except for his eyes which seethed with emotion. 'What are you trying to say, *Lisa?*' he asked silkily. He stood up and took a step closer to the bed. 'Are you disappointed you haven't got laid?'

'No!' Lisa shrank from him. 'I'm not just talking about sex! I mean the small things, the casual touches of affection, the caring gestures, *the little things* I've seen my parents do a thousand times over the years!'

Dan understood what she was talking about because he'd seen his own parents do the same things, but hearing Lisa mention parents she didn't have infuriated him. When would she give up this act?

He moved right up to the edge of the bed. Lisa fell onto her back and Dan followed her, flattening his palms on either side of her shoulders, his weight braced on his outstretched arms as he gazed down into her shocked face. 'Sorry, I'm all out of tenderness, but if it's mindless sex you're after I'm your man,' he said bitterly.

Lisa pressed her fists against her breasts and stared at him uncomprehendingly. 'Dan? What are you doing?'

For several heartbeats he continued to watch her before closing his eyes and swearing softly. When he opened them again, Lisa saw self-loathing and revulsion in them before he tried to jerk away. She grabbed his biceps and hung on.

Dan jerked upright, pulling her with him. 'I'm sorry! Just let me go.'

His pain made her want to cry. She clutched him tighter. 'Dan. Really, it's OK. You've been badly hurt by somebody you loved and trusted. You've every right to be angry and defensive.'

He took hold of her wrist and carefully removed her hand from his upper arm. 'Let go of me, Lisa,' he said stonily and reached for her other hand.

She hung on stubbornly. 'Dan, please listen to me! I *am not* Linda! Linda is *dead! Your wife is dead.*'

He didn't seem to hear. 'I've never treated a woman the way I just treated you.'

'Dan, *please* give me a chance.'

'I have nothing left to give,' Dan told her flatly. 'I can take you to bed and we can screw one another's brains out, but that's all it will be — sex. If that's what you want then I'm your man, but just be clear that's *all* I have to offer you. I used everything up on Linda. This time round I'd be the one doing the taking.'

'I don't believe that,' Lisa whispered.

'Then you're a fool.'

She dragged herself backwards across the bed, the rough edge of her cast catching the bedcover, so it rucked up beneath her. 'Why? Why did you tell me about Linda's affair and the baby when you've never mentioned it before?'

'Because I thought you might get to hear about it from the police or in court.'

Lisa recalled what he'd said about the police calling. 'Court? I'll have to go to court?'

He nodded. 'A woman died, Lisa.

She wanted to yell, *Yes! Me!*

Instead, she nodded wearily and took a shuddering breath. 'Can you leave now, please?'

She wouldn't let herself cry until he'd gone. Dan hesitated, his expression bleak.

Lisa concentrated on staring at her cast.

His eyes followed the restless movement of her fingers pleating and unpleating the bedcover. He felt as if he'd just dealt her a mortal blow, an injury almost as bad as those she'd sustained in the car crash. Reluctantly, he went to the door.

'Dan?'

He paused with his hand on the door handle. 'Yes?'

'Was Linda unfaithful a lot?'

His raised his shoulders, let them fall. 'Just this one guy ... I think.'

Lisa wanted to lessen his pain. 'She didn't want to go. She

was meant to come back instead of me. But there was a mix-up. You got the wrong woman back.'

The hairs rose on the back of Dan's neck. He hated it when she talked like this. Her blue eyes suddenly seemed old and indescribably sad. Dan had the feeling she'd seen things he couldn't begin to imagine or understand.

He quietly let himself out of the room.

☆

Dan was waiting for the telltale sound of Lisa walking in her sleep. He found her on the patio at the back of the house. She'd managed to open one of the doors and was wandering towards the fence at the bottom of the garden. The cliff edge was a short distance away, bordered by a wooden fence and manuka and pohutukawa trees. A sliver of moon provided a faint light. The sea

was an inky, black expanse of nothingness beneath it, the distant sound of the surf falling onto the nearby beach loud in the quiet, still night air. Dan had to run to catch her. He grabbed her so roughly that Lisa jerked awake and screamed.

'You're sleepwalking again!' He held her against his chest as she struggled against him, frightened and disorientated. 'Sssh...it's okay. It's Dan.'

She slumped against him.

This was his fault. If he hadn't argued with her earlier, she wouldn't have walked in her sleep. He'd come to realize there was a pattern to Lisa's nocturnal wanderings. If she was upset or stressed, she sleepwalked. On the days he returned home and found her looking relaxed, she remained in bed. In fact, the night after they almost made love in the kitchen she slept the whole night through, which made his decision to keep his hands and the rest of himself away from her damned hard to stick to when he knew she was every bit as hungry for him.

Even without the added worry of Lisa sleepwalking off the cliff or down the street and being hit by a car, Dan doubted he'd have managed more than a few hours' rest thanks to the dreams he kept having about her: naked, hot, sweaty dreams where they were wrapped around each other like a pair of eels.

Naked on the beach.

Naked on the rug in front of the fire in the lounge.

That particular one would have made sitting in the lounge at night with her an exercise in self-control if she didn't go straight to her room after she'd tidied the kitchen each night.

Naked in his car.

It had certainly livened up the tedium of sitting in the traffic on the drive over the Harbour Bridge to and from the hospital. She'd even turned up in one dream as his scrub nurse. When he'd held out his hand for the bone drill, there she was, buck naked except for a mask and surgical cap, her long-lashed eyes half-lidded and sultry. 'One screw or two, Mr Brogan?' she'd asked huskily in her cute Kiwi accent. Dan looked about frantically at the rest of the surgical team, but nobody else seemed to notice anything was wrong.

He woke up with his cock making a tent pole in the middle of the covers and his eyes gritty from lack of sleep. That day he was uncharacteristically grumpy in the OR, or theatre as it was called in New Zealand, earning himself several surprised looks from the nursing staff with whom he was usually a favourite.

When Lisa hadn't sleepwalked in over a week, Dan began to hope she'd stopped. She said she thought it was because she was so worn out hopping around on crutches all day and didn't have the energy to climb out of bed in the middle of the night. Dan hoped it was because they'd settled into a pattern of sorts, but he'd blown that to hell last night with his uncharacteristic outburst, although he'd meant every word.

Lisa began to shiver. She still preferred to wear his old cotton T-shirts as nightdresses, which Dan found oddly touching. He wore a pair of the pyjama pants he'd been forced to buy so he didn't leap out of bed naked on his nightly rescue missions.

When Lisa clumsily attempted to push him away, Dan loosened his grip but continued to guide her inside. 'I'll take you back to bed.'

'No!' She shoved against him, encountered his bare chest and snatched her hands away.

Dan wasn't sure if he imagined it but for a moment her touch gentled to a caress before she curled her hands into fists against her breasts. He imagined how they looked beneath the soft cotton fabric.

'I'm awake. I can manage by myself,' Lisa insisted.

Dan dropped his hands and stepped back.

He wanted to carry her back to the big bed, strip her naked and spend the rest of the night investigating every inch of her beautiful body. She'd been so incredibly responsive in the kitchen. He'd been bemused by the tentative, endearing way she'd touched him, as if he was a present she wasn't quite certain she was allowed to unwrap. Her touch wasn't the touch of a woman who'd made love to the same man for the past eight years, who knew his body as well as her own.

He followed behind her, keeping close enough to catch

her if she tripped. She was always groggy and disorientated if she woke up while she was sleepwalking. She hopped inside, stumbling twice before reaching her bedroom. Dan watched from the shadows of the doorway as she climbed beneath the covers and rolled on her side with her back towards him.

'Can you shut the door, please?' she asked quietly.

They had an agreement to leave their bedroom doors open so he could hear her. Feeling as if he had lost something he might never get back, Dan slowly closed the door.

★

The next morning Lisa rang Sherry and asked if she could move in with her.

'What happened?' Sherry demanded.

'Nothing. I just ... want to be with you.'

There was a long pause. 'I can't do that.'

Her tone put Lisa on the alert. 'What's wrong?'

Sherry sighed. 'It's Mum. She tried to go back to work but she keeps losing it.'

Lisa struggled to keep her voice steady. 'Now isn't a good time?'

Would it ever be? Sherry wondered.

'If you want to come over here, then pack your bags and I'll come and get you right now.'

'But I'd have to hide, Sherry, and I don't think I could stand it,' Lisa replied, fighting back tears.

'What's happened, Lisa? Has he hurt you? Something's wrong, isn't it?'

'Of course something's wrong! I'm living in another woman's body!'

'*What's happened?*' Sherry insisted.

'Nothing.' Lisa swiped her eyes and blotted her nose with a tissue. 'Nothing *new*. Dan's very kind to me. If I had to live with a stranger, I couldn't have found anyone more decent. I'll be OK.'

'You don't sound OK.'

'I am. Really, I am. I'm just ... missing you all.'

Lisa's contact with Sherry and her visits to see her father at the garden centre were all that kept her sane. Her dad smiled whenever Lisa arrived, bringing him yet another distressed plant in a plastic bag for him to doctor.

'Another one?' he scratched his head. 'Are these *all* your plants?'

Lisa said her name was Lisa and she was rescuing her neighbours' plants. She refused to call him Brian and several times almost called him Dad. His gentle, kind presence soothed her.

'You're a regular Red Cross for plants aren't you?' he observed.

Sherry's angry voice dragged Lisa back to the present. 'I hate this! It's all wrong!'

She let loose a hiccuping laugh. 'Tell me about it.'

'Lees?'

'Yes?'

'Dillon has been trying to contact you. He needs to take your statement about the accident.'

Lisa chewed her lip. 'Dan told me about it last night when I got home. God, Sherry! What do I say to him?'

'I don't know. I really don't know.'

Chapter 17

Dan insisted on being present at the interview. Despite the distance between them since the night Dan told her about Linda's miscarriage, Lisa was glad he was there.

It was a bizarre experience. First, she totally freaked out Officer Dillon Taylor by opening the door, smiling widely, and calling him by the name her the family used to tease him. 'Hi, Dilly!'

Dillon's face froze beneath his police cap. 'I beg your pardon?'

Dan had managed to hand over an out-patients' clinic to his registrar so he could make it home in time. He came up behind Lisa at the front door and gently moved her out of the way so Dillon could come in.

'Officer?' He reached out and shook Dillon's hand. 'I'm Dan Brogan. This is ... Linda, my wife. Please come in.'

It was the first time Lisa had heard Dan introduce her as his wife. It made her feel uneasy, and at the same time it made her belly flip with excitement.

Dillon followed Dan into the house, giving Lisa a long, puzzled look as he went by.

They assembled in the lounge where Dillon took out a pad and began to take Lisa's statement. She was unnerved by his professional, unsmiling manner. The Dillon Taylor she knew came to her parents' house for barbecues and to watch rugby. If he occasionally drank too much when he watched a game, he slept overnight on the couch.

Dan sat beside Lisa, not touching her but there if she needed him.

Dillon started out by asking Lisa her full name. She looked at Dan helplessly.

'Linda Elizabeth Brogan née Mulholland,' he said.

Dillon looked at them both strangely and wrote it down. 'Date of birth?'

'June the . . .' Lisa tried to remember what Dan had said in the coffee shop the first time he took her to Browns Bay. 'Sixth?'

He nodded.

Dillon raised his brows.

Lisa knew him well enough to know he thought they were nuts. She felt a bubble of laughter work its way up her throat and disguised it with a cough. Dan shifted, sprawling more comfortably on the sofa, and bringing his thigh into contact with hers. Lisa felt the firm, sharp nudge of warning and sat up straight. She concentrated on Dillon and his new haircut. It suited him.

It was Dan's thigh digging into her again that drew her attention to the expectant expression on Dillon's face. 'Sorry. Could you repeat the question?'

She applied pressure to Dan's leg to get him to move it. He responded by letting his long legs sprawl even wider, crowding her space even more. I'll kill him when Dillon's gone, Lisa thought irritably.

Dillon repeated the question.

It went on like this for over an hour.

Lisa did her best, but she couldn't answer the questions— at least not from Linda Brogan's point of view.

'Did you have a driver's license in the States?'

'No,' Lisa replied, relieved she could answer truthfully.

Dillon checked to see if Dan agreed before scribbling some- thing on his report.

'Were you aware you were driving illegally without a New Zealand license on the evening of March 24?'

'No.'

Dillon stared. 'Are you sure about that?'

Dan's thigh went rigid with tension.

'You thought that when you were driving,' Dillon paused to check his notes, 'Mr Jack Millar's blue Triumph convertible the day of your accident you were licensed to do so?'

What should she say? What *could* she say?

Lisa clutched her hands in her lap and remembered the sight of the little blue car racing towards her. She remembered the bang when it hit her Mazda and the awful sound of glass breaking and the door buckling as the blue car hit, pushing her and her car sideways. There was another horrendous crashing noise on the other side. A noise like a roar of destruction, tearing at her ears, making her scream with fright. And the pain, the dreadful, dreadful pain in her right side.

She clapped her hands over her ears and wailed, 'It hit me! The blue car hit me! It caved in the door and then the other door caved in . . .'

Suddenly, Dan was there, forcing her hands down from her ears and scooping her against his chest. 'Sssh! It's over...it's over.' He pressed his lips against her hair. Lisa heard him say, 'I think my wife has had enough, officer.'

'She needs to sign her statement.'

'I'll sign it for her,' Dan said quickly, and when Dillon began to protest added, 'My wife is dyslexic, Officer Taylor. Writing is difficult for her, particularly since her head injury.'

Lisa felt him nuzzle the top of her hair.

'Is that OK, honey? Can you tell the officer it's OK?'

She raised her head and looked at Dillon. 'I'm sorry, Dillon.'

He stared at her in confusion. 'Have we met before?'

Her eyes filled with tears. This was the way it would always be. She'd be a stranger to her friends. 'No,' she said dully and held out her hands. 'I'll sign the form.'

Dillon looked suspicious when Dan protested.

Lisa gave Dan's arm a reassuring squeeze. She knew that he was frightened she'd sign herself as Lisa Jackson. Gripping Dillon's pen tightly she managed to sign Linda Brogan's name. and was embarrassed by her untidy scribble. 'Sorry. It's not very legible is it?'

'That's OK,' Dillon retrieved his pen and packed his things away.

After he'd gone, Lisa sat at the breakfast bar in the kitchen while Dan made coffee.

'When do you think the court case will be?' she asked when he carried the delicate mugs over to the counter. They looked out of place in his big hands.

He sat next to her. 'I don't know. They'll tell us.'

Lisa toyed with the handle of her mug. 'Thanks for being here. I appreciate it.'

'I wasn't going to leave you to cope on your own. It was tough for you.'

'And you, your leg was working overtime for a while there.' She raised her mug in a mock salute. 'And good try at signing for me. You were petrified I was going to sign as Lisa Jackson, weren't you?'

He frowned into his coffee.

'I probably would have if you hadn't reminded me. Thanks.'

He didn't answer.

They sipped their coffee in silence.

'You don't remember driving the blue car, do you?' Dan asked quietly.

Lisa shook her head.

'You remember being hit by the blue car, don't you?' He watched her hands go still on the china mug, and said gently, 'Tell me what you remember, Lisa.'

After wanting to tell him for so long what had happened to her, Lisa didn't know where to begin. 'I ... I ... remember slowing down. . . to give way to the car on my right.'

She pressed her chin against her chest. Dan had to bend forward to hear her muffled voice.

'The sunstrike was really bad. You know how it is? When it's so bright you're dazzled and can't even see the car in front of you?'

He nodded, his clear grey eyes watching her patiently.

'I'd seen Janice Millar that afternoon and she'd told me I had to have a hysterectomy.'

Dan frowned. 'Why?'

'I had endometriosis. None of the treatments had worked for me.'

His gaze flickered, but he said nothing.

'I remember looking to my right and seeing the little blue car coming towards me. The driver had long, dark hair blowing in the wind. It was going fast but there was another car on her right that was pulling up to the roundabout, so I ... I didn't bother to give way like I should have. I thought she'd stop for the other car.

'I pulled out and heard a car's brakes squeal and the honk of a horn. When I looked over, I saw the driver of the blue car hadn't stopped and the other car had stopped to miss it. She came at me so fast!' Lisa's breathing became ragged. She didn't realize she'd started to cry.

'She hit me so ... so *hard* that it pushed me and my old Mazda right across the road. The noise was terrible! It was so loud! Like a monster roaring. And the blue car just kept coming at me. The door on my side was caving in and there was glass smashing but the other car kept on coming, and then...and then there was another big crash on the other side and that door began to cave in, too!'

Lisa dug her fingers into her right side beneath her breast. 'The pain was so bad! Sharp and awful and ... and . . .' She turned to Dan her eyes huge. 'I didn't give way, Dan! Everybody keeps blaming your wife, but *I* didn't give way like I should have!'

Dan's heart was pounding so hard it was like a drum in his ears. Lisa's hands were pressed over the region of her liver. The woman in the other car bled to death from a lacerated liver.

He dragged her against his chest. 'Stop it! You don't have to say anything more.'

She turned into him and wound her arms about his neck. 'I'm not sorry you asked! I've wanted to tell you for so weeks, but I didn't think you'd listen.' She shuddered. 'You might as well hear the rest now ... but it'll upset you.'

'Upset me?' Dan doubted anything could upset him more than imagining her terror as a car caved in around her.

'It's about Linda,' she said quietly.

She told him about the waiting room and Moira and George. And about Linda and her baby.

And how George had sent her back in Linda's place.

When she'd finished, she waited silently, still huddled against him.

'That's quite ... a story,' he said at last.

Lisa's heart sank. He didn't believe her. She began to pull away.

Dan tightened his hold. 'Where are you going?'

'I want to get down.'

He refused to let her go. 'How did you know the police officer?'

She blinked up at him in surprise, her face inches from his. 'Dillon? He's a friend of my sister Sherry; she's a cop too. I went out with him for a while.'

'You mean you dated him?'

'For almost two years. But my endometriosis got so bad that in the end I broke it off.' She tried to smile. 'It's not a condition that lends itself to romance.'

Dan felt a surge of jealousy. Was that a polite way of saying she'd stopped sleeping with the guy? He gave himself a mental shake, feeling yet again as if he was picking his way through a minefield blindfolded. 'Sherry's the woman you shouted at in the car park?'

She nodded.

'I saw her at the hospital the day of the accident. She was in the Emergency Department. I thought she was waiting to interview me.'

Lisa refrained from mentioning she'd also seen Sherry as she passed by on her way into Linda's body.

Dan took a deep breath that expanded his chest, lifting Lisa up where she lay against him. As he exhaled, she rode the movement gently down again. He stroked the fingertips of one hand around her brow and cheekbone. 'You truly believe you're Lisa Jackson, don't you?'

Lisa stiffened and pulled away.

'Lisa . . .' Dan sighed and reluctantly let her go.

She slid clumsily from the tall chair. 'Please, just forget it — forget everything I said.'

'How on earth do you expect me to do that?' he demanded.

'I don't know — that's your problem. I have enough of my own.' She didn't look back as she hopped towards her bedroom. When she reached it, she shut the door firmly behind her and sat on the bed shivering.

She was an idiot to think that he'd believe her. If somebody had spun her the story she'd told Dan, she wouldn't have believed them either. The only reason Sherry believed her was because Lisa was able to tell her things that only she would know. She shared a history with Sherry, but none with Dan.

The situation would almost be funny if it weren't so painful. If she were in Dan's shoes, the first thing she'd have done was remove any sharp objects from the area right after she asked for her shoelaces.

She sucked in a breath as something new occurred to her.

What would happen if Dan told Craig Fergusson?

☆

'There's a sausage going spare!' Sherry yelled. '*Has anybody not had their sausage?*' Under her breath, she muttered, 'That has got to be a first.'

The sausages were Brenda's contribution to the barbecue Ben had organized. Brenda always brought vegetarian sausages, one for each person, once she'd found out how people many were expected. Sherry was outraged that it was possible to buy vegetarian sausages in the first place and that Brenda could arrive carrying a big bag of food without breaking her housekeeping budget for the week.

However, Ben overcompensated by buying heaps of booze, which put Brenda in a bad mood for the night.

Sherry was annoyed that they were having a barbecue when it was well past summer and the nights were getting cold, but a meeting had been called to discuss the wedding. There was no way Brenda would fork out for a cooked meal for so many, and no way Sherry would let her mother cook for Brenda's horrible family.

The wind suddenly kicked up and Sherry snuggled more deeply into her big white sweater decorated with tea roses.

She'd never known Brenda to miscalculate on the sausage count before — well, certainly not in a *positive* way. She supposed she'd have to put it down to wedding nerves. The thought made her shudder. She wished Lisa was here to snigger with her over the extra sausage and roll her eyes at the idea of Ben marrying Brenda instead of living with Dan Brogan. She pushed the sausages around the grill and thought about the phone call Lisa had made asking if she could come and live with her. It had kept her awake at night ever since, worrying. For all Lisa's assertions to the contrary, Brogan could be a pervert and wife-beater.

Brenda glowered at Sherry through the glass doors that led from the dining room to the decked barbecue area in the back garden. In reply, Sherry hoisted the lone sausage from the hot plate with the barbecue tongs and bared her teeth in a cheesy, insincere grin. Brenda stomped into the kitchen and out of sight.

Sherry waved the sausage and yelled, 'No takers on the sausage?'

Ben stalked outside and snatched the tongs and sausage from her. 'Will you pack it in?'

She gazed at him innocently. 'But Brenda went to all the

trouble of bringing them. It seems a shame to let it go to waste.'

He glared at her.

She glared back.

Ben looked away and took a sip from his can of beer. She knew the purpose of the barbecue was to discuss the wedding and that it was his way of pushing their mother and father towards regaining some normality, some *happiness,* in their lives. Having something to plan helped him to take his mind off Lisa's absence as well.

'I wanted to talk to you about something,' Sherry said.

'Is that right?' Ben replied acerbically. 'I thought you just wanted to piss Brenda off.'

'She's a tightarse, Ben.'

'She's *careful* with her money.'

'She's a tightarse, Ben,' Sherry repeated. 'And not just with her money but with yours too.'

'She can't help it,' he said at last. 'You've seen what her family's like.'

Sherry glanced up at the deck where their parents and Raylene and Denny Buckner were sitting in green canvas chairs sharing a drink. She noticed Brenda's parents had already hoovered up most of the chips and dips her mother had made. Christine was hunched on a bench in the corner of the deck, looking bored and picking at her fingernails. Sherry was convinced she'd only come along because she'd been hoping for an argument to break out. Christine knew how much Sherry loathed Brenda.

'So because she was brought up by the Munsters, Brenda should be excused for being a bludger and a user?' She asked.

'That's *enough,* Sherry!'

She decided it was time to back off. Ben was so laidback he was almost horizontal, but like a lot of easy-going people, he was a force to be reckoned with if he was pushed too far.

She turned to switch the burners off on the barbecue. 'I do need to talk to you.'

'The wedding is off-limits, Sherry.'

'It's not about the wedding,' Sherry replied quietly. 'It's about Lisa.'

His expression turned bleak, but she knew he wouldn't refuse to listen to her. He probably thought she needed to offload some of her grief. He nodded at the five-finger tree. 'We can sit out here with our plates.'

Raylene, Denny, and Christine were the first to the dining-room table when the meat, salads and garlic bread had been laid out. Sherry always made a point of posting herself at the head of the table with the tongs to stop the Buckners cleaning out the meat before anybody else got a look-in. Lisa used to run point on the salad bowls to ensure they didn't run into the same problem there.

'There's a sausage for you, Denny pet!' Sherry squeezed so hard on the tongs the sausage between split in half. 'Damn! They're tender! Where *do* you get them, Brenda?' She transferred half a sausage and the smallest piece of marinated chicken and steak she could find to Brenda's father's plate.

Denny looked between Sherry and his plate, scowling. He was an overweight, stubby man with yellow teeth and a habit of boasting to people that he hadn't bought a new shirt in twenty years. Tonight, he was wearing a pair of brown polyester trousers that were too small for him and a bright-blue-and-yellow Hawaiian-style shirt that strained across his hairy belly. He reminded Sherry of a pink, hairy pig.

His wife stood behind him, a picture in a rayon dress the colour of baby kaka and a bilious green cardigan buttoned at the neck. Raylene, or 'Ray' as she was known, had about as much shape as an oil tanker and stood several inches taller than her husband. Sherry couldn't recall ever seeing her smile. 'And what can I get for you, Ray?' she asked.

'I'd rather serve myself,' Brenda's mother replied irritably.

'Nonsense!' Sherry cried. 'You're our guests and we so seldom get to see you.'

Ray glowered at the morsel of meat placed on her plate and followed her husband in the direction of the salad bowls. 'I'm sure she does it on purpose, Den! Stuck-up cow! Neither of them Jackson girls ever made us feel welcome.'

Denny concentrated on scooping huge dollops of pasta salad onto his plate. In the past, Ben's other sister had manned the salad bowls and had once even whacked him on the back of the hand with a serving spoon when he'd tried to filch a few extra tomatoes from a bowl with his fingers. Denny loved coming to the Jackson's barbecues because Jill and the girls were such good cooks. Which was more than could be said for Ray and his girls.

It was a while before Sherry could get Ben to herself out in the garden. They took their plates to the wooden seat under the big five-finger tree and sat down to eat.

'If this is about calling off the wedding, you're wasting your time.' Ben warned.

'It's not. I told you, it's about Lisa.'

He peered at her in the gathering dark. 'OK. I'm listening.'

Sherry pushed pasta shells about her plate nervously.

Ben was puzzled. It wasn't like his eldest sister to be so

hesitant.

'You remember I said I wanted to see Linda Brogan?' she said at last.

He groaned. 'What have you done now?'

'Not what you think!' she snapped. '*She* came and found *me.*'

This was met with incredulous silence. 'Linda Brogan came to see you?'

Sherry nodded and realized Ben couldn't see her. 'Yes.'

'Beeennn!' Brenda suddenly whined from the deck. 'How can you see out there to eat? Aren't you cold?'

'Won't be long, Brenda!' He called back.

Sherry seethed. Brenda hated it when Ben spent any time with his mother or sisters. She seemed to see them as competition.

'Didn't you know, Brenda?' she called tartly. 'Ben's got x-ray vision! He can see through anything!'

'Sherry...' Ben growled.

Brenda stomped across the deck and into the house.

'So what happened?' He demanded curtly.

'She came to the garden centre to see Dad, and I happened to be there. It was the day Dad gave Ray Tanner his final warning. She was the customer he swore in front of.'

Ben was shocked. 'What did she want to see Dad for? How did she know who he was?'

Sherry stared at the outline of his face in the dark. 'She knew him. She knew me, too.'

'What do you mean she *knew* you and Dad?'

Her hands were shaking. She clasped them together between her thighs. 'Please, Ben, just hear me out.' She took a deep breath, let it out. 'We went to a café.'

'You went for a cup of tea with the woman who killed Lisa?'

'I said hear me out!'

Their mother appeared on the deck, hugging herself against the cool night air. 'You two aren't fighting, are you?'

'No!' Sherry barked.

Ben fumed silently until she kicked him. '*Ow!* No!'

Jill peered at their shadowy figures beneath the tree. 'Well it sounds like it to me. I'm dishing up the pavlova. If you want any, you'd better get in quick.'

She headed back into the house, her shoulders drooping wearily.

Ben watched her go. 'She's tired.'

'She's always tired.'

He shifted on the bench. 'I'd better get inside.'

'No!' Sherry clutched his arm. 'Let me finish.'

'I don't want to hear about Linda Brogan, Sherry,' he said coldly.

'You will when you hear what I have to say.'

She proceeded to tell him the entire events of the day she had met Lisa.

'That is *bullshit!*' Ben exploded when she finished. 'I can't believe you of all people were sucked in by her! Can you *hear* what you're saying?' He sprang up from the bench.

Sherry grabbed his arm again. 'Ben, listen to me! I know how crazy it sounds! Doesn't it tell you something if she convinced *me?* She's Lisa, Ben! If you'd just meet her, I know you'd believe her too!'

He shook her off. 'What's got into you, Sher? I miss Lisa every day. But you can't bring her back from the dead! She's gone! She's in a hole at the cemetery.'

'Her *body* might be!' Sherry insisted stubbornly. 'But her

soul came back! She got *sent* back, Ben!'

'What the fuck have you been drinking?' He snarled.

Sherry blinked. She'd never seen Ben in a rage before. He looked surprisingly big and intimidating; her soft little brother wasn't so soft after all.

'Beeennn!' Brenda called impatiently from the deck. 'We want to talk about the wedding arrangements. Are you coming in?'

'Yeah! Coming!'

'Ask Brenda what happened in the two-dollar shop a few days before your birthday! Ask her about the woman with the broken leg who yelled at her for buying your birthday presents there!' Sherry cried.

'Shut up, Sherry! That's old news from last year!'

'It's not! Brenda tried to pull the same trick again this year, but Lisa saw her and followed her into the shop and reminded her she'd warned her about pulling a stunt like that *last year*.'

Ben hesitated. 'I don't believe you.'

'Ask Brenda.'

He turned away. 'I will not.'

'How did Linda Brogan know what happened last year, Ben? Because I sure as hell didn't tell her!'

Sherry watched helplessly as Ben towards the house and up the steps to the deck, his thick-soled boat shoes thumping aggressively on the wooden boards.

Brenda immediately stuck herself to his side like a sink plunger. Sherry heard her ask, 'What was all that about?'

'Nothing.' Ben replied tersely.

Together they walked into the house.

Sherry sat on the bench, shaking with fury and frustration.

Who would have guessed Ben would be such a hard nut to crack? Everybody automatically pointed the finger at her when it came to naming the stubborn, cynical member of the family.

Brian eventually came out to find her.

He sat down beside Sherry on the bench. 'Your mum said she thought you and Ben had been fighting.'

Sherry shrugged, not trusting herself to speak.

'There's no point pretending you haven't. Ben walked in with a face like a slapped arse.'

She smiled reluctantly. It was one of her father's favourite sayings.

Brian reached out and stroked her hair. 'What's the matter, love?'

She shocked him by burying her face in his shoulder. It wasn't like Sherry to show any sign of vulnerability, to reach out for comfort. Brian closed his arms about her. 'I know, love, I know,' he said softly.

'Dad?'

'Yes?'

'Do you remember the woman who came to the plant centre the day Ray went off the deep end?'

'The one he swore at?'

Sherry nodded against his shoulder.

'The one with the broken leg?'

She nodded again.

He paused. 'She's not much of a gardener. She keeps bringing dying plants to me for advice on how to save them.'

Sherry lifted her head and enquired tartly, 'Does she now?'

'Mmm. She reminds me a bit of you. Pretty and same colouring.'

Sherry was struck by the irony of his observation. He was right. She'd never thought about it until now, but Lisa looked more like her sister now than she did before.

'Why?' Brian asked. 'Do you know her? I meant to ask you but got sidetracked by the business with Ray. You seemed to have a lot to talk about.'

'We sure did,' she agreed wryly.

'Is she alright? I mean about what happened with Ray. I didn't feel comfortable bringing it up when she comes in.'

'She's fine.'

'Is she a friend of yours?'

Sherry wished she could tell her father the truth. 'Yes, she's a friend.'

Jill stuck her head out the doors to the deck. 'Brian!'

'Looks like your mother's calling for reinforcements.' Brian remarked dryly.

Sherry recalled the Buckners were still inside and scowled. 'How bad is it?'

'Well, before I came out to find you, Denny was talking about a wedding he went to where they ran out of food at the reception and the guests had a whip-round and went to the nearest KFC.'

She shook her head in disgust. 'Has Brenda mentioned the bridesmaids' dresses?'

'Ray offered to make them to save money. Brenda said something about green satin.'

'Please god, no! Not the green satin!

'July is still a way off.'

Sherry peered at the outline of his face. It was the closest she'd ever heard either of her parents come to admitting they weren't too crazy about Ben's fiancée. 'We have to stop him, Dad. He's going to make the biggest mistake of his life if he marries Brenda.'

'We can't interfere, Sherry. It's not our choice.' Brian got to his feet, pulling Sherry with him.

'But Dad! He'll eventually share our genes with that family! They'll have babies with bri-nylon baby-gros. Toddlers with polyester short sets. It won't matter if they turn out as nice-looking as Ben. Do you honestly want to have a Grandad's Brag Book with photos of grandchildren dressed by Brenda and RayRay?'

Brian chuckled. 'We'll cross that bridge when we come to it. Although, I have to admit that the Buckners wouldn't exactly be top of my list if I was looking to graft my family tree.'

Sherry laughed. She couldn't have put it better herself.

Chapter 18

Dan didn't doubt Lisa's sincerity. He was certain she believed every word she said. Hell, it would certainly explain a lot of the bizarre things that had happened since she'd woken up. However, his head told him a different story.

He understood how awkward it must be for her to be living with him. He was a stranger, not because she'd lost her memory, but because she'd never set eyes on him before she saw him at the hospital. She wasn't the only one who felt awkward. He'd tried hard not to cause her any embarrassment because she didn't know him while he'd been one hundred per cent sure he knew *her*. But her revelations had pulled the rug right out from under his feet.

Dan felt like he was on a never-ending first date. But instead of the flirting and getting-to-know-one-another period they'd moved in together right after the first drink had been bought. He was living with a beautiful woman about whom he knew nothing. He didn't know what her favourite colour was, what her favourite food was, what music she liked — all the intimate little details dating revealed along the way.

'I'm the one who's going bonkers,' he muttered, borrowing one of Lisa's favourite sayings.

Now, when he recalled the look on her face when he unpacked her underwear into her locker on his nightly visits to the hospital, he winced. And when he thought of how often he'd wandered round the house dressed in a pair of Speedos after returning from windsurfing and how Lisa almost dropped the basket of cutlery she was unloading from the dishwasher, he groaned. He'd been so engrossed on heading to the laundry to rinse his wetsuit, it never occurred to him that he might be the cause of her clumsiness or why she refused any help picking up the knives and forks.

He needed to take control of the situation, to make some *sense* of it all. So Dan did what he was trained to do. He researched the facts.

Lisa had mentioned she'd had surgery on her foot as a child. When Dan asked her about it, she answered his questions warily, but she seemed to speak truthfully. As soon as he had a spare moment at the hospital, he called the patient records department and asked how far the archives went back. He knew what he was about to do was unethical, but he was desperate.

'We keep medical records for about twenty-five years, Mr Brogan,' the clerk told him.

'Then what happens to them?'

'They're destroyed or, if you're lucky, they might have been transferred onto microfilm.'

'Would you mind taking a look for me?'

'Of course, tell me what you need.'

The clerk called Dan back later that morning. 'You're in luck, we still have those records. Did you realize Lisa Jackson is deceased? The notes would have been destroyed if it weren't for the fact her death has been referred to the coroner and the notes might be needed for reference.'

Dan was unnerved by the casual way the woman spoke about Lisa Jackson's death. He managed to thank her without revealing how much her reply had distressed him. *He* didn't understand why it upset him. Apart from her date of birth and that she was the woman who died in the other car involved in Linda's accident, he didn't know who Lisa Jackson was.

Lisa said she was twenty-seven when the accident happened and that she'd been born at National Women's Hospital almost two months' premature and lived her entire life at the same address in Browns Bay.

Lisa Louise Jackson's medical records went right back to the date of her birth twenty-seven years ago on 22 February, just like she said. There were two thick yellow folders of ink-filled notes held together with a thick elastic band. A bright yellow Post-it note was tucked under the band upon which somebody had written: *Deceased 24 March. Coroner's Case.*

Dan stared at the date and shivered. He felt like somebody had walked over his grave.

The records told the story of a baby girl born almost two months premature. She was the second child of Jill and Brian Jackson of Beach Road, Browns Bay. She had one older sibling who was also a girl. The baby spent weeks in the neonatal and special baby care units at the hospital before being released home weighing five and a half pounds. There were brief mentions of a left club-foot deformity, but it was way down the list of concerns in those early months. She returned to hospital for surgery and plaster casts and ongoing physiotherapy until she was four years old. Her sunny nature was often mentioned. *In some pain last night. Responded well to change in analgesia. Woke up smiling as usual this morning. Happy little girl.*

Dan came across a child's painting showing the usual stick figures, one of which had one big, fat leg and one skinny one and a big smile on the stick figure's face.

Somebody had written across the top in black felt-tip: *To Mr Wrigley from Lisa Jackson aged three and three quarters*. Wrigley had been the surgeon caring for Lisa. She'd signed her name with a backward L and a wonky S.

His heart throbbed. Dan smoothed his finger across the childish writing before folding it up and putting it away in his briefcase. The earlier notes ended when Lisa was seen for the last time in the out-patients' department. She was thriving and enjoying school and there was now a third child in the family, a brother who was two years younger. Dan felt the familiar prickling begin in his scalp. The boy's name wasn't mentioned, but he just knew it would be Ben.

He leaned back in his chair, cupped his head in his hands and closed his eyes. It was dark outside. Usually, he'd have been home by now. He should call Lisa and tell her not to worry, not that she ever complained or questioned his erratic schedule. Dan guessed she didn't think she had any right to. The thought depressed him.

He rubbed his eyes wearily. He'd been in surgery until one o'clock and then on a ward round until he was called down to the children's emergency department to see a child involved in a car accident with hip and leg injuries. It resulted in another stint in theatre that hadn't ended until seven o'clock. He really should go home but, tired as he was, he couldn't tear himself away from Lisa Jackson's clinical records. It was like peeling layers from an onion. He was drawn to this cheerful, brave little girl who'd fought the odds and survived. The love and commitment of her parents was there in the surgeon's notes which ended when she was five and a half.

Lisa said Janice Millar was treating her for endometriosis.

Turning to his computer, Dan keyed in her National Health Index number and began a search. In a matter of minutes, Lisa's name appeared on the screen along with her most recent medical history. Dan scrolled quickly past the last entry of her admission on 24 March and the time of her death. Seeing it made his skin crawl. He searched further back and grunted when Janice Millar's name came up as the treating physician. It was an ironic coincidence that Jack Millar's wife had been Lisa's gynaecologist.

The skin prickled on Dan's scalp when he saw that Lisa's occupation was listed as primary school teacher and that the last notes written by Janice Millar concluded that due to Lisa's poor response to treatment and the severity of her endometriosis the only answer was a hysterectomy. Dan sensed Janice's frustration and reluctance to perform such a final procedure on a young woman.

I have discussed a hysterectomy with Lisa. Understandably, she is reluctant to proceed with this unless absolutely necessary. States she had always wanted children. Explained it is now the only way to manage her chronic pain. Lisa's general health continues to decline ...

Lisa's blood results showed she was anaemic. Dan read on: *Conservative management of her endometriosis has proven ineffective.*

He stared at the computer screen. Everything Lisa had told him about herself was there in Janice's notes.

★

Apart from one visit to his office to offer her heart-broken apologies for what had happened, Janice had pretty much avoided Dan since the accident. He felt sorry for her. She was yet another woman sucked in by Jack Millar's practiced charm and commitment to his own selfish pleasures. Janice was a shy, awkward woman with a nervous manner. Her looks were pleasant but nothing out of the ordinary, and she always looked worried. She was besotted with Jack and devoted to their three children.

Dan recognized a fellow introvert when he saw one, particularly one who hadn't found a way around her shyness. Janice had a reputation as an excellent doctor and was highly regarded by her patients and colleagues. Dan was mystified what an intelligent woman saw in a shallow bastard like Jack.

She seemed shocked when he knocked on the door of her office at the main hospital the following day. Her brown eyes widened, and she clutched the edge of her desk. 'D-Dan!' she spluttered in her pronounced Texan drawl.

He smiled reassuringly from the doorway, the knuckles of one hand still resting on door. 'Hi, Janice. Sorry to bust in on you like this.'

She shook her head. 'No ... no, that's OK. What can I do for you?'

'You've finished your clinic?'

She nodded apprehensively.

Dan closed the door behind him and leaned against it. Janice's eyes flickered to him and away again. He could tell she was dreading what he would say and decided to put her out of her misery and come straight to the point. 'Were you treating a young woman called Lisa Jackson for endometriosis?'

Clearly, it wasn't what she was expecting him to say. No surprises there.

'Yes.' She frowned. 'How did you know?'

'I looked at her records.'

'Why?'

They both knew he shouldn't have done it.

'Lisa Jackson was the driver of the other car in the accident.'

Janice dipped her head and fiddled with some forms on the desk. 'Yes. I know. She died.'

Dan flinched. Why did he find it easier to cope with the idea of Linda's death than Lisa's? 'I know this will seem like a weird question but,' he cleared his throat. 'What was she like?'

She raised her head and stared at him. 'What she was like?'

'Yes.' He tried to think of an explanation and settled for, 'It's been bothering me.'

Janice sighed heavily. 'It's been bothering me, too.'

He waited.

'Damn, I want a cigarette!' she cried irritably. 'I keep trying to give up but something always tips me over.'

'It's tough.'

In Dan's opinion, anybody married to a weasel like Jack Millar would have to resort to nicotine, booze or Class A drugs to dull the pain.

'I don't suppose I have to be concerned about patient confidentiality under the circumstances.' Janice raised a questioning brow.

He nodded reassuringly.

'I'd been treating Lisa for several years for endometriosis. Her case was hard to manage, the endometrial tissue was all through her pelvic area and she was in a lot of pain. I'd tried all the usual conservative treatments and an IUD, but she only improved for a brief period of time. She had to give up her job as a full-time teacher and become a relief teacher. I'd reached the end of the line and a hysterectomy was all that was left.' Janice gave Dan a wry smile. '*Not* one of my success stories.'

'We've all been there,' he murmured. 'What was she like?'

'Sweet, cute, *nice*. I really liked Lisa. She had a really kooky sense of humour and used to floor me with the way she managed to stay so positive. It wasn't until I told her that she needed a hysterectomy that she fell to pieces. I remember her saying that last day that she'd always believed she'd end up with a husband and the 2.4 kids. She loved her job, but she wasn't a new millennium career woman.' Janice sighed deeply. 'She was only twenty-seven when she died, Dan. She'd been handed so much shit, but she kept coming into my office each month determined to see her life as a bunch of roses. Don't get me wrong: she wasn't stupid, but she was *very* determined.'

The description pretty much fitted the Lisa Dan knew. 'What did she look like?'

Janice's brows rose in surprise. 'She was small — only a couple inches over five feet and very petite. She wasn't beautiful, but pretty in a cute kind of way.' She gestured to her hair. 'She had short, curly fair hair and blue eyes. She was a preemie and had to have corrective surgery for talipes.'

Dan thought about Lisa's comment in the supermarket about how great it was to be tall.

'Dan?'

He brought his wandering thoughts back to Janice. 'Yes?'

'Is it true that Linda has been suffering from amnesia since she regained consciousness?'

'Yes.'

'I'm so sorry. That must be dreadful for you ... and her,' she added belatedly.

Dan straightened and reached for the door handle. 'We'll get by.'

☆

When he got home, he was tempted to tell Lisa that he'd read her notes and spoken to Janice Millar. But he didn't.

The whole idea of her being Lisa Jackson and not Linda was preposterous. His head told him so — even if his heart said otherwise. The awkwardness Dan had felt so far when they were together was multiplied a hundredfold. Before, he'd believed that despite her bizarre behaviour, Lisa was still Linda and the truth would eventually out. Even if she didn't remember him, he had memories of her. The past few days had shot that theory to hell and back.

A stranger was living in his house. They hadn't had time to get to know each other except in the most superficial sense before being thrown together in the most intimate way possible – as husband and wife. Dan pitied Lisa when he realized it had been like this for her right from the moment she woke up. The only way he could keep his sanity was by staying away from her, which nagged at his instinctive urge to protect and support her. He made a point of setting the table for their evening meal, so he didn't have to sit beside her and relive the night they almost had sex on the counter. If he came away from the table with indigestion from eating too fast, it was a small price to pay for keeping his hands to himself.

He stopped strolling through the house in his Speedos when he got back from windsurfing. Instead, he wore his wetsuit inside and showered it clean along with himself. He reverted to the old-fashioned manners his mother and father had taught him and treated Lisa like she was his maiden aunt.

Lisa acted as if she hated him. She hid in her room and hardly spoke to him. From what Dan could see, she had longer conversations with Slade than any she shared with him. He knew he was bungling the situation but didn't know how to make things better. Dan hated the how things had turned out. He missed her quirky sense of humour and her laughter but didn't know what else to do.

It was a relief when he spotted a sheet of paper next to Lisa's purse a few days after he visited Janice. He went looking for Lisa and found her ferociously scrubbing a pot in the kitchen.

'Lisa?'

She looked at him over her shoulder, her arms elbow deep in soapy water, and asked rudely, 'What?'

He'd noticed that her rudeness had increased in proportion to his politeness. 'I see you have an appointment to have your cast removed.'

She turned back to the sink and attacked the pot again. 'Yes.'

Dan studied the curve of her bottom beneath the long denim skirt she was wearing. He didn't recognize the skirt as one of Linda's. In fact, Lisa had been wearing a few things lately that he'd never seen before — simpler, more functional items of clothing that suited Lisa but would never have been Linda's taste. After eight years of marriage, Dan knew what expensive women's clothing looked like, and the denim skirt and the other new things weren't designer items. Lisa's ability to manage on the miniscule amount of money she accepted from him, simultaneously astounded and annoyed him.

'It's tomorrow morning.'

She kept her back turned. 'I know.'

Dan gritted his teeth. 'How were you going to get there?'

'I dunno. Shanks's pony.'

'Pardon me?'

'Walk, bus, whatever. Don't worry, I'll be there.'

'I'll take you.'

She stopped scrubbing the pot and frowned at him over her shoulder. 'The appointment isn't until ten-thirty. You're usually gone by seven.'

'You can wait in my office until your appointment is due.'

Lisa regarded him suspiciously. 'Why?'

He frowned. 'Why what?'

'Why the sudden urge to escort me? Don't you think I can be relied on to turn up? Believe me, I'm *dying*—'

They both winced.

'I mean I *really* want this thing off.'

Dan ground his teeth. Why couldn't she just accept his offer? Because he'd been behaving like a total asshole, that's why.

'They won't give me another one, will they?' Lisa asked anxiously.

'Another what?'

'Another cast? I won't need another one, will I?'

'Hopefully not,' He paused. 'But if you do, you'll need a ride home.'

Dan watched her face fall and felt like the worst kind of a heel. It was unlikely the cast would be replaced. Her injury had been a straightforward fracture and should have healed enough to get rid of the cast.

Lisa looked upset. 'I am not having another cast! I don't care what *anybody* says!'

His lips twitched. She reminded him of one of the kids at the hospital throwing a tantrum about their treatment. *I don't want another plaster, Dr Dan! It itches and I hate it!*

Usually, he could talk them around. He wasn't so sure about Lisa.

'I'm sure you won't. Just be ready to leave at seven.'

'Alright,' she agreed grumpily and returned to her pots and pans.

☆

They barely spoke on the drive to the hospital the next morning.

Lisa stared out of the window at the slow-moving rows of traffic fighting to get down the Northern motorway and across the Harbour Bridge into the city, feeling thankful they were travelling at a crawling pace.

Dan's hope that they might be able to return to their former easy footing and enjoy the kind of lively conversation they'd had in the past was ruined by the memory of a dream about Lisa sitting stark-naked in his car on the journey into work. It had woken him at two o'clock in the morning with an erection and his breath rasping in and out of his lungs like an old asthmatic.

He could barely think straight, let alone speak.

After depositing Lisa in his office, he departed for the operating theatre. He'd asked her to wait for him after her appointment so that when he finished his theatre list so he could drive her home.

'I can get the bus,' She insisted.

'There's no need,' Dan snapped and departed.

Lisa surveyed the mess on his desk. It looked a lot like his bedroom used to.

She was hurt at the way he kept blowing hot and cold and

regretted ever telling him her story. Ever since, he'd treated her like an alien being and was as twitchy as a drug addict going cold turkey when he was around her. She hated it. She wanted to hate *him*. But whenever she heard his car drive into the garage and saw his square-jawed face and those wary grey eyes as he asked her about her day, she'd remember how he'd held her and shielded her from pain and ridicule. And her heart would squeeze in her chest and blow a raspberry in the direction of her brain.

Her heart was most definitely running the show; aided and abetted by her hormones. Both deserved to be locked up for inciting the roaring desire she felt whenever she imagined getting herself wrapped around that tall, fit-looking body.

Sherry had no difficulty identifying the reason for Lisa's crabbiness or the cure. 'Sleep with him.'

Lisa was appalled that it was so obvious and outraged that Sherry made the answer sound so simple. 'I will not! What do you take me for?'

'A horny, pathetic slapper. *Sleep with him.*'

She sighed and gave up pretending. 'He wouldn't touch me with a ten-foot pole.'

'Maybe not a pole but I'm sure there's something else he'd be happy to touch you with.'

'You can be *so* crude sometimes, Sherry!'

'And sexually satisfied,' Sherry retorted. 'I sleep *well* at night, Lisa. Do you?'

She stared at her shoes and muttered, 'I don't know what to do.'

Sherry was incredulous. '*You don't know what to do? Are you serious?*'

'He goes hot and cold,' Lisa explained miserably. 'He can

be as unreachable as the Southern Alps when it suits him.'

'For God's sake, Lisa! When it comes to sex, men aren't complicated and I'm sure that includes the good doctor. Work it out, girl!'

She gazed back helplessly. 'What do I do? What would *you* do?'

Sherry had the grace to blush. 'I'm sure if you got naked and climbed into bed with him during the night he wouldn't fight you off. You'll soon get over him once you realize he's just the same as any of the other men you've gone to bed with.' She paused. '*Both* of them.'

Lisa scowled. This was her reward for confiding in her sister. Where had her pride gone? Up in smoke the moment Dan Brogan strolled into the kitchen in his Speedos. 'I wouldn't bet on that,'

'Will you shut up? You're starting to piss me off. Just remember one thing.'

'What?'

'A condom.'

Lisa almost laughed herself sick when she imagined creeping — well, maybe not creeping, more like *thumping* with the plaster cast on her leg — into Dan's bedroom naked and clutching a condom. She pictured herself sliding into bed beside him and running her hand across the warm skin of his naked shoulder. Did he sleep naked? He always seemed to have something on when he rescued her from her sleepwalking episodes.

'*Dan?*' she'd husk. '*Dan?*'

Husking sounded so much better than her Kiwi twang.

It was about then that he reared up and looked over his shoulder at her with an appalled expression on his face as Lisa stroked a foil-covered condom teasingly down his arm and husked again, *'I've come prepared, Dan. Prepared to come.'*

He leapt out of bed and told her to fuck off. It wasn't the climax she'd been hoping for.

☆

Lisa found her way up to the main block to see Rob the plaster technician at the appointed time and waited an extra three-quarters of an hour because the clinic was running late. After Rob had cut off her plaster, he sent her to the radiology department to get in the queue for an x-ray. After that, she got in the queue to wait for the orthopaedic surgeon to look at her films. By then, Lisa was sweating at the thought of being told she would have to have another cast put on.

When she went in to see the surgeon, the first thing he asked her was, 'How's Dan?'

'Er ... fine,' Lisa muttered. What about her? What about her leg?

'Haven't seen him for a while,' Boneman put the x-ray onto the light box and squinting at the bright white bones in Lisa's leg.

Lisa squinted with him. All she could see was a fluffy kind of lump around the two bones. Was that normal? She wished Dan were here. He would know. It occurred to her the man in front of her would too.

'How does it—' she began just as Dan walked in wearing dark-green theatre scrubs. He even looked handsome in them. She bet the nurses just about wet their pants watching him scrub up.

'Speak of the devil!' Boneman leapt to his feet to shake Dan's hand. 'I was just asking ... your wife how you were.'

Her lip curled in disgust. The moron couldn't even

remember her name. Perhaps that was just as well, the name on the big brown envelope of x-rays was Linda Brogan.

'How are things looking, Mark?'

'Good! I hear you're up for one of the Quality in Health Awards.'

Lisa listened with interest. Was he?

'Maybe,' Dan studied at the film on the light box. 'How's Lisa's leg?'

Mark didn't notice the name Dan used was different to the one on the Xrays. He tapped the box with his knuckle. 'It's looking great. We'll put her into a double Tubigrip for a few more weeks and she can start weight-bearing. She'll need to keep up the physio for a little longer.'

Lisa listened anxiously. Was a Tubigrip another name for a cast?

'I hear you're doing some great work with the Ilizarov splints down the hill,' Mark continued. 'I'll be at the awards evening. I'm looking forward to seeing your presentation.'

Dan nodded. 'Do you want to see Lisa again?'

Mark blinked and looked at Lisa glowering in her chair as if he'd just remembered she was the reason he was there. He looked at the name on the notes and x-rays. 'Lisa? I thought your name was Linda.'

'She prefers to be known as Lisa,' Dan replied smoothly.

'What's a Tubigrip?' Lisa asked as she hopped along the corridor after the appointment.

Dan walked slowly by her side. 'A stretchy white stocking that goes from your knee to your toes. It's a little like a surgical stocking.'

She sighed with relief. 'I'm good with a surgical stocking, even if I do end up looking like a Nana Doris.'

'A Nana Doris?'

'An old lady.'

He snorted.

'It isn't funny.'

He snorted again. 'The Tubigrip will be a piece of cake after the caste. It's only for a few more weeks, and you can take it off to shower and before you go to bed.'

She regarded him suspiciously. 'You're not winding me up?'

His lips twitched. 'I'm not winding you up.'

'What about the crutches?'

'You can start weight-bearing gradually.'

She beamed at him.

It was Dan who measured and applied the stretchy white stocking to her leg. Lisa was mortified by its' hairy, white condition but Dan didn't seem to notice. He was more interested in making sure there weren't any wrinkles in the stocking and that it was the right size. The feel of his big, steady hands on her bare skin set parts of her body tingling that really needed to butt out. He got her to practice walking a few steps with the crutches while he looked on, his arms crossed over his green scrub shirt. He wasn't impressed when Lisa almost tripped over the crutches. 'Pay attention to what you're doing!'

She was *trying* but kept getting distracted by the sight of his chest and throat above the V of the green shirt.

'OK?' he asked.

'It's a bit overwhelming.'

'You'll soon get used to it.'

She wasn't talking about the stocking or the crutches. 'Why didn't I get somebody like you to look after me instead of Mighty Mark?'

'You're too old for me.'

'Gee, thanks.'

He smiled. 'I know he doesn't have the greatest bedside manner but he's a good surgeon. I'd let him work on me.'

Lisa took another slow circuit past him. 'Go ahead! Sign up.'

Dan chuckled and turned red when Lisa stopped walking and stared.

He took her up to the theatre floor and found her a seat outside while he went back in to change his clothes. Lisa was touched when he explained in the elevator that his morning list had run over, which was why he had run down still wearing his scrubs because he was worried she'd think he'd forgotten her.

'Are you hungry?' he asked when he returned wearing his dark-blue suit and with his hair mussed from dressing in a hurry.

'A bit.'

Recalling Sherry's advice, Lisa grabbed the lapel of his suit and went up on tiptoe to smooth his hair flat.

Dan's brows rose, but he didn't pull away. He slowly tipped his head to make it easier for her to reach and took hold of her elbows to steady her while his eyes searched her face.

Lisa allowed her fingers to linger in the silky thickness of his hair for a few seconds longer than necessary, until she realized she was standing in a public building stroking him. She cleared her throat nervously and stepped back. 'That's better. You looked like Dennis the Menace.'

'Gee, thanks.'

She laughed.

Dan took Lisa to lunch at a nearby café, walking slowly

beside her in the sunshine. She felt as if a bottle of champagne had been opened inside her; bubbles of joy kept surfacing and popping all over her body. Dan looked the most relaxed she'd seen him in weeks.

After lunch they returned to the hospital. Lisa was prepared to catch a bus home, thinking Dan had used up his entire lunchbreak and wouldn't have time to drive her back. He delighted her by asking if she wanted to come up to the ward and meet some of the children while he did a quick ward round.

'I'd love to!'

☆

The first thing Lisa noticed when she walked into the ward were the colourful pictures on the walls, the cheerful prints on the beds and curtains, and the bright sunshine flooding the rooms from the big windows. Most of the rooms held four beds with a few single and twin-bedded side rooms.

The children's faces lit up when Dan walked in.

'Hi, Doctor Dan!'

'What tie have you got on today, Dr Dan?'

His Pokemon tie got the stamp of approval. He let a small boy hold the end of hit and inspect Pikachu.

'Cooool...'

He introduced Lisa to the children simply as 'Lisa' and began explaining the metal frames some of them had attached to their legs. They were the Ilizarov splints Mark had mentioned during her appointment.

Lisa eyed them warily. They weren't a sight for the fainthearted. A round metal frame stretched the length of the child's limb with slim metal rods thrust through the leg and out the other side again. The rods were then attached to the frame by screws. They looked like a human form of shish kebab.

Dan checked one of the older boys. 'Are you turning the screws regularly, Baron?'

'Yeah, Dr Dan,' Baron produced a small silver tool from his bedside drawer and a list with times and dates on it. 'See? And I've been cleaning the pin sites myself too.'

I think I'm going to be sick, Lisa thought, smiling until her face hurt. How can they be so brave?

Baron's leg had a few more centimetres to go before it matched his uninjured one. He was being discharged at the end of the week and would carry on turning the screws on his frame four times a day for as long as it took to grow the soft spongy bone at the fracture site.

Lisa studied the children lying on their beds with their legs propped on pillows and listened to them discussing how much their legs had grown, how much more they needed to grow and how often they'd turned their screws that day. Dan went from bed to bed wearing a smile, speaking in his quiet, kind voice, congratulating most and raising his brows at the ones who weren't doing what they should be. Those raised eyebrows seemed to be all they needed to get out their little silver tools and get to work on the screws.

A small girl called, 'Hey, Dr Dan!'

'Hey there, Moana,' Dan replied easily as he scribbled on some notes.

'Could grow our legs as tall as yours?' she asked cheekily.

This was greeted by a burst of laughter from the children, who rolled around their beds giggling.

He shook his head, smiling. 'I want to get you home sooner than that, Moana.'

Moana studied Lisa. 'Are you Dr Dan's girlfriend?'

Lisa hesitated. She didn't wear any wedding rings, so it was a natural enough assumption. 'Er ... no.'

'This is Lisa,' Dan repeated, just as he had when he brought her into every room.

Moana wasn't satisfied with his answer. 'Are you Dr Dan's wife?'

Lisa was accustomed to dealing with kids and their awkward questions but didn't have a clue how to answer. 'Er ...'

Dan had Moana's chart braced on his raised thigh while he wrote on it. Without raising his head, he said, 'Yes, Moana, you nosy little monkey, Lisa's my wife.' He finished with the chart and sent Moana a look from beneath raised brows which clearly said *Behave*.

She grinned and buried her nose in a raggedy old doll.

Lisa leaned on her crutches, feeling awkward and wondering why Dan wasn't as perturbed as she was by Moana's questions. He'd moved on to the girl in the next bed and was examining her foot.

Baron reclaimed her attention. 'What happened to you? Did Dr Dan operate on your leg too?'

This brought another round of laughter.

Lisa relaxed and smiled. 'No. But I did break my leg.'

'When?'

'March.'

'How?'

'In a car accident.'

'Who was driving?' Baron asked.

Dan lifted his head. '*Baron.*'

'I was,' Lisa replied.

Baron thought about this for a moment. 'Well, that was

dumb.'

Lisa burst out laughing, along with the children. Dan rolled his eyes and shook his head.

'Not as dumb as playing on the roof of your uncle's shed and falling through, Baron!' Moana retorted.

Baron shrugged and grinned.

'They're great.' Lisa said as they left the ward.

Dan smiled and nodded. 'Sometimes it's hard to keep my poker face, especially when I have to get tough on them.'

'Oh, yeah. I can see you're real tough, Dr Dan. I'd be quaking in my splint if I had you sorting me out.'

He smiled again and checked his watch. 'If I give you a ride home now, I'll be back in time for my out-patients clinic.'

'You're sure?'

'I'm sure.'

In the car, Lisa asked, 'What are the awards Mark was talking about?'

'Nothing special. They're awards for clinical excellence — innovation — that kind of thing. They're held every year.'

'And you're one of the finalists?'

'Not just me, the whole team working on the Ilizarov programme.'

Lisa eyed him with amusement. 'Well, I hope you win. After what I saw today, you deserve to.'

'You haven't seen the other finalists. They're doing some amazing things. Non-invasive surgery, studies into medication levels in psychotic admissions in the ER — all sorts of things that are incredibly important.'

As they crossed the Harbour Bridge to the North Shore, Lisa fiddled with the top of her white stocking and watched the boats on the Waitemata Harbour. The ocean glittered in the sunshine, sailing boats carving the surface on their way towards the islands scattered about the Hauraki Gulf.

'It's three weeks this Saturday night. Would you like to come?'

She looked at Dan in surprise. Her first instinct was to decline, fearing he was only asking her out of politeness, until Sherry's sardonic voice intruded on her thoughts. Why not? What did she have to lose? Your pride, your self-esteem, your marbles, the sensible part of her brain replied tartly.

'I'd like that.'

Chapter 19

Lisa was determined to put a stop to her sleepwalking — or at least to Dan having to chase her around the house in the middle of the night. He seemed to take it in his stride, but she was acutely aware there were dark circles under his eyes most mornings and that he was going into the operating theatre without the benefit of a good night's sleep. So, on the Friday night following the removal of her cast, she took what seemed to be the only sensible course of action...and tied herself to the bed.

It had seemed like a good idea the night before as she knotted the silk sash of Linda's white robe around her wrist and the other end around the wooden headboard, leaving herself enough slack to lie down but not get out of the bed. In the morning, she awoke with pins and needles in her hand. During the night she'd obviously tried to get out of bed a few times and each time she climbed or tripped back in, the sash had twisted turning the knot into a hard little nut of material and the slack she'd allowed herself to disappear.

Lisa struggled to her knees, and she tried to loosen the knot, but it wouldn't budge. To make matters worse, she was dying to go to the toilet. She clamped her knees together, jiggled on the mattress and called tentatively for Dan, hoping that he'd understand why she'd tied herself to the bed. After several unanswered and increasingly frantic calls for help, Lisa realised he'd probably risen early, and gone for a ride on his mountain bike or down to the beach with his windsurfer.

She whimpered. Her bladder felt like it was going to burst. Sweat broke out on her forehead as she watched the tips of her fingers turn from purple to white. What if her hand had to be amputated through lack of blood flow? Most people lost limbs doing something heroic like getting lost in a blizzard and succumbing to frostbite, not tying themselves up to a bed.

The little silver mobile phone Dan had given her suddenly began to vibrate on the bedside table. With a cry of triumph, Lisa leapt for it, crashed into the table, and knocked the phone across the carpet. It came to a halt when it hit the wall beneath the window.

Eyes glued to the phone, Lisa held her breath and waited. When it buzzed again, she gave a sigh of relief, slid from the bed and extending her good leg as far as she could tried to stab the answer button with her big toe.

'Hello? Hello? Can you hear me? Whoever this is *please come quick!* To the house! I'm ... I'm trapped in my bedroom and ...*the situation is desperate! I need help!*'

She tried to hook the phone towards her with her toes and howled in frustration when she managed to slam her foot onto the keypad instead and cut the caller off. 'Oh shit! Oh shit! Oh shit!'

Lisa tucked her heel beneath her bottom and rocked back and forth on the carpet. The pain in her bladder was excruciating. She pressed her forehead against the mattress and mumbled, '*I will not pee on the carpet... I will not pee on the carpet...*'

Five minutes later, she heard Dan pull into the garage.

'Dan! Dan!! DANNN!'

Dan cut the engine and heard Lisa shout his name. He'd been out on his windsurfer, leaving her fast asleep at the house. So far, she'd never walked in her sleep in the morning, so he felt confident about leaving her for an early-morning trip to the beach.

Her frantic calls sent his heartbeat into overdrive. Leaping from the car, he raced into the house, still wearing his black wetsuit, and burst into her bedroom. She wasn't in the bed. Dan's gaze tangled with Lisa's blue eyes watching him anxiously over the edge of the mattress and one arm tethered to the headboard. 'What the—?'

'Hurry up!' She tugged frantically at the stripe of material tethering her to the bed. 'I'm busting to go to the loo!'

Dan stared. 'You tied yourself to the bed?'

She pressed her sweaty forehead against the mattress. 'For God's sake cut the small talk and untie me!'

He scooted around the bed and examined the knot. 'What the hell have you been doing?' he demanded, feeling torn between disbelief and amusement at her latest escapade.

'I was trying to stop sleepwalking, You never get a good night's sleep.' She wriggled anxiously and moaned. 'Hurry up, Dan! I can't hold on much longer!'

'OK! OK!' He set to work on the knot. 'I'll be as quick as I can.'

☆

Neither of them heard another car pull into the driveway, or footsteps hurrying through the garage and into the house.

'Dan!' Lisa wailed loudly, convinced she was about to disgrace herself on the bedroom floor. She would *die* if she humiliated herself like that in front of him.

He swore at the knot, which refused to budge. 'I'll have

to cut it.'

'You're not cutting anything!' A voice snarled.

They looked up in astonishment at the woman standing in the doorway to the bedroom, her long legs spread, her weight balanced on the balls of her feet as if she were getting ready to spring.

Lisa saw her sister.

Dan saw the woman from the supermarket car park.

Sherry saw the fruitcake that sounded but didn't look like her sister tied to a bed at the feet of the big American doctor who was dressed in a black Neoprene wetsuit and tying her to the bed.

'Get away from her!'

Dan frowned and demanded, 'What the hell are *you* doing here?'

Sherry couldn't answer that. She'd heard Lisa's tormented cries over her mobile phone, leapt in her car and headed for the Brogan house. She'd given up trying to tell herself that it was impossible Lisa was alive and well inside Linda Brogan's body.

'Sherry, it isn't like that—' Lisa began in a tortured voice.

Dan suddenly marched out of the bedroom.

She blinked in astonishment. He was *leaving* her? *Abandoning* her at a time like this?

The pain in her bladder was killing her. The dam gates were about to burst. 'I can't ... hold on ... any longer ...'

Sherry tried to work the knot on the white silk free. 'What has that bastard been doing to you?'

Lisa rocked back and forth, moaning, 'No ... no ...'

Dan walked back in carrying a pair of scissors. He held them out to Sherry and said curtly, 'You'll need these.'

Sherry narrowed her eyes at him as Lisa sank from view

onto the carpet.

'You'd better hurry,' he advised crisply. 'She's about to pee on the carpet.'

Snatching the scissors from him, Sherry snipped the taut fabric in half and jumped backwards as Lisa launched herself from the floor and raced towards the bathroom with her hands clamped between her thighs.

Sherry and Dan glared at each other and tried to ignore the sound of Lisa attending to nature.

The noise from the bathroom went on . . .

And on . . .

Their brows rose in unison as their faces turned towards the bathroom door wearing matching expressions of fascinated disbelief.

The noise stopped.

Dan grunted.

And started again.

Sherry's eyes popped wide open.

They waited tensely until at last all was silent, and Lisa reappeared, the white silk sash hanging from her wrist.

She refused to look at Dan. 'What are you doing here, Sherry?'

It was clear that her sister had flung on her clothes without taking time to ensure her usual high standards of grooming.

'I'm here because I heard you yelling for help on your mobile,' Sherry sent Dan a look cold enough to freeze him into a large Popsicle. 'What were you doing to her?'

Dan ignored Sherry and cut across Lisa's clumsy attempts to explain. 'Perhaps you could introduce us, Lisa?' he suggested sardonically.

Lisa glanced warily between them. She was stuck

between Dan, the rock, and Sherry, the hard place. 'Dan, this is my sister, Sherry Jackson. Sherry, this is Dan Brogan, my . . .' She ground to a halt and shrugged.

Dan waited; one brow raised in query. When it became clear Lisa didn't have anything further to say, he turned a cool gaze on Sherry and repeated, 'Your sister?'

'Yes,' Lisa insisted defensively.

He studied Sherry. 'Is that so?'

Sherry ignored him. 'What were you doing to her?'

'Sherry!' Lisa cried reproachfully.

On the rare occasion she'd allowed herself to imagine what it would be like to introduce Dan and a member of her family to each other, it wasn't like this. They both looked pissed that she was in the house. 'Why are you two behaving like this?' she exclaimed.

Dan wasn't listening. 'What do you mean, *what was I doing to her?*'

'It isn't what you think, Sherry!'

Sherry curled her lip. 'And that would be what? That the good doctor likes to dress up in rubber suits and tie you to the bedpost?'

'Of course not!'

'So, *you* like him to dress up in rubber suits and tie you to the bedpost?'

Under different circumstances Dan would have laughed, but there was nothing about this situation that was remotely amusing. He was disturbed that Lisa Jackson's sister was in his house treating his wife like she was someone she couldn't be.

'That's not funny, Sherry!' Lisa fumed.

Sherry dropped the scissors on the bedside table with a clatter. 'What the hell were you *doing*, Lees?'

Lisa limped towards the bed. Sherry saw that her injured leg was bare beneath the knee-length T-shirt she wore as a nightdress. She watched a tight-lipped Dan Brogan take Lisa's elbow and help her onto the bed. 'Your cast is gone.'

Dan disappeared from the room and returned carrying a long white piece of material. Kneeling in front of Lisa, he folded it in half and despite her murmured protests pulled it gently over her instep to her knee. Lisa momentarily braced her hand on one of his shoulders when she lifted her leg to help and let go again quickly.

Sherry arched a brow and surveyed the sleek, black Neoprene-covered back and the wide shoulders topping it. The good doctor was extremely well put together.

Lisa caught sight of her perusal of Dan's back and glared at her over his shoulder.

Sherry smirked and shrugged.

Dan climbed to his feet. 'I'm going to take a shower and change into my bondage gear. Lisa, go find the whips and handcuffs.'

He stalked into the bathroom and closed the door.

Sherry laughed.

'Don't look at him like that!' Lisa hissed.

'Like what?'

'You know what I mean, like he's a piece of rump steak on your personal barbecue.'

'I have to admit he does have a nice rump,'

Lisa reacted like a cat whose fur had just been stroked the wrong way. 'Dan is nothing like the guys you date! He's a gentleman.'

Sherry snorted. 'For your sake, I hope not. I can't imagine anything more boring than making out with a *gentleman.*'

'I'm not making—' Lisa clamped her lips together.

'You mean you're *still* not? Why? When it's obvious you're both dying to?'

Lisa refused to be drawn. 'Why did you call me?'

'I wanted to know how your appointment at the hospital went.'

'They took my cast off.'

'I can see that,' Sherry replied impatiently. 'I also wanted to know what the hell you think you're doing taking Dad a never- ending supply of sick plants. I thought we agreed that Mum and Dad were strictly off-limits to you for the foreseeable future.'

'No, *we* didn't. *You* did. How else am I supposed to get to see Dad?'

'That's the point — you aren't!'

'You're not going to stop me from seeing him.' Lisa replied stubbornly. 'Anyway, it's a bit late now.'

Sherry scowled, but it was obvious Lisa wasn't about to back down. 'Tell me why you tied yourself to the bed.'

When Lisa finished explaining about her sleepwalking, Sherry decided she'd never heard anything more stupid. 'You're sleeping in separate rooms?'

'Of course, we are.'

Sherry pressed her fingertips to her eyelids, muttering.

'What?' Lisa demanded.

'Let me get this straight. You're sleepwalking, Brogan's having to dive out of bed to rescue you, and you're both clearly dying to jump each other's bones —'

'We're *not* – '

'- but you're sleeping in separate rooms.' Sherry eyed Lisa with disgust. 'That's about the stupidest thing I've ever heard.'

It was freaky being in Dan and Linda Brogan's house, freaky having a conversation with her sister when she looked nothing like herself. Sherry sympathized with Dan Brogan's hostile attitude; she felt the same way about him. Lisa didn't understand why she refused to stay for coffee and took herself off to the bathroom to shower.

Sherry saw the hurt and disappointment on her face and hesitated to leave.

Dan Brogan told her bluntly, 'Leave now. I'll take care of her.'

She was about to depart when she caught sight of the back garden and the cliff edge through the vast living-room windows. Sherry stopped so suddenly Dan almost crashed into her back.

'What now?' he demanded.

She pointed at the view. 'Is that pathetic excuse for a fence all that separates your garden from the cliff edge?'

Dan glanced at the fence and back again. He knew exactly where this conversation was going. 'Yes.'

Sherry struggled to contain her anger and fear. He might not be a great host, but he certainly wasn't an idiot. Or at least that's what she'd thought until now.

She tried not to imagine Lisa's battered body at the bottom of the cliff being swept out by the tide. 'Lisa has been known to unlock doors and climb out windows when she's sleepwalking. So yonder little fence isn't going to stop her from falling off the damned cliff one night!'

'I keep a close eye on her,' Dan replied tightly.

Sherry lost her temper. 'Bullshit! If you were keeping such a close eye on her she wouldn't feel the need to tie herself to the bedpost, would she? Lisa's frightened, Brogan! She knows how vulnerable she is but being Lisa she's more worried about disturbing *you*. She didn't survive that car crash to fall to her death from that cliff!'

Dan was sickened by the images she was painting in his head. He went on the attack. 'Back off! She *isn't* your damned sister.'

Sherry took a step closer, her eyes like blue flames. 'You think I'm comfortable with this? You think any of this makes sense to me? I'm as freaked by the idea as you are.' She glared up at him, a tall woman with a will of iron. 'But just answer me this: can you say with *absolute certainty* that the woman you're living with is your wife?'

Dan glared back, unable to answer her.

'I thought not. It's your job to keep her safe so do it!'

Later that night, when Dan found Lisa wandering in the back yard, he gently steered her back into the house, but this time he put her back in his bed, deciding he'd figure out a way to explain things to her in the morning. She slept like a baby for the rest of the night.

Lisa woke on Sunday morning feeling more refreshed than she had in months. She uncurled between the sheets, stretching her arms and legs until the sole of her foot encountered a warm, hairy leg. She shot upright in the bed, clutching the bedcovers.

Dan looked up blearily from beside her, one arm tucked beneath his pillow and mumbled, 'Morning,'

She stared at him, at the stubble on his chin and the tuft of dark hair in his armpit before looking around the room. 'This is your bedroom. I'm in your bedroom.'

'That's right and before you jump to any conclusions: nothing happened.' He sat up and propped himself against the pillows.

His chest and shoulders were bare. Was he naked? Her

eyes were drawn to outline of his genitals beneath the sheet. It certainly looked like it. She looked up to find Dan watching her and closed her eyes. He had just caught her checking out his dick.

Dan raised a knee and adjusted the sheets. 'I'm wearing pyjama bottoms.'

Lisa nodded jerkily, stretched out a foot and began to slide out of the bed.

'Don't you want to know how you got here?'

She hovered by the side of the bed, tugging the bottom of his old University of Colorado T-shirt lower on her thighs. 'I...walked in my sleep and you brought me here?'

Dan couldn't figure out why she was acting so jittery - like a teenage virgin - or how he was going to get out of bed without revealing the erection he'd got when she'd looked at his dick. The fact *he'd* reacted like a horny teenager made it even more imperative that he explain that having sex with her wasn't the reason he'd decided to bring her into his bed. That it hadn't even entered the equation.

Like that was the truth.

'We both needed to get some sleep and this way I should be able to stop you getting out of bed in the first place.'

'Uh huh,' She sidled around the foot of the bed towards the bathroom door.

'If you'd prefer to sleep in your own room, I'll understand.'

'No, no ... this is fine. I'm fine.'

She didn't sound fine.

'You're sure?'

She fumbled for the bathroom-door handle, nodding vigorously. 'Yes, absolutely ... makes sense.'

He felt like a pervert. 'I can keep my hands to myself. You

haven't got to worry on that score.'

'Never crossed my mind, never in a million years.' Lisa opened the door to the bathroom. 'I just need to ... you know ...'

'Go right ahead,' Dan said testily.

She bolted through the door.

'Way to go, Brogan,' he muttered sourly. 'You handled that real well.'

Chapter 20

Lisa didn't have a problem about sleeping with Dan. The problem she had was sharing a bed with him and *not* sleeping with him. She wasn't a teenager in the throes of a crush. She was a mature woman with a once healthy, active sex life, and what she felt for Dan was sexual desire wrapped up in a lot of other emotions she didn't want to explore. She pictured him naked, imagining how it would feel to have the weight of that long, lean body pressing her into the mattress. But Dan had made it clear that he'd brought her into his bed as a last resort, that he was tired and at the end of his tether, *not* because he was attracted to her. When she sometimes thought he looked at her with frustrated sexual desire, it really was just frustration.

They reached an unspoken agreement when it came to bedtime. Lisa went to bed first and either fell asleep or pretended to be asleep when Dan came to bed. He kept to his side of the bed and fell asleep on his side, facing away from her. The problem was that Lisa was a snuggler. As soon as she fell into a deep sleep, she drifted across the bed to spend the night curled against Dan's back while he lay tense and sweating, feeling every breath and hearing every sigh. Linda had liked to be held but she'd never been able to fall asleep wrapped in his arms. He suspected Lisa could spend the entire night cuddled against his chest if he gave in to the urge to roll over and pull her into his arms. Instead, he rose before she awakened and stood under a cold shower, his hands braced against the wall, wondering how the hell he was going to get through another night without touching her.

Lisa tried to sleepwalk on the first two nights and each time Dan gently eased her back into bed and held her until she settled again. Once she had, he made himself roll over and let her tuck herself against his back. By the end of the week, lack of sleep and sex turned him into the taciturn, short-tempered human equivalent of a bear with a sore head. He snapped at everything and everybody except the kids at the hospital. If he'd been back home in the States, he probably could have looked up an old girlfriend and got laid but he didn't have the luxury of old acquaintances in New Zealand. And besides, he didn't want to sleep with just anybody. He wanted to sleep with Lisa, who looked clear-eyed and as fresh as a daisy since she'd moved into his room whereas Dan was certain the sprinkling of grey hairs at his temples had increased.

When he came home one night to discover Lisa sitting in the living room playing a guitar for a left-handed player and singing a Dixie Chicks song to herself, Dan demanded to know where she'd found the guitar and who'd taught her to play.

'It belongs to Slade and I was taught to play by my brother Ben.'

'You *don't* have a brother called Ben!' Dan shouted. 'And by the way, tomorrow is your thirtieth birthday.'

Lisa took a deep breath and counted to ten. Her clear eyes and fresh-as-a-daisy appearance were a sham. She might appear to be sleeping at night, but whatever she was dreaming about was exhausting her. 'Yes, I do,' she replied firmly. 'And tomorrow *is not* my birthday.'

Dan glared at her. 'I'm going to bed.'

On Wednesday morning, Lisa woke in the middle of a

wonderful dream to discover she wasn't dreaming after all, and that Dan's hands really were on her breasts, and he really was delivering delicious little nips to the spot where her neck met her shoulder. She moaned and arched her back to give him better access. Dan ground his pelvis against the soft curve of her buttocks. Surely that wasn't *all* him? She didn't have a chance to find out because he suddenly stopped, swore, and erupted from the bed as if it was on fire.

'Keep on your damned side of the bed!' he yelled and stormed into the bathroom.

Lisa tried to return to her own bed that night, but Dan wouldn't hear of it. 'I'm not scraping you off the bottom of the cliffs tomorrow morning.'

They spent another tense, restless night on opposite sides of the bed.

It was a block of butter that finally brought everything to a head at breakfast on Saturday morning. Lisa dropped one on the floor and Dan stepped on it and skidded across the kitchen and crashed into the sink.

She rushed towards him where he lay sprawled on the tiled floor. 'Are you alright?'

Dan boiled over. He raved and ranted and generally made a complete ass of himself.

Lisa waited until he finally ran out of steam, her lower lip trembling. '*Arsehole!*' she cried and marched out of the kitchen.

He stared at the spot where she'd been standing, feeling disgusted at his show of temper and sickened by the stricken look on Lisa's face. When he went to find her, she wasn't in the house. He slammed the laundry door and ran out of the garage in time to see her disappearing up the street as fast as she could limp. Dan ran after her, his long legs making short work of catching up with her. 'Lisa!'

She put her head down and broke into an awkward trot. 'Go away and leave me alone!'

He easily kept pace with her. 'I'm sorry! I shouldn't have spoken to you like that. I know I've been an asshole this past week.' He tried to catch her wrist.

Lisa snatched her hand away and stopped to kick him in the shin for good measure.

'*Ow!* Shit!' Dan was more surprised than hurt. 'Guess I deserved that.'

Her eyes flashed. 'Oh, do you? What about this then?' She punched him in the arm.

It had about as much impact as a fly landing on a horse, but Lisa had put so much effort into, Dan felt he owed it to her to at least pretend it hurt. 'Ouch,' he said and rubbed his arm. About two seconds too late.

Lisa was furious. She jabbed her hands into his chest and shoved as hard as she could. He obligingly shuffled back a few steps. 'Bastard! You're just making fun of me!' She aimed her good foot at his shin again.

Dan caught her wrists, jerked her against him and kissed her right there on the footpath. When he lifted his head, Lisa blinked up at him and gulped. 'If you don't have sex with me, I swear it will be you they'll be scraping off the cliffs in the morning!'

The moment was interrupted by a grey head suddenly popping up above the white fence beside them. It belonged to an elderly man wielding garden shears Dan vaguely recognized as one of his plant-toting neighbours.

'Hello, Mr Benns,' Lisa said in a strangled tone.

''Lo Lisa,' Mr Benns gazed shifted between her and Dan. 'I've been meaning to call you to say you can pick your gardenia up,' she continued brightly while trying to discreetly remove Dan's hand from her butt. He refused to let go.

'It sounds like you have more pressing matters needing your attention at the moment,' Mr Benns observed dryly.

Lisa squirmed.

Dan nodded. 'Nice talking to you.'

He scooped Lisa up, marched back to the house, and discovered he'd managed to lock them out.

'Oh no ... oh no, no, no, no . . .' Lisa buried her face in his chest. 'What are you trying to do to me?'

'Sssh! I'm thinking!'

'Think *faster!*'

Dan dropped her onto the hood of his car and pressed the wall switch to lower the garage door. Why hadn't he noticed before how long it took to close? He returned to where Lisa was perched on the silver hood. 'Take your clothes off.'

'*Here?*' she squeaked. '*Now?*'

He hooked his fingers under the coral-red sweater she was wearing and tugged it over her head. 'I've got one thing to say to you, Lisa. *Cliffs.*'

'But it's freezing in here.' Her nipples were sticking out, but not from cold.

Dan stared at them. 'I'll warm you up.' He yanked his sweatshirt over his head.

Lisa sucked in a breath. Those shoulders and that chest were finally hers for the licking. Within seconds, her clothes were flying about the garage like they were inside a tumble dryer.

When she was finally naked on the car, Dan's face contorted with an almost pained expression. God, she was beautiful.

Lisa watched him and shivered.

He gathered her up and slid her beneath him and he braced a knee on the front bumper of the car. Bending his head, he stroked her breasts with his tongue and smoothed his palms down the chilled flesh of her outer thighs. His penis was hammering at his fly like a Labrador panting to be let out to play. He wasn't sure how long he'd be able to devote to foreplay before he came in his underwear.

Lisa seemed to be in no better state. Her pupils were dilated with passion and her beautiful breasts were rising and falling rapidly. 'I can't wait ... I...'

Dan hooked his fingers around her ankles and began to push her knees upwards and apart.

Her eyes widened. She tried to clamp her legs together, but Dan bent down and kissed her again, sliding his tongue into the warm cavern of her mouth and crushing her breasts against his bare chest. 'Don't go all shy on me. You're beautiful down there.'

She let him spread her ankles apart, watching his face apprehensively as he lowered his eyes. 'Damn, you're pretty, Mona Lisa,' he murmured as he looked at the hot, slick centre of her.

Lisa watched him bemusedly, wondering, as so many women had before her, how anybody could call *that* beautiful. The fact she suddenly couldn't wait to see his penis wasn't the same.

Dan unzipped his fly and reached into his underwear.

Suddenly she was scampering backwards on her hands and feet towards the windscreen. 'We can't ... we'll never fit!'

He closed his eyes, tried to count to ten, but only made it to three. Why the hell did women get such a surprise when they saw him naked? He was six feet five inches tall. What did they expect? A weenie? He struggled for patience. 'Lisa, honey, I promise we'll fit.' He hesitated. 'Our bodies have done this before.'

She stared at his erection for several moments and slowly slid back down the car towards him.

Dan took the time to arouse her to her earlier feverish state, even though he was certain he was going to disgrace himself on the hood of his car at any moment. Lisa purred, stroked, and rubbed herself like a sensuous little cat all over him until he began to slowly push himself inside her.

She tensed, staring up at him apprehensively.

'I promise I'll stop any time you want me to.'

Please don't ask me to.

It wasn't an easy fit. He tilted her hips and rocked against her, easing home a little at a time, gritting his teeth against the overwhelming urge to drive into her and pound himself senseless. Gradually Lisa softened beneath him and began to sigh. She wrapped her legs about Dan's waist, cupped his buttocks in her hands and began to slowly rotate her hips against him. When he finally slid home, she gasped and arched beneath him. As Dan picked up the tempo, Lisa unwound a leg from his waist, braced her foot on the metal hood and met him thrust for thrust. He felt her get hotter and hotter before she convulsed around him at the same time as he emptied himself into her.

Lisa came back down to earth as softly as a feather. She was vaguely aware when Dan withdrew from her body and slid her palm down the length of his arm as he stepped away from the car.

'I didn't use a condom.'

She stroked his arm and murmured, 'You didn't use a

condom,' She shot upright. 'Oh! *You didn't use a condom!* It never occurred to me to ask. I haven't had sex in three years and my endometriosis meant I had about as much chance of getting pregnant as climbing Mount Everest.'

Dan zipped his fly, feeling the familiar pressure begin to build behind his eyes.

'But I guess I can now, can't I?' She gazed at him wonderingly. 'Get pregnant, I mean?'

Her nonchalant response and the panic he felt at her getting pregnant hit Dan between the eyes like a jackhammer. He recalled all the times he'd broached the subject of having children with Linda and her horrified response. But now she was lounging naked on the hood of his car looking sexually satiated and awestruck at the thought of being pregnant, and so damned desirable his dick was beginning to stand up and wave like a conductor's baton all over again.

'When did you last have a period?' he asked tightly.

'Last week.' She looked hurt. 'It should be alright, shouldn't it?'

He raked a hand through his hair. 'What? For you to *be* pregnant or *not* be pregnant? I guess we'll just have to wait and see.'

Lisa hugged her arms around her bent knees. She realized he was being sensible, but did he have to look so grim? 'Would it be so bad?' she murmured.

Dan didn't know what to say, so he changed the subject. 'If you want to do this again, I need to get some condoms.'

'I want to do it again.'

'Then I'd better hit the supermarket.'

They scrambled around the garage finding Lisa's clothes and locating a spare set of keys Dan kept hidden in the car.

Lisa clutching her clothes against her bare breasts shivering. 'I can't find my panties.'

'Your knickers?' Dan scanned the garage. 'Just put your skirt on. Nobody will know you're bare-assed beneath it.' Apart from him.

As they accelerated away from the house, he spotted something white fluttering from the wing mirror on the driver's side right before it flew off. 'I think I just found your knickers.'

'You have? Where?'

'They just blew off the wing mirror and onto the road behind us.'

'*What?*' Lisa squawked. 'Stop! I need to go back and get them!'

Dan hit the brakes and pulled over. 'You really want to go back there and pick your underwear up off the street?'

She craned her neck to look out the back window. 'Yes.' She cringed when she spotted them lying in the road. 'No.'

He took pity on her. 'Stay there. I'll get 'em.'

He'd just scooped the panties from the road when he sensed he was being watched. It was karma that Mr Benns should be the one staring at him across the hedge he was trimming, the clippers frozen in space. He looked at Dan and the white lacy underwear in his hand.

Dan cleared his throat. 'Flew off the wing mirror. Lucky I saw 'em.'

Mr Benns nodded slowly. 'Are they yours?'

He frowned. 'No.'

'Well, I guess that's something.'

Dan refused to hand them over to Lisa when he returned to the car. 'Nuh uh.' He stuffed them into the pocket of his jeans. 'Finders keepers.'

'But I want to put them on!'

'You owe me,' Dan grumbled. '*Boy*, do you owe me.'

He thought about her bare ass on the drive to the supermarket, and he thought about it at the supermarket while he made his selection from the comprehensive range of condoms on sale.

'Put some back!' Lisa darted embarrassed looks up and down the aisle. 'People will think we're sex-starved!'

'I am,' He headed towards the checkouts at the front, his big hands overflowing with boxes.

Mortified, Lisa trailed behind him. Why couldn't he be a little more discreet and carry a placard instead?

The little checkout girl blushed crimson and kept sneaking looks at them as she passed the boxes across the electronic scanner and into plastic bags. Lisa hid behind Dan while he took his time paying and collecting the two overflowing bags.

She was convinced he'd purposely tried to embarrass her by buying so many at once and told him so on the way to the car. 'That poor girl didn't know where to look. She was only a student.'

'Letting her see that adults are practicing safe sex is my contribution to adolescent sex education,' He casually swung one of the bags over his shoulder and a box of Ribbed Riders came tumbling out.

Lisa snatched it from the asphalt. 'Do you have to practice it so publicly?'

'I shut the garage door.'

'That's not what I meant!'

He laughed down at her, looking rumpled and relaxed, the lines of tension gone from beside his mouth and beneath his eyes, and his dark hair standing on end where she'd dragged her fingers through it. Lisa felt an answering smile curve her lips. 'You have no shame, Daniel Brogan.'

'Not when it comes to sex. Guess it's a guy thing.' He paused to give the hood of the car an affectionate stroke and unlocked the doors.

On the way home, he glanced across at Lisa and said, 'Slide your skirt up.'

'What?'

'I said . . .' His voice dropped an octave. 'Slide your skirt up.'

She swallowed and shook her head.

'Go on, I dare you. *Please.*'

She clutched a handful of skirt and slowly pulled it up.

Dan glanced at her bare knees and smiled. 'Nice.' Stopped at the traffic lights he studied her from beneath his lashes and coaxed, 'Higher.'

Lisa blinked at him, fighting equal measures of excitement and embarrassment. Excitement won out. She slid the skirt to the middle of her thighs. Folds of material fell between them making her breath hitch when it touched the throbbing flesh between her legs.

'Come on, Lisa,' Dan chided softly, pulling away from the traffic lights. 'You can do better than that. You know you want to.'

She gulped, raised her hands and felt cool air against her heat.

The car swerved. Lisa shrieked and Dan cried hoarsely, 'No! Don't ... I mean. . . *sorry!* You're safe, honey, I won't lose control of the car, I promise.'

He wasn't so sure he could say the same about himself.

Lisa slowly relaxed and began to enjoy herself. She rearranged her skirt and, watching Dan from beneath her lashes, slid her palms along her naked thighs.

'Holy shit...'

Encouraged by his response, she parted her thighs and trailed her fingers back up along the insides of them, stopping just short of the black curls at the top.

'Go on,' Dan urged in a low voice. 'I dare you.'

Lisa hesitated.

He smirked. 'Knew you wouldn't do — *holy shit!*'

The moment the garage door closed behind the car, Dan grabbed a condom from one of the boxes, unzipped his fly and rolled it on. He helped Lisa scramble across the handbrake and onto his lap facing him. She gasped as she eased herself slowly downwards at the same time Dan thrust upwards into her.

'You OK?' he asked raggedly.

'Oh, yeah,' she clutched his shoulders and began to rise and fall against him. Her head fell back, and her eyes closed. 'Are you?'

Dan's eyes drifted shut. 'You're without a doubt, the nicest seatbelt I've ever had.'

☆

The week that followed was one of the happiest of Lisa's life.

They were so engrossed in each other they barely noticed the rest of the world. They couldn't keep their hands off each other and spent each night twined together like a pair of eels, waking regularly to make love before tumbling back to sleep again. Dan kissed Lisa awake each morning, sometimes pulling her into the shower with him to make love again. The boxes of condoms were emptying out fast.

Knowing how hard he worked, Lisa tried to exercise restraint and not dive on him the moment he stepped through the door at night and asked about his day and told him what was for dinner.

Dan had different ideas about the kind of welcome home he wanted. He'd back Lisa against the kitchen counter and nuzzle her neck. 'Sounds great, but you taste better.'

'Aren't you tired?' Her hands would steal inside his suit jacket and begin tugging his shirt from his trousers. 'You hardly got any sleep last night.'

He'd wrench off his jacket and fling it across the kitchen, knocking over the fruit bowl or caddy of kitchen utensils in the process. 'If I'm tired, it's due to a lack of sexual fitness. I need to work out more.'

'OK,' Lisa would agree eagerly dragging his Thomas the Tank Engine/Wallace and Gromit/Fred Flintstone tie over his head. 'I'll be your personal trainer.'

She'd read about being in love, heard other people talk about it and even fancied herself in love with Dillon. But nothing, *nothing* prepared her for the way she felt about Dan. She didn't hold anything back. She gave every particle of herself and wanted to share everything about herself with him.

Dan couldn't believe the gift he'd been given. Lisa filled up all the empty spaces inside him. For the first time in years, he didn't need to bury himself in his work to escape the pain of his failed marriage. He dragged his feet each morning when it was time to leave and called her during the day to tell her something funny one of the kids had said or done, knowing she'd appreciate the story.

Lisa loved Dan's wry sense of humour and watching his usually serious face dissolve into laughter. He enjoyed teasing her until she either laughed or leapt on him, hitting him with her girly fists. 'Pathetic. You need to work out more.'

She did. But it wasn't her abs, pecs or glutes that got a workout.

Now, when Dan went to the beach to windsurf Lisa sat on the sand with a picnic, wrapped up against the winter wind, not caring that it was tossing sand into her sandwiches. He promised to teach her how to surf as soon as her leg was stronger. She promised to teach him how to play the guitar in his office.

Their relationship was almost perfect. Almost.

Dan still wouldn't accept Lisa was who she claimed to be. Whenever she spoke about something that had happened to her in the past, he listened in silence then changed the subject.

It hurt. Dan had opened up a whole new dimension in her life. But there was one aching, empty part of her he would never be able to fill and that was the place in her heart her family would always occupy. If Lisa tried to share a story or memory with him, he distracted her with sex. She pretended it didn't matter, but each time it happened, a few more weeds grew in their paradise.

Dan was grappling with his own demons. He felt as if he was waiting for the other shoe to drop. There was always the chance that Linda would resurface if Lisa regained her memory, and he didn't know what he'd do if that day ever came. The feelings he had for Lisa were far more profound than what he'd felt for Linda, even at the beginning of their marriage. She understood him in ways Linda never had. Lisa had self-esteem and courage.

Watching her struggle the past few months had shown she would never allow herself to be a victim. He'd taken over the flash cards from Slade. Lisa got annoyed then laughed at her mistakes, and kept at it until the night she managed to read an entire article from the daily newspaper out loud to Dan.

'I did it!' she yahooed, waving the paper in the air.

She was pale with exhaustion. Dan didn't think he'd ever seen her look more beautiful. He thought he'd burst with pride at her achievement. Swooping on her, he caught her about the hips, lifted her high against his chest and spun her around the kitchen.

She shrieked, clutching his shoulders, and ducking the light fitting. 'Hey, this is great! I'm in giant land!'

Laughing, he took her to bed. When he finally ran out of stamina and condoms, Lisa mumbled, 'If I'd known this was going to be my reward, I would've done it weeks ago.'

Dan was still preoccupied by the possibility she might be pregnant. While the logical, sane part of him knew an unplanned pregnancy would be a disaster because Lisa was still recovering from her accident, he was gripped by a powerful desire to bind her to in the most elemental way possible.

As the awards night drew closer, Lisa became obsessed with making Dan see her as herself. She decided to get her hair cut and enlisted Sherry's advice on choosing the style and which of Linda Brogan's clothes she should wear.

'You're beautiful,' Sherry assured Lisa over the phone. 'You could wear a sack and shave your head and you'd still look good.'

'I need your help!' Lisa insisted. 'You have to come!'

She kept the visit quiet, mindful of Dan's hostile reception the last time Sherry had come to the house.

Sherry wasn't keen on being in the Brogan house either or touching Linda Brogan's clothes. She chose a black, tight-sleeved jersey-knit dress with an asymmetrical hem and deep V-back. 'The hem will cover that ugly bandage. Have a look at her bras, but I doubt you'll be able to wear one.' She ran a critical eye over Lisa and pointed at the white Tubigrip on her leg. 'Do you *have* to wear that thing all the time?'

'I take it off when I go to bed or have a shower.'

'Lose it tomorrow night.'

'Dan won't like it.'

'*Dan's* not the one wearing it.'

Lisa tugged her hair. 'What about this?'

Sherry pursed her lips and considered. 'You *really* want to look different?'

She nodded emphatically.

'Then cut it off.'

'All of it?'

Sherry fished in her handbag and handed Lisa a card. 'Ask for Russell. And while you're there, ask if Lauren can give you an eyebrow tidy; they look like a pair of caterpillars.'

'Flatterer,' Lisa muttered.

Sherry cast a final, linger look over the racks of gorgeous clothes and shoes and shouldered her bag. 'I'm out of here.'

As they walked to her black SUV, Slade pulled into the neighbouring driveway on his motorbike. Lisa's heart sank. Slade was sweet but not the most discreet of souls and she *really* didn't want Dan to know about Sherry's visit.

'Hi, Lisa,' he called with a curious glance at Sherry.

Sherry frowned. 'Hey, aren't you the kid who works a—'

Lisa jabbed her in the side with her elbow and smiled at Slade. 'Hi, Slade. How's it going?'

'Cool,' he stared at Sherry. 'Isn't your dad Mr Jackson at the garden centre?'

She snapped her fingers and pointed at Slade. 'I knew I recognized your face. You work there on weekends, don't you?'

Slade nodded. 'Lisa said she knew Mr Jackson.'

Sherry made a noncommittal sound, said goodbye, and drove away.

Lisa hovered beside Slade, twisting her fingers. 'Ah, Slade? Can you *not* mention to Dan that you saw my sis— I mean, my friend? They don't get along very well.'

'Oh? *Oh!*' Slade bobbed his head in understanding. 'Of course. I know how to keep my mouth shut.'

Lisa smiled weakly and patted his shoulder. She seriously doubted that.

When Dan saw Lisa's new haircut, his jaw just about hit the floor.

She smoothed a hand self-consciously across the feathery strands lying against the nape of her neck. She guessed that like most men, Dan liked long hair.

He continued to stare. 'You've been ... busy.'

She ducked her head and turned away to open the oven door. He hated it. 'Dinner's ready.'

Dan murmured agreement and continued to watch her warily.

Lisa retrieved a casserole dish from the oven and banged the oven door shut with her elbow. 'I couldn't wear plaits for the rest of my life.' She said resentfully.

He looked confused. 'Plaits?'

Oh hell, what did Americans call them?

'Braids?' she tried. 'Pigtails?'

His expression cleared, but he knew he wasn't out of the woods yet.

'I looked like a schoolgirl,' She slapped beef casserole

onto two plates so forcefully Dan was surprised they didn't break in half. 'People will start wondering if you're some sort of a pervert.'

'*Me?*' How did her wearing braids make him a pervert? 'You cut it for *my* sake?'

'No, *mine*.' She dumped the plates on the dining-room table. 'And if you don't like it, it's ... tough!'

'I do! You look cute.' Dan moved cautiously towards the table, his stomach growling, wishing he could pull Lisa into his arms and kiss her like he usually did. 'I like it,' He insisted.

She seemed unconvinced.

He kept sneaking looks across the table at her while they ate. She *did* look cute. And sexy too. The cropped, feathered cut drew attention to her long, white neck and high cheekbones. Her big, cornflower-blue eyes watched him through the wispy fringe. He'd always loved Linda's long hair. She'd been particularly vain about it, so it disturbed him that Lisa had cut it. Linda would never have contemplated cutting her hair. Not in a million years.

Chapter 21

The morning of the awards dinner, Dan saw Slade wheeling his motorbike out of the next-door garage when he went to collect the newspaper from the letterbox.

'Hi, Slade.'

'Hey, Mr Brogan.'

No matter how often Dan told Slade he could call him Dan, the boy couldn't seem to bring himself to do it.

Slade kicked the bike onto its stand and began to strap on his helmet. He wore his favourite leather trousers and a black leather jacket with silver chain draped across the back. 'Lisa said you're going to an awards dinner tonight.'

'That's right.'

Dan was on his way to the hospital to check on some children he'd operated on the previous day and wanted to get a move on. But he liked Slade and appreciated the way he'd befriended Lisa. There'd been times he felt jealous of him too.

'She was really worried about getting her hair cut and what to wear,' Slade continued.

It irritated him that the boy living next door still knew more about the things that worried Lisa than he did. 'I think her hair looks great.'

'Yeah, me too.' Slade reached for his leather gloves making the silver chain resting on his narrow back clink. 'It was nice of her friend to help her pick out some clothes.'

'What friend?'

Slade froze.

'What friend?' Dan repeated.

'Um . . .'

He stared hard at the boy. 'Which of Lisa's friends came to see her?'

Slade made a big production of checking the straps on his boots while he tried and failed to remember the name of Lisa's friend. 'I didn't get a name.'

Dan told himself he was being paranoid, but all he could think about was Jack Millar coming to see Lisa — no, *Linda* — while the coast was clear. Maybe the new haircut had been for his benefit.

Slade looked panicked. 'It was a woman!' He insisted.

Dan eyed him stonily. He knew how loyal Slade was to Lisa and how strong their unlikely friendship had become.

'Have a nice day, Simon.'

He stalked to his car.

Dan stayed late at the hospital. When he finally came home to change, he was in a filthy mood. Throughout the day he'd brooded over just who Lisa's friend might be. Slade was probably telling the truth, but memories of Linda's betrayal and the night he'd found her wrapped around Jack Millar filled his thoughts. To make matters worse, he found out that Janice and Jack Millar were attending the dinner as well. Perhaps it wouldn't be such a bad thing to see just how Lisa behaved around him.

He could tell she was excited by the glow in her cheeks when she finally came out to where he sat waiting in the lounge, pretending to watch a rugby match on the television. He wore black trousers and a black rollneck sweater beneath a dark, beautifully cut blazer with a fine, beige check. Dan studied Lisa's slinky, black dress with its long sleeves, high neck and crooked skirt. He couldn't recall seeing it before, but Linda had so many clothes that wasn't unusual. He didn't like the dress or the way it clung to her breasts and hips.

'Aren't you going to wear a bra?'

Her face fell. She hunched her shoulders. 'I can't.'

'What do you mean, you can't?'

She silently turned to show him her back. The dress dipped in a wide V all the way to her waist.

'You'll freeze,' Dan said curtly.

Lisa felt crushed, and angry. Why was he acting like this? All day, she'd looked forward to showing him how good *she* could look. Not Linda. *Her. Lisa.* And he was ruining it, sitting there looking handsome as sin and radiating disapproval.

It was a couple of seconds before she realized he was speaking again. 'Pardon?'

'I said: where's your Tubigrip?'

Lisa stared at him. She was wearing a gorgeous, sexy dress and all he cared about was an ugly elastic support sock. 'I took it off.'

'Put it back on.'

She gritted her teeth. 'No.'

His gaze dropped to shoes. 'What are you doing wearing high heels? You've only just got out of plaster. Are you mad?' He stopped abruptly.

Lisa looked stricken.

Dan flushed. 'I'm sorry. That came out wrong.'

An understatement if ever she'd heard one.

'Dan?'

He eyed her warily. Yes?'

'Get stuffed.'

Fighting tears, Lisa walked carefully back to her

bedroom to remove her makeup and clothes, leaving Dan in a state of shock at what she'd just said to him.

He laughed for the first time that day, got to his feet and went to make some sort of peace.

Lisa gave in because she wasn't prepared to let him ruin her night. She hadn't been out at night for months. She didn't understand what had put him in such a bad mood and racked her brain for a reason. Dan wasn't a moody person; he was even-tempered and easy-going. Perhaps he was just tired.

Or perhaps he was losing interest in her.

☆

The dinner was being held at the nearby North Harbour Sports Stadium. They hardly spoke in the car on the way. Dan silently switched on the car heater when Lisa began to shiver. Once inside, he kept a firm grip on her elbow as she navigated her way in the high heels and tried to ignore the way her nipples were poking the front of the silky black dress.

There were a lot of people crowding a large upstairs room, which was filled with boards displaying posters about the different projects up for awards. People could cast a vote on the poster they thought was the best and the winner of each category would be announced later that night.

Several people called out Dan's name and came across to talk to him. Each time they looked at Lisa, he said simply, 'This is Lisa.'

Not, this is my wife.

Lisa gasped when she spotted a familiar face.

'What?' Dan asked sharply and turned his head to see what she was looking at.

'I've just seen Janice Millar!' She craned her neck to keep

the other woman in sight.

'So? What's it to you?'

Where Janice was, her husband wouldn't be far behind. Dan spied Jack Millar watching Lisa with a hungry, intense expression on his face. He resented the effect Millar *and* Lisa had on him. Millar was skating on thin, fucking ice. Jack looked into Dan's cold, unblinking stare and disappeared into the crowd with his wife.

Lisa was baffled by the fierce look on Dan's face and the hostile way he'd spoken to her. Why had mentioning mild-mannered Dr. Millar made him so angry? She tried to break the tension by making a joke. 'I've been used to seeing that woman's head between my knees for the past five years. I hope she isn't sitting opposite me at the dinner table.'

Dan felt the beginnings of a headache. Janice Millar had never treated Linda. She'd been as healthy as the proverbial horse until her accident. And he didn't want to think about Janice's association with Lisa Jackson. He caught Lisa's elbow and said brusquely, 'I think we'd better go in.'

She allowed him to escort her into the room where the awards ceremony was to be held, wondering at his sudden coldness. He'd been acting out of character ever since he arrived home. The night loomed in front of them as a potential disaster.

When they found their places in the dining room, she was disconcerted to find Craig Fergusson seated at the same table. And at the opposite end of the table sat Janice Millar and a man Lisa presumed must be her husband, who kept staring at her like he wanted to put her on his empty plate and gobble her up. When Lisa looked at him, he lowered his lids and gave her a creepy smile.

She looked away, feeling repulsed. She must be the only

woman in the world unlucky enough to share a table with her gynaecologist *and* her psychiatrist. She liked Dr. Millar, but she wouldn't remember her and seemed to be avoiding looking at her. Lisa wondered glumly what Linda had done to upset a gentle soul like Janice Millar.

By contrast, Craig seemed delighted to see her. 'It's nice to see you.'

'Thanks,' she replied in a lukewarm tone as Dan took the seat beside her.

'How have you been?' Craig asked pointedly.

Lisa had missed their last appointment. 'Oh the usual, a woman trapped in a stranger's body.'

Dan stiffened. Craig's brows rose but he refrained from comment. Instead, he introduced his date, Rebecca, who was staring at Lisa as if she'd just sprouted another head.

'I'm one of Craig's patients,' Lisa leaned across the table and patted Rebecca's hand. 'It's OK, I only need locking up when it's a full moon.'

Rebecca smiled uncertainly at Craig, who sipped his wine.

Dan clasped one of Lisa's hands, leaned in and murmured, 'It's a full moon tonight. *Behave.*'

Enveloped in the light, clean scent of his cologne, Lisa's fit of pique dissolved. She looked into the grey eyes inches from hers and dropped her gaze his mouth.

'Stop that,' He muttered and released her hand.

Her misery returned. She caught Craig Fergusson watching them curiously from his side of the table. She wanted to stick her tongue out at him but settled for scowling instead.

Craig laughed and looked at Dan. 'When are you up?'

Dan started. 'Huh?'

'I said, when are you up?'

He reddened.

Craig snorted.

Third,' Dan snapped.

Craig's eyes twinkled behind his glasses. 'Then I'm after you. I think laparoscopic removal of gallstones is first, followed by the community skin lesions project.'

Rebecca's face twisted with revulsion.

'Oh, that'll be nice. Do we get the gallstones for the entrée or the main course?' Lisa enquired sarcastically.

A waiter appeared at the table with a silver dish of nuts. 'Nuts, ladies?'

Lisa choked back laughter.

Craig sniggered.

Dan smiled reluctantly.

Rebecca looked bewildered.

'What's going on down there?' Janice Millar's husband called. 'I feel like we're missing out.'

Lisa didn't notice the icy look Dan gave Jack Millar. Craig did.

'Hand 'em over,' he said cheerfully to the confused waiter, ignoring Jack. 'Look, Becca, they're your favourite kind, green pistachios.'

Becca was looking greener than the nuts.

Over the next hour and a half, dinner was served, and the projects were beamed to them in all their technicolour glory via a big screen at the back of the stage. Lisa couldn't believe they were expected to eat to the accompaniment of colour pictures of gallstones. She looked at the crumbed potato balls on her plate and felt her stomach heave.

Rebecca didn't seem to be doing any better. It was easy to spot the non-medical people in the room. They ate less as the night progressed and rolled their eyes like frightened horses at the more lurid shots while Dan, Craig and the other health professionals worked their way through their meals without blinking an eye.

By unspoken agreement, Lisa and Rebecca decided to drink instead. The young waiter recognized their strategy and brought a bottle of wine for them to share. Dan and Craig were so engrossed in the presentations that it was a while before they realized that their dates were getting drunk.

Dan regarded Lisa as if she were an alien being freshly sprung from John Hurt's android abdomen. Before he brought her home from the hospital, he'd never seen his wife touch alcohol and he'd *never* seen her drunk.

'Gary?' Lisa squinted at the name badge clipped to the front of their waiter's black waistcoat. 'It is Gary, isn't it?'

'My name's Rory.'

'Is it?' She blinked and smiled sweetly at him. 'Did you know SpongeBob SquarePants has got a cat called Gary?'

'I do,' Rory agreed with a grin. 'It's my favourite cartoon.'

'Me, too,' Lisa beamed and peered at his name badge. 'Why doesn't it say Rory?'

'It does,' Rory replied patiently and replaced the empty bottle of Cloudy Bay.

'Does it?' Lisa was so surprised she failed to notice the meaningful look Dan gave the waiter.

Rory smiled and moved the bottle beyond Lisa's and Rebecca's reach.

'Sorry 'bout that. I'm dyslexic.'

Dan sucked in a breath. Linda struggled to talk to *him* about her dyslexia let alone announce it to a table full of strangers. He stared at the inebriated woman beside him in bewilderment, wishing she wouldn't keep throwing these curve balls at him. He refused to give credence to her story that she wasn't Linda, even if Lisa was far nicer than Linda had ever been — funnier, warmer, sweeter, kinder ... and hornier. Beneath the table, his body responded. He focused on the table arrangement, dreading getting to his feet when it was his turn to take the stage and make his presentation.

Rebecca peeped at the screen and gagged. 'Oh...my...god.'

Lisa looked up and recoiled. 'Is this your first date?' she asked.

'No, second. And the last, I think.'

Dan snorted at Craig's offended expression before returning his attention to the woman at the podium describing the lurid photos of various skin diseases.

Rebecca rested her chin on her hand. 'I guess being married to a surgeon you're used to this sort of thing.'

'Oh yeah, I'm an old hand.' Lisa nudged Dan. 'Can I have my wine back?'

'No, you're smashed.' He applied himself to the coffee torte on his plate.

She checked the screen and said plaintively, 'I need to be.'

His name was finally called to present the Ilizarov project. Lisa felt a thrill of pride watching him make his way to the stage. He had the attention of every woman in the room, and she didn't think it was due to any deep interest in orthopaedic surgery.

Rebecca whispered across the table, 'Is this going to be gory?'

Recalling the kids she'd seen at the hospital, Lisa nodded apologetically. 'Not as bad as the skin lesions and gallstones

— think human shish kebabs and that should give you some idea.'

Rebecca narrowed her eyes at Craig. 'If you don't want me to run screaming from the room, I suggest you get Rory over here with another bottle of wine — *pronto*.'

Dan's presentation was the best of the night. The pictures of the kids charmed and moved the audience, but the big American surgeon moved them even more with his self-deprecating manner and modest charm. The passion he felt for his subject and the way he talked about his patients made his listeners feel they were a part of what they saw happening on the screen. When he finished, Lisa was certain the applause was louder than for any of the other projects. And hers was the loudest of all.

'You were brilliant!' she cried when he returned to his seat. 'I bet you win!'

Her unbridled enthusiasm thawed some of his frostiness. 'I wouldn't be too sure about that. The competition is pretty stiff.'

Lisa was thrilled when Dan's presentation won the award for innovation at the end of the night. She clambered to her feet to applaud and hug him before he even made it out of his chair. He grinned and went on stage to accept a glass trophy and give a short speech of thanks that gave the impression everybody else was responsible for the project's success but him.

As Lisa watched him walk back to the table, she acknowledged the emotion filling her heart. She loved Dan. She'd fallen in love with Linda Brogan's husband.

★

The following morning, Lisa woke with a hangover and stayed in bed feeling sorry for herself. 'Remind me never to drink again,' she moaned.

Dan lay on his side, watching her pensively. 'Any sign of your period yet?'

Her eyes clouded. His concern about the possibility of her being pregnant was sensible, but it still hurt. 'No, it's too soon. I don't get much warning anymore.' She paused, 'Not like before.'

His lips tightened.

For once Lisa refused to take the hint. 'Sometimes I used to spend all month in bed.'

Silence.

'Janice Millar put in an IUD but that didn't work, and when she did a laparoscopy, it showed my pelvis was riddled.' She wondered if Dan realized his grip on her arm had tightened. 'She thought the IUD would work but—'

'—it didn't help,' He released her arm, sat up and punched the pillows into shape behind his back.

Lisa stared. 'How do you know that?'

'I read Lisa Jackson's case notes.'

'You read my case notes? *When? When* did you read them?'

'Weeks ago,' he muttered.

'Weeks ago?' Lisa searched his face for a clue to what he was thinking. 'Why didn't you tell me?'

'I didn't see the point.'

Her temper started to simmer. 'You didn't see the point? Tell me, if it was such a *pointless* exercise why did you go to the trouble of reading the notes of a dead woman you'd never met? What prompted you to do that, Dan?'

He set his jaw and stared at the wall.

'You arrogant prick!' She shot up, clutching the bedcovers to her breasts. 'How *dare* you! All this time I've been telling you things about myself like having a club foot when I was little, and my endometriosis and you already knew! You'd read all about me so you *knew* only Lisa Jackson — or somebody close to her — could know all those details!'

'I read the notes of Lisa Louise Jackson. You *are not* Lisa Louise Jackson.'

She hauled back and took a clumsy swing at him.

Dan caught her wrist before her palm connected with his face. He stared at her, seeing flashes of the old Linda. '*Stop it! Calm down!*'

When she threw herself at him again, Dan caught her and rolled on top of her, trapping her beneath him. Lisa tried to buck him off, but it was hopeless. She could see all her foolish dreams for the future dissolving into thin air. '*Why* can't you believe me?'

He gazed down at her in sorrow and frustration. 'I just can't! Christ! *Nobody* could, Lisa! Nobody goes to heaven and gets sent back in another person's body by some rookie angel. Not unless they're from the cast of *Charmed*.'

Lisa paled. 'Get off me,' she said tonelessly.

Dan hesitated. 'Lisa . . .'

'Don't you mean *Linda?*' She shoved him in the chest. 'Get off me.'

He reluctantly complied, sitting back on his heels.

Lisa slowly climbed off the bed, her movements like those of a woman twice her age. She wound the sheet around her and stepped backwards, tugging it from where it was anchored beneath the mattress.

Dan swallowed and rubbed his chest. The fact she needed to cover herself made his heart hurt, which was stupid — how could his heart hurt? Or was the pain of watching a relationship disintegrate similar to having a heart attack?

Lisa backed away, pulling the sheet with her and leaving Dan sitting naked on the bed, his big, solid body so beautiful she had to swallow the lump in her throat. She wished she could tell him she hated him, but she couldn't lie.

'Where are you going?'

'Back to my old room.'

'Don't do this, Lisa,' Dan pleaded. 'Please. We can work this out.'

'No. I don't think we can,' She headed to the door, trailing the sheet behind her. 'I can't pretend to be somebody I'm not - not even for you.'

Later that night, Lisa walked in her sleep. She was surprised she slept at all, but at some point, her mind and body simply shut down.

Dan wasn't so lucky. He lay in his big, empty bed, recalling the anguish in her eyes and how beaten she looked, as if the stuffing has been knocked out of her. He wasn't surprised when he heard the bang of something hitting the floor and the rattle of the things on top of the chest of drawers in Lisa's room as she bumped into them. He'd been expecting her to sleepwalk. She always did when she was upset. But when Dan went to her room to check on her, Lisa had locked the door.

★

Lisa stayed in her room all day Sunday and was in bed on Monday morning when Dan left for work. She didn't respond when he knocked softly on her door before he departed. The less she saw of him, the less it would hurt when she left, and she knew she had to leave.

She sensed him lingering in the hallway before she

finally heard his car pull out of the garage. The tears began to leak from the corners of her eyes again. She wondered where her body stored them all.

The phone rang several times, but Lisa didn't answer it. Around noon, she finally dragged herself from bed and into the shower and cried all over again as she washed the smell of Dan and their lovemaking on Saturday night from her skin. Watching the soapsuds slide down the drain seemed symbolic of their relationship. Lisa reminded herself that Dan had never really been hers in the first place; she only got him by default.

Just before three o'clock, there was a knock on the front door. Lisa answered it looking and feeling like death warmed up. She was wearing her well-washed denim skirt, an olive polo-neck sweater that had lost its shape, with a black long-sleeved shirt of Dan's over the top. The sleeves were rolled up to fit her arms, and the hem hung to the back of her knees. There was no reason for her to wear it apart from the fact that it smelt of him. Lisa was certainly not looking like a showstopper. Misery had made her eyes swollen and bloodshot, and the end of her nose was red enough to give Rudolph the reindeer a run for his money.

A man stood on the doorstep dressed in an expensive charcoal suit and polished loafers, the teal-blue silk handkerchief spilling elegantly from the breast pocket of his jacket perfectly matching his blue-and-grey-striped tie. His blonde hair was carefully styled and brushed behind his ears and his eyes were a surprising shade of nutmeg brown.

It took Lisa a couple of moments to recognise Janice Millar's husband. She assumed he must be looking for Dan. 'Dan isn't here,' she said listlessly. 'He's at the hospital.'

Jack Millar looked appalled. 'Linda! What has that

bastard done to you?'

Her brow creased as a suspicion began to form that Jack might not be here to see Dan. 'I beg your pardon?'

'You look terrible, darling. Are you sick?' He reached out to touch her cheek.

Lisa pulled away before he could touch her.

The *darling* was the first indication that perhaps Jack and Linda Brogan had been more than passing acquaintances. Lisa studied Jack's features and was suddenly reminded of the baby boy in the waiting room. Her stomach heaved. Linda had been having an affair with Janice Millar's husband. He was the father of her baby.

'I think you'd better go.'

She tried to shut the door, but Jack stopped her by putting his foot in the opening.

'Linda, it's me! Jack!'

She put her shoulder to the door and shoved but he forced it open again.

'Linda! What are you doing?'

'Please go!'

Lisa tried to gather her wits. What would Sherry do in a situation like this? Probably kick him in the balls.

'But we need to speak! You can't imagine what it was like knowing you were with Dan and how much you hated him. So many times I wanted to come and take you away.'

His criticism of Dan sparked her temper. 'I don't hate Dan! What I don't understand is how Linda could ever have preferred you over him. She must have been nuts.'

'What?' Jack seemed stunned.

'If you don't leave, I'll call the police.'

'What's happened to you? You've changed!' he frowned. 'I don't like what you've done to your hair either.'

'*You think I care?*' Lisa yelled. 'Get out! Or I'll call the police!'

They were both so intent upon each other they didn't notice a car pull into the driveway.

Lisa snatched the phone from the table by the front door and began to dial 111. When Jack realized she was making good on her threat, he followed her and tried to wrench the phone from her hand. They were tussling for possession when Dan suddenly appeared, his expression lethal when he saw Lisa struggling with Jack Millar, who was winning the battle for the phone.

Lisa saw him and sagged with relief. 'Dan!'

Jack looked up and blanched.

Dan grabbed the collar of Millar's immaculate grey jacket, hauled back, and punched him in the face. There was a satisfying crunch as his nose broke and bled all over his silk tie. Jack dropped like a stone onto the tiled floor and curled up, clutching his nose.

Lisa blinked. She looked from Dan's snarling face to Jack's prostrate form and back again. 'Have you killed him?' she whispered.

'I should be so lucky,' Dan rubbed his knuckles. 'Get up, Millar!'

Jack cowered beneath an arm and tried to staunch his nose with his tie. 'Gno. You'll only hnit me agnain.'

Lisa gasped when she saw Dan's knuckles were skinned. 'Your hand!'

He jerked away when she tried to touch him.

'Hnith hnand! Wha about muh fucking gnose?'

She turned on Millar and snapped, 'Get yourself a plastic surgeon! And see if he can do some work on your morals while he's at it.'

'Gnu bitch.'

'Open the door,' Dan growled.

Lisa hastened to swing the door open. Dan scooped Jack off the floor and flung him outside. When she turned back after slamming the door, Dan was gone. She found him in the bathroom soaking a facecloth in cold water for his hand.

She felt drained and shaken. 'Will it be alright?'

Dan didn't look up. 'Fine,' he replied curtly, wrapping the facecloth about his hand.

'Here, let me help—'

The coldness in his eyes stopped her. Lisa stepped back and hugged her arms about her waist. 'What are you doing home so early?' She hoped it was because he wanted to straighten things out between them.

His lips twisted. 'Yeah, sorry about that, did I ruin the big reunion?'

Her hope shriveled and was replaced by razor-sharp pain. 'Did that look like a reunion to you?'

'How would I know? Perhaps you and Millar get a kick out of tearing each other to shreds before you get down to business.'

Lisa swallowed a sob. She'd fooled herself. He couldn't care - not *really* care - if he could casually talk about her having sex with another man. However, where Dan was concerned, she was a masochist, so she tried again to make him see the truth. 'I didn't invite him here. He just arrived on the doorstep. At first, I didn't even know who he was.'

His eyes glittered with suppressed fury. 'But you worked it out, didn't you?'

Lisa shook her head frantically. 'Please don't do this, Dan! I know we have a lot of things we need to work through, but I want to be with *you*.' She swallowed and whispered, 'I love you.'

He stilled. 'Don't give me that crap!'

'It's *not* crap!' She closed the distance between them to look up into his face. 'I'll do anything! *Anything!* Just give me a chance!'

He stared hard at her. 'Anything?'

She nodded, her lips forming a silent yes.

He stalked towards the bedroom.

Lisa followed him into the big walk-in wardrobe that contained Linda's clothes and watched Dan open the black-lacquered jewelry case on one of the shelves. He scooped something into his palm, turned, and held out his hand. 'Put them on.'

Linda's diamond engagement ring and platinum wedding band lay in the palm of his hand. Lisa stared at them, her eyes huge and her heart sinking as tears turned her vision blurry.

'You won't, will you?' Dan taunted. 'I'll do *anything*, you said, but that doesn't include wearing a sign of your commitment.'

She swiped at the tears rolling down her cheeks. It was hopeless.

'How can they be a sign of *my* commitment? They belong to Linda, they're a symbol of your marriage to her, not me. You're not being fair.'

His mouth twisted. 'Hell. Who said life was fair?'

It was two days before Lisa left Dan's house. Two days before she found somewhere to go.

Sherry would have taken her in, but it would have been far too awkward for her sister to explain the presence of Linda Brogan in her house and Lisa didn't want to put her into the position of having to try.

It was Edie Cruickshank who solved her predicament when Lisa went to her in desperation and said, 'Edie, I really need your help. I need to get away and I have nowhere to go.'

Edie took one look at her wan face and unkempt appearance and ushered her into her brown-and-orange lounge.

'I know just the place,' she said.

It took Lisa the best part of a day to write Dan the letter telling him she was leaving and thanking him for everything he'd done for her. Her dyslexia made letter-writing hard, and she'd never written a Dear John letter before.

She hesitated a long time before deciding to leave the small gift she'd bought for his birthday the following week. A chance phone call from Dan's brother, Glenn, had yielded the information that Dan's birthday was coming up on July first. Lisa had gone to great lengths to find just the right gift for him.

When she'd spoken to Glenn Brogan, Lisa decided she could have liked him if she'd had the chance to get to know him better. He sounded a lot like Dan, but she got the feeling a far more flamboyant personality lurked beneath the cool, polite voice on the other end of the phone. Lisa liked Glenn because he seemed to care about his brother and didn't like Linda. She told Dan about the call and what she thought about Glenn when he got home but didn't mention she knew about his birthday.

She left the small, gift-wrapped package and the yellow envelope containing Dan's birthday card next to his computer along with her front-door key.

And her heart.

Chapter 22

Esmeralda Moody was Edie's younger sister by three years, but she was in worse shape than her big sister and couldn't walk without the aid of a walking frame due to arthritis in her knees. Lisa knew about Esme, as she was known, because Edie had called her to locate the birthday present Lisa wanted for Dan.

'I'm on the waiting list for a knee replacement, but who knows when that'll be,' Esme confessed.

She was a small, frail woman with a bubble perm dyed ginger-brown and eyebrows she drew on each morning with a matching ginger-brown pencil. 'I may be old and crippled, but I like to keep myself looking nice.'

If she weren't so miserable, Lisa would have laughed when she saw Esme's little two-bedroom house. The front garden was filled with gnomes of every description engaged in a variety of activities. In the past, she and Sherry had speculated about who the house's manic gnome owner might be. Sherry thought the owner was a mad axe murderer who buried the bodies of victims under the gnomes. Each time a new gnome appeared, she promised she was going to knock on the door and ask to interview the owner. She'd die laughing if she knew Lisa had moved into the gnome house.

The interior was filled with lots of little ornaments collecting dust, and Esme's prized collection of Disneyland statues lived in the back garden. She saw Lisa staring at Snow White and the Seven Dwarves, Bambi, Thumper, Flower, and several of the characters from *Cinderella* and announced proudly, 'They're collector's items, you know.'

'I'll bet there are.'

'All I need is the wicked stepmother to finish off my Cinderella collection and then I'm going to make a start on Sleeping Beauty. I've seen Prince Charming on Trade Me.'

'You don't say?' Lisa stepped carefully around Sleepy and Doc while trying to decide what worried her most: walking in her sleep and falling over Sneezy and breaking her neck or knocking Snow White on her concrete bum.

She arranged to rent Esme's small, spare bedroom and agreed to do shopping and the household chores that Esme found too difficult, to top up the token amount of rent she was asking. Fortunately, the jobs didn't include dusting because in Lisa's current mood, the ornaments would have come off second best. The only things she'd taken from Dan's house were the clothes she'd bought during her stay and Linda Brogan's passport because it held a work permit.

The morning after she moved into Esme's, Lisa got a job as a waitress at Flavasum, the café attached to the garden centre. It was only for thirty hours a week, and the pay wasn't great, but it was enough to cover her rent and food provided she was careful, and Esme's house was close enough she could walk to work.

Flavasum was owned by a husband-and-wife team named Anton and Susie who'd just had their first baby, a boy named Joey. Lisa's biggest fear was that her dyslexia would make her too slow to write down the orders legibly in a busy café. At her interview, sensing Anton was about to offer her the job, she blurted out she was dyslexic.

'Me, too. Can you start—' Anton replied without missing a beat.

'But I might not be able to write down the orders fast

enough! In fact, I might not be able to write them down at all.'

'Sure you will. We've got a system.' He pointed at the menu chalked on the blackboard covering one wall. 'See? A star and a hook for vegetable frittata, a moon means a side salad, muffins are circles, a circle with a dot is a scone.' He shrugged. 'Easy.'

Lisa stared at the menu. There was a God.

'You'll soon memorize the symbols. There's a prize of a latte and muffin for whoever thinks up something for anything new we add.' His smile held a wealth of understanding. 'So, do you want the job?'

'Yes! *Yes, please!*'

Edie had shared enough about Lisa's situation for Esme to know she needed to give her new boarder some space. The old lady's heart went out to the lovely young woman with her big, sad, blue eyes and lost expression. Esme still missed her husband, Leonard, even though he'd died over forty years ago. For the first time it occurred to her that being parted by death might be better than being rejected by the living.

Working at the café and Esme's kindness were all that kept Lisa putting one foot in front of the other in the early days after she left Dan. Anton was struggling to run the café and help Susie out at home with their new son, so everybody took turns looking after Joey, who spent some of the time asleep in his pushchair in a corner of the café when Susie came in to cook. Lisa was always the first to offer to take the baby for a walk when he or his mother got too cranky.

She struck up a friendship with Starr Warrender, one of the other waitresses. Starr was a tiny elf of a girl with cropped mahogany-coloured hair she wore gelled into tiny spikes all over her head. Her huge eyes were a gorgeous shade of lavender-blue and framed by thick black lashes. She wore a tiny silver stud in one nostril, shiny black Doc Martens on her little feet and rode a motorbike. She was studying to be a midwife, and waitressing helped pay for her tuition and books.

Lisa worked hard because exhaustion made it easier for her to fall asleep at night. Starr and Anton insisted she sit down at least once a day and tackle some of the rich café food, while privately wondering about who had caused the dark circles under Lisa's eyes and the forlorn droop to her mouth.

'I'd like to get my hands on him,' Starr muttered to Anton as she cleaned tables. 'Lisa's as nice on the inside as she is on the outside.'

'It might not be a man,' Anton pointed out.

'Lisa's not a lesbian,' Starr replied firmly.

'How would you know?'

'Because my mother is.'

Whilst Lisa was grateful for their kindness, the greatest comfort working at Flavasum gave her was being close to her father. The café had bi-fold doors that opened onto the plant-filled courtyard at the back of the shop. In good weather patrons sat beneath umbrellas at tables, enjoying the smell of the food and the sight of the plants and water fountain with its four small rearing horses spouting water from their mouths.

Brian seemed pleased to see Lisa. He looked at her black skirt and the long black apron tied about her waist and raised a brow. 'Working at the café now, eh?'

Lisa smiled and nodded. Just seeing his kind, misty-blue eyes and calm face eased some of the emptiness in her chest.

She watched him transferring seedlings from trays into individual pots.

'Given up saving all your neighbours' dying plants, then?'

Mention of her former neighbours made her eyes fill. She wished she could lay her head on her father's shoulder and cuddle into him as she'd done so many times before.

Brian's smile faded. 'Are you alright, love?'

Lisa bit her lip and nodded. 'Yes.' She shook her head. 'I don't know.' She swiped her eyes with the heels of her hands and swallowed. 'I've just had some things happen lately.'

He nodded sympathetically.

She looked at the seedlings. 'Have you got a school visit?'

Brian gazed at her in surprise. 'Yes.' He always presented each child with a seedling to take away and nurture. 'How did you know that?' he asked, a seedling suspended over one of the small black pots filled with potting mix.

'Lucky guess.'

Lisa leaned across the potting table, slid her little finger into the soil in one of the pots and pulled it out again, leaving a perfect-sized channel for the seedling just the way Brian had taught her, Sherry and Ben when they were small.

Brian stared down at the little pot before slowly raising his eyes to Lisa's face. 'Why did you do that?' he asked unsteadily.

'Because that's the way I was taught to do it.' Lisa replied softly.

She wiped her hands on apron and walked slowly back to the café, leaving him staring after her.

★

There weren't any other high points during that first week when Lisa walked about in a daze.

Time became her nanny. It told her when to get up and when to go to bed, when to take a shower and, less successfully, when it was time to eat. Esme was a good, plain cook and enjoyed having somebody to fuss over, but Lisa only picked at her culinary efforts. She continued to lose weight and began walking in her sleep again, which alarmed Esme and unnerved Lisa whenever she looked at all the little ornaments. Esme was no Dan; she didn't have his strength or tolerance for dealing with Lisa's nocturnal wanderings.

Fearing she might smash some of Esme's prized ornaments, or even worse a gnome and get evicted before the week was out, Lisa made an appointment to see a doctor to get some sleeping tablets. She avoided visiting her own family doctor, because her mother worked as his medical receptionist, and Lisa knew she'd fall apart if she saw her.

She was lucky enough to get an appointment at another practice on the same day she called. When Lisa told the receptionist she hadn't visited the doctor before she was given a registration form to fill out. The receptionist had bleached-blonde hair and a fake tan that made her look as if she'd been left out in the sun too long. Her name badge read *Lexie*.

'If you've moved house or married recently make sure you put down your old address and maiden name,' she told Lisa.

Lisa wondered what Lexie would think if she gave the details surrounding her recent changes of address and "marriage".

After she'd completed the form, she took it to the counter and returned to her seat in the crowded waiting area to try and get interested in a woman's magazine. Yet another movie star was pregnant. Lisa stared at the photos and sadly thought about the pregnancy Dan had been so worried about. The arrival of her period the day before had been another reason to cry.

Lexie was busy entering Lisa's details into the computer and called across the waiting room, 'Are you sure your name is Lisa Brogan? We have a Mrs *Linda* Brogan registered at your old address.'

Lisa sighed. It was just her luck to pick the doctor Linda had registered with. So much for patient confidentiality; the entire waiting room was listening in on their conversation. She shook her head. 'No, that's not me.'

Lexie frowned. 'That's strange.' She moved the mouse and clicked. 'Next of kin Daniel Kelly Brogan?'

Dan's middle name was Kelly. Hearing his name made her tear ducts spout. She blinked rapidly and repeated firmly, 'No, that isn't me.'

Lexie studied the registration form as the door opened. 'No, I suppose not. Your next of kin is Sherry Ann Jackson.'

Lisa glanced at the door and froze.

Her mother stood in the doorway with a deep frown etched between her brows.

Lisa's heart somersaulted. She was shocked by the change in her mother's appearance. Jill's blonde hair was streaked with grey and in need of a cut, and there were new lines around her blue-grey eyes and bracketing her mouth. She looked thin and brittle and indescribably sad. Lisa fought the urge to fling herself into those comforting arms.

Jill was staring at Lisa as if she'd grown horns.

'You can see the doctor now,' Lexie said. 'By the way, it's a locum. Dr Peachgrove is away today.'

Lisa fled in the direction of the consulting room.

Jill Jackson stared after the black-haired woman. She

had a bad feeling in the pit of her stomach, like her intestines were tying themselves in knots, but she'd felt that way a lot since Lisa's accident. Jill still thought of it as her *accident*. She couldn't bring herself to call it her death.

Something about the woman and the way she'd looked at her had given Jill goosebumps. The family liked to tease her about her 'feelings'; they called her a witch and had gone through a period of buying her brooms and even a cat named Salem for her birthday. But Jill had learned that ignoring her gut instinct, premonitions or whatever you wanted to call it, was a big mistake, and right now her instinct was screaming that the lovely, black-haired woman with the imploring eyes held some special meaning for her.

She'd been a medical receptionist long enough to know the importance of maintaining patient confidentiality, which was more than could be said for Lexie Bartlett, who'd called Jill for help when the other receptionist called in sick that morning. Jill was happy to oblige on her day off; she hated them and weekends because it gave her too much time to think.

'Who was that?' she asked Lexie quietly as she stowed her handbag beneath the reception desk.

'Lisa Brogan,' Lexie replied at the top of her voice. 'It's really weird, she says she's a new patient, but we have a Linda Brogan registered at her old address. But she's given a different next of kin and date of birth.' She frowned at the computer screen. 'I hate it when things like this happen. It gets messy.'

Jill stopped listening and stared at Lisa Brogan's date of birth. It was the same as *her* Lisa's. She shook her head in confusion.

'Guess what?' Lexie cried. 'Her next of kin is Sherry Ann

Jackson. That wouldn't be your Sherry, would it?'

Jill mumbled an excuse about feeling sick, grabbed her bag and fled.

She was still lying on the bed when Brian got home from the garden centre later that night. The bedroom curtains were drawn, and dinner wasn't started.

Brian paused in the darkened doorway to the bedroom they'd shared for over thirty years. 'Jill?' he asked uncertainly, dreading what he would see in her face. She'd only just returned to work and begun to cope with performing the simple task of preparing their evening meal in recent weeks. His shoulders slumped with relief when she spoke.

'Something strange happened today.'

He approached the bed cautiously. 'Did it? What?'

'A woman came to Dr Peachgrove's practice today. I've never seen her before, she was a complete stranger.' Jill rolled her head on the pillow so she could look at her husband. 'Her name was Lisa and she looked nothing like *our* Lisa, but when she looked at me . . .' She swallowed and took a deep breath. 'When she *looked* at me, she looked just the way Lisa did when she was scared, or her endometriosis had got the better of her. I swear to God, Brian...' Jill held back a sob with her hand. 'She *looked* at me with Lisa's eyes and the same expression. I know you all think I'm just being maudlin and you all make fun of me when I get these funny feelings, but . . .'

Brian lowered himself carefully to the side of the bed, too shaken by her words to trust his legs to support him. 'What did she look like?'

Jill gazed at him in surprise.

'What did she look like?' he repeated.

'She ... she had black hair and blue eyes, and she was very pretty. . . like Sherry.' She paused. 'Why do you ask?'

'Did she limp?'

Jill frowned in confusion. 'I'm not sure. I think she had a bandage on one leg. Brian? *Do you know this woman?*'

He nodded slowly. 'I think so.'

He told her about the seedlings and the other times Lisa Brogan had come to see him for help with plants. Jill listened intently. When he'd finished, she sat up and switched on the lamp on the bedside table.

They blinked at each other in the light.

'Brian, what's going on?' she whispered.

'I don't know, love. But I've had exactly the same feeling whenever I see her. She reminds me so much of our Lisa—' His voice broke.

Jill stroked his arm and said firmly, 'We need to get to the bottom of this.'

He stared at her in bewilderment. 'How?'

'Well, for a start we need to speak to Sherry,' She replied tartly. 'Because guess what? She's listed as Lisa Brogan's next of kin.'

★

Dan let the dishes pile up in the sink and his dirty clothes clog the laundry basket.

He couldn't believe Lisa had actually gone and left him. Although, if he were honest, he knew she didn't have much choice after he'd given her the ultimatum about Linda's wedding ring. He'd deliberately tried to drive her away, never thinking she'd actually go. She'd said she *loved* him, for crissakes.

The birthday present and card she left behind had nearly been his undoing. What woman in her right mind walks out on a guy and leaves behind a present for his birthday? When Dan opened the gift, the grief and pain was so bad he felt as if his chest would crack open. She'd bought him a tie for his collection. It was decorated with the donkey character from *Shrek* which he'd mentioned to her an eternity ago.

'Ah Lisa . . .' he murmured, stroking the donkey's toothy face.

Dan tried to convince himself that he was better off without her, but by the third day when he still hadn't heard from her, he was frantic with worry. Where had she gone? Was she taking care of herself? Was her leg giving her any problems? He worried about her sleepwalking and hurting herself. He wondered how she was surviving financially. Thinking about her was driving him crazy. He drove past the Jackson house so many times he was surprised one of the family didn't notice and call the police, but there was no sign of Lisa. It was foolish to think the Jacksons would take in the woman who had crashed her car into their daughter's and killed her.

Somehow that argument had worn thin.

When Lisa didn't keep an appointment with Craig Fergusson, Dan was so distraught he poured out Lisa's story and that she'd left, and he didn't know where she'd gone.

Craig was alarmed by Dan's bizarre story and Lisa's disappearance. 'You *have* to find her. She's in no state to be on her own!'

Dan scowled. 'I *know that.* But I don't know where to look.'

'Didn't you say Lisa Jackson's sister was a police officer?'
'Yes.'

'Do you have any idea where she works?'

Dan stared at Craig. Why hadn't it occurred to him to

contact Sherry Jackson?

'Why don't you give her a call? Lisa may have tried to contact her and, even if she hasn't, it might be prudent to let the Jackson family know.'

Craig's logic made him feel uncomfortable because it made Lisa sound like she was crazy, which wasn't the case. Eventually, desperation drove him to get hold of Sherry Jackson's number and call her.

'When did you last see her?' she asked after a prolonged silence.

'Ten days ago.'

There was another silence. 'You'd better come over.'

Dan felt hopeful for the first time in days and made the short journey to Sherry's Torbay home in record time. However, the first thing the tall cop said when she opened the door was, 'I don't know where Lisa is, Brogan.'

He felt like he'd been kicked in the guts. He stood on the doorstep for several moments, staring blankly at the spot where Sherry had been before he realized she'd gone inside, leaving the door open behind her.

Dan found his way into a welcoming kitchen painted lemon-yellow with handcrafted wooden cabinets. Sherry was perched on one of the chairs at the bleached-pine kitchen table, with her long legs stretched out before her and her hands clasped loosely between her knees. She waved Dan towards one of the chairs.

Despite her masculine pose, Sherry Jackson managed to make black sweatpants and her matching black hoody look elegant. He wondered why a woman with the body and face of a model chose to be a cop. She looked like she belonged on the cover of *Vogue* or *Sports Illustrated*.

Sherry took in the stubble on his jaw and shadows

beneath his eyes. 'I've had a couple of calls from her.'

The relief Dan felt at hearing Lisa was okay was swiftly followed by resentment that she'd reached out to Sherry instead of him. 'She left her cellphone behind. Do you have her number?' he demanded.

The disparaging arch of Sherry's brow told him he'd just asked a really stupid question.

'So you *do* know where she is?'

'No, I *don't* know where she is,' She retorted. 'She's my sister, not a criminal, and she'll *tell* me where she is when she's good and ready.'

Dan was flooded with rage just like the day he discovered Jack fighting with Lisa. That day, he'd wanted to rip Millar's balls out through his throat, whereas on the night he caught Jack fondling Linda by the pool, he'd felt revulsion and disgust before he walked away, not anger. But even the threat of a firing squad couldn't have made him walk away when he saw Lisa and Jack at his house. His fury and frustration must have shown because Sherry's gaze sharpened.

Dan realised he was glaring at her, and she was preparing to defend herself. Considering she stood about six feet tall in her bare feet and had the toned body of an athlete, Dan was pretty sure Sherry Jackson wouldn't be a pushover in a fight. 'Don't worry,' he said roughly. 'I'm not going to lose it.'

'That's good,' she replied calmly. 'Because I'm really not in the mood to arrest you.'

Dan attempted to dredge up a smile. 'What did Lisa say when she called you? Did she sound alright?'

'No, she sounded like shit.'

He scowled.

'What did you expect? Admit it, you'd be gutted if I said she sounded like she was having a great time. But she sounded as miserable as you look.' His expression tugged at Sherry's conscience. She unbent enough to tell him that Lisa had found somewhere to live and a job.

'A job?' He was astonished. 'Lisa's got a job?'

'How else do you think she's going to support herself?' Sherry inquired sarcastically.

'I would have given her money! She didn't need to find a job!'

'Oh, get *over* yourself! It's exactly what Lisa needed to do. She needs to get out from under your wing and stand on her own two feet.'

He glared at her. 'Is that so?'

'*Yes.*' Sherry glared right back. '*That is so.*'

'Who's she living with?'

'An old lady.'

'An old lady? What old lady?'

'Are you deaf, Brogan? *I ... don't ... know.*'

Having hit a dead end, Dan set off down the highway that led to his other concern. 'Why do you say she's your sister? You know she isn't. She's Linda Brogan. *My* wife.'

Sherry snorted. 'Tell me, Daniel...'

She sounded so much like Lisa, Dan got goosebumps.

'Does she *seem* like your esteemed wife? Try and be honest when you answer.'

He wouldn't answer.

Sherry laughed mirthlessly and got to her feet. She moved to the door that concealed the pantry and gave it a tug. The door stuck on the linoleum at the bottom edge. When she closed it again Dan saw a scuff mark worn into the surface of the black-and-white checkered floor tiles.

'See how this door sticks?'

He nodded, wondering what a wonky pantry door had to do with Lisa.

'My brother Ben built this house for me and it's about as perfect as you can get, because he's one of those pain in the arse perfectionists.' Sherry applied some upward pressure to the door and eased it smoothly across the floor. 'This one door drives him nuts. He's always trying to get in here to fix it. Our parents and Lisa and I tease him about it, it's one of our family jokes.' She pushed the door closed. 'The first time Lisa came to see me, she helped herself to the tissues I always keep in this cupboard. If that wasn't freaky enough, when she opened this door—' Sherry pulled it open again '— she knew just how to lift it, so it didn't stick.' She stared at Dan. 'Without me saying a word, she knew where I kept the tissues and how to open and close this door. Strangers always struggle with it.'

Dan felt the familiar prickling begin at the back of his neck.

Like him, Sherry Jackson was a person who dealt in facts. Yet she seemed to believe that his wife Linda was her sister Lisa.

Sherry pulled a yellow envelope of photographs from one of the kitchen drawers, flipped through the contents and extracted a photo. She held it out to him.

He eyed it warily. 'What's that?'

'It's a photo of Lisa.'

Dan stared at the photograph as if Sherry was offering him a hand grenade with the pin removed.

'Don't tell me you haven't wondered what she used to look like?' she taunted.

He reached out slowly to take the photo and lowered his

eyes.

It was a head-and-shoulders shot of Sherry with a man and woman. She was in the middle of the trio, an arm hooked about the necks of the other two. They were all grinning at the camera and holding up cans of beer in a toast. Dan glanced fleetingly at the dark-haired man whom he didn't recognize and focused his attention on the girl snuggled up to Sherry, laughing. She was petite, only just reaching Sherry's shoulder, and the sleeveless white tank-top she wore revealed small breasts and fragile clavicles. Her eyes were a misty blue, her delicate chin pointed, and her short hair blonde and curly. She was cute rather than beautiful, with a radiant smile. Dan noticed the shadows beneath her big eyes and the thinness of her cheeks, the telltale signs of somebody with a chronic illness suffering constant pain. And he noticed the way she smiled with her whole face — the way Lisa had smiled at him so often in the past months.

'Are you okay?' Sherry murmured.

Dan swiped a hand across his face and swallowed. 'Yeah. You'll ... uh ... keep me posted?'

'Next time she calls, I'll let her know I saw you.'

There was a knock on the front door.

Taking it as his cue to leave, Dan followed Sherry into the hallway when she went to answer it.

A middle-aged couple stood on the doorstep. It was an indication of just how distracted Jill Jackson was that she stepped over the threshold without noticing Dan Brogan's towering figure in Sherry's hallway.

'Why has a woman called Lisa Brogan got you listed as her next of kin at Dr Peachgrove's surgery?' Jill demanded.

Dan felt as if he'd been punched in the gut. Lisa had been

to see a doctor?

He studied the man and woman, guessing they must be Sherry's parents, and, if she were to be believed, Lisa's mother and father. He almost felt sorry for Sherry; she was stuck between a rock and a hard place. The sensible thing was to get the hell out before the proverbial manure hit the proverbial fan.

Sherry wanted to get the hell out too. It was one thing to lie to Dan Brogan about not knowing Lisa's whereabouts, but another thing entirely when it came to her parents. Beside her the big American tensed like a guard dog preparing to attack, while her mother bristled like a curly-haired poodle. What on earth had Lisa done now? She glanced at her normally placid father, but he was every bit as wound-up as the other two.

'How do you know Lisa's been to see a doctor? Is she sick?' Dan demanded.

Jill drew back in shock. 'Who are you?'

'I'm Lisa's husband,' he replied brusquely.

'No, you're not!' Sherry shot back. 'You're *Linda Brogan's* husband.'

Jill gasped. 'Linda Brogan? That's the woman who killed my daughter!'

'Jill, you can't keep saying things like that,' Brian said wearily. 'Sherry told you that Lisa didn't give way at the roundabout.'

She thrust a finger at Dan. 'His wife never had a driver's license!'

Dan's scalp started to itch. Lisa told him she hadn't given way. She'd as good as admitted she'd caused the accident.

Sherry dug the heels of her hands into her eyes. She was due on the nightshift in a few hours and could really do without this.

Dan was trying to think of a reason Lisa needed to see a doctor and could only come up with two: either her leg was giving her problems, or she was pregnant. He ignored the tiny voice of reason telling him an unplanned pregnancy would be the worst possible way to get Lisa to come back to him, but he didn't care. He'd take whatever cards fate dealt him if it meant getting her to come home.

He was rudely jolted from his thoughts when Sherry suddenly took hold of his arm, pressed her knee into the back of his knee, and shoved him towards the open door.

Jill and Brian Jackson jumped back as he stumbled past them.

'Hold on a mo—' he protested, before finding himself outside the front door.

'I have three crazy people in my house which is one more than I can deal with at a time,' Sherry snapped. 'I'll speak to Lisa when she calls and tell her you want to see her but until then, Brogan, go home and leave me alone. I need to talk to my parents.'

She closed the door in Dan's shocked face.

Sherry led her parents to the kitchen and pulled out a couple of chairs from her kitchen table. 'You better get comfortable,' she advised. 'It's a long story.'

Chapter 23

Dan's visit to Sherry left him feeling even more angry and frustrated. His reaction to Lisa Jackson's photo unnerved him, because on some elemental level he *recognized* her — a woman he'd never met and who'd been dead for over three months. Lisa might be pregnant. And if she was, why hadn't she called him?

He'd used the arrival of Sherry's parents to slip the photo into his jacket pocket. When he got home, he sat at his desk in the study, staring at the photo and stroking a finger across Lisa's smiling face. He was going out of his mind. He opened a bottle of whiskey and proceeded to get blind drunk.

The phone rang. Dan considered ignoring it but the faint chance it might be Lisa or Sherry Jackson with some news made him pick up. 'What?' he snarled.

He was met by silence.

'Is anybody there? Because if you don't speak up in the next five seconds I'm hanging up!'

'What the fuck is wrong with you?' his brother asked.

Apart from Craig, Glenn was the only person Dan had opened up to about what had happened since Linda had woken up at the hospital and become Lisa. After Lisa and Sherry, Glenn was the person Dan most wanted to speak to, although he hadn't realized it until that exact moment.

'Lisa's left me,' he said.

There was a long exhalation. 'What happened?'

When Dan had finished, Glenn was quiet for so long Dan thought the connection had been cut. 'Glenn? Are you still there?'

'Uh huh. Sorry, I'm stunned. You mean you hit the guy?'

'Yeah,' Dan muttered.

'You really *hit* the guy?' Glenn was having great difficulty reconciling his peace-loving, dedicated doctor brother with the lunatic who'd raved and ranted for the past ten minutes.

'Yes! I fucking hit the guy!'

'No shit?' Glenn murmured. 'Hell ... I can hardly believe it.'

'That's rich coming from you! You've spent most of your adult life beating guys up on the basketball court and you have the gall to be shocked when I deck a guy who was sleeping with my wife!'

'I thought you said Linda — I mean, *Lisa* — was fighting with him.'

'She was!' Dan yelled. 'What I *meant* was, he's slept with her in the past.'

'In the past,' Glenn repeated.

'That's what I said!'

'But you didn't want to beat his brains out when you saw him making out with Linda by the pool, did you?'

'No.'

'But seeing him arguing with Lisa sent you off like a rocket?'

'When the little shitbag called her a bitch I nearly hit him again.'

Silence.

'*Shit*. She's got you good,'

'Fuck off,' Dan snarled.

'That's two fucks in the space of one conversation. I haven't heard you swear so much since high school.'

'What the fuck is it to you? I don't recall you ever being

the pin-up boy for the morally correct and self-righteous.' Dan waved his glass about and swore some more when whiskey splashed across the computer keyboard. 'Got any advice on how to deal with a wife who thinks she's been reincarnated?'

'I'm probably the last person to advise you. Linda and I couldn't stand to be in the same room together.'

Dan sighed. 'I know. When Linda answered a call from you she threw the phone at me as if it was a live snake, and you were no better.'

'This is all just too weird for me,' Glenn remembered how different Lisa had sounded to Linda the time he spoke to her. She had the cutest accent and was so excited when she heard about Dan's birthday. Glenn recalled he'd been offhand with her to the point of rudeness.

'Tell me about it,' Dan agreed bitterly. 'You wanna hear something really strange?'

'Stranger than what you already told me?'

'No.'

'Lisa likes you. You know why she likes you?'

'No.'

'Because I told her you didn't like the way Linda used to treat me. She said that meant you must be a good brother.'

Glenn was speechless.

Dan took a swig of whiskey and grimaced at the sour taste in his mouth. 'There's something else.'

'Let's have it.'

'I think she's pregnant.'

'You've knocked her up?' Gleen sounded shocked.

'I'm not sure. I found out today she's been to see a doctor. She might not be, it was only one time without a condom,' Dan mumbled defensively.

'That's generally all it takes, brother,' he replied sarcastically. 'I'm sure you got taught that in med school. Did you find out from the sister where Lisa is?'

'She doesn't know.'

'Trust me, she knows.'

'No, she doesn't,' Dan protested. 'Why do you say that?'

'Because women always have a best friend or a sister or someone they confide in. Believe me, Shirley knows where Lisa is. Go back and get the truth. I've watched women fall for your knight-in-shining-armour, honest-guy shit like apples from a tree.'

'Her name's Sherry and believe me, she isn't your average woman. She threw me out of her house.'

Glenn snorted. 'What you *mean* is you *left*. You're too damned polite.'

'No. I *mean* she manhandled me out the front door.'

There was a pause while Glenn digested this piece of information. 'What is she? Atilla the Hun?'

'She's six feet tall and looks like a supermodel.'

'Really? Which supermodel are we talking about?'

'For fuck's sake, get your brain out of your pants!' Dan snapped. 'She's a cop. That must be why she managed to shove me out the door.'

'Or you're getting soft in your old age.'

'What?'

'I said, you'd better get off your sorry ass, find Lisa and find out if she's pregnant. I'm not having my niece or nephew raised by some nutcase who thinks she's been reincarnated.'

'Don't say that, Glenn. Lisa isn't a nutcase.'

Dan couldn't recall much of the conversation after that. When he woke the next morning, he had the mother of all hangovers and discovered he'd used the keyboard as a pillow and the right side of his face was covered with small square indentations.

☆

It was Edie Cruickshank who told Dan where to find Lisa. He'd tried pumping her grandson for information, but Slade had been tight-lipped and disapproving, and even though Dan outweighed him by more than a hundred pounds the younger man refused to give in.

'You've really hurt her, you know,' he told Dan.

'I know, Slade, that's why I want to talk to her,

Slade sniffed. 'I'll tell her what you said.'

Dan ground his teeth and considered following Slade as he departed on his motorbike, but it was impossible to trail a vehicle that never went faster than fifty kilometres an hour without alerting Slade to what he was doing and holding up traffic.

He was standing in the Cruickshanks' driveway staring down the road after Slade when Edie shuffled out to her letterbox to collect the morning paper. 'Morning, Dan.'

'Morning, Edie,' he replied dispiritedly and climbed into his car to make the journey across the Harbour Bridge to the hospital.

Later that night, as he was contemplating another evening in the company of a bottle of spirits, Edie suddenly arrived in Dan's living room with a look of disapproval reminiscent of her grandson's.

Dan nearly dropped the bottle of vodka in his hand. He hated vodka but it was all that was left in his rapidly shrinking supply of booze. 'Fuck! Edie! How the hell did you get in here?'

She fixed him with a beady stare. 'I don't appreciate

being sworn at, Dan.'

'Sorry.'

Dan wondered fleetingly why he was apologizing when Edie had waltzed into his house uninvited. He noticed she was eyeing the layer of dust coating the living-room furniture and the cups and plates littering the side tables.

'Look at this place,' she tutted. 'Lisa would be disgusted if she could see it.'

Hearing her name hurt so much Dan forgot all his manners.

'Is that so?' he hissed. 'Well, in case you hadn't noticed, Lisa doesn't live here anymore.'

'Just as well. It's a pigsty.'

Dan glared at her. 'Listen lady—'

'I'm no lady, son. And don't think you can frighten me by looking mean and towering over me.' Edie sniffed. 'I never took you for a wallower.'

'A *what?*'

'A wallower. Somebody who wallows in self-pity because things haven't gone their way.' Edie shook her head. 'After all you've been through with that wife of yours — I mean the *first* one, not Lisa — and then *with* Lisa. I thought you had balls. But obviously I was wrong.'

Dan blinked. She was talking about his *balls*. And speaking about Lisa as if she had nothing to do with Linda.

'If you miss her so much, *do* something about it, but don't wallow. I can't stand wallowers.'

'How can I do something about it when I don't know where the hell she is?' Dan roared.

Edie looked surprised. 'I'm not deaf, you know. Why didn't you come and ask if you didn't know?'

He frowned. '*You* know where Lisa is?'

'Of course I do. She's staying with my sister.'

'Staying with ... staying with your . . .' Dan couldn't get the words out.

Edie shook her head and turned to leave. 'Leave your door key under the mat by our front door and I'll come in and clean up tomorrow.'

'Edie!' Dan stalked grimly after her. 'I want your sister's address and telephone number.'

'In the morning,' she tossed over her shoulder as she marched in the direction of the garage. Dan realized he'd left the garage door up and that's how she got in. 'I'll give it to you in the morning *after* you've tidied yourself up. The way you look at the moment would probably send the poor girl running for the hills.'

'But—'

Edie gave him a hard look. 'In the morning, Daniel.'

'You promise?'

She smiled kindly. 'I promise.'

☆

She'd been right under his nose all the time. Smack bang in the middle of Browns Bay in the house with all the gnomes.

The little old lady who opened the front door didn't look like Edie Cruickshank, unless you counted the disapproving way she looked Dan up and down. 'I s'pose you must be Lisa's husband?' she asked doubtfully.

'Yes, ma'am,' Dan fought the urge to bend his knees as he looked down into Esmeralda Moody's small, wizened face.

'Edie told me you'd be turning up. I hope you're not going to upset Lisa; she's not been well.'

'She hasn't?' Dan queried sharply. 'What's wrong with

her?'

She pressed her lips together. 'That's Lisa's business.'

He almost hugged her. Lisa was pregnant. He beamed at Esme. 'The last thing I want to do is upset her, Mrs Moody.'

'Looking like you do, it's a foregone conclusion.'

Dan couldn't decide if he'd been insulted or complimented, and frankly he didn't care. He wanted to punch the air in jubilation. He gave in to impulse, bent down and kissed Esme on her powdery cheek. 'Thank you for looking after her.'

'Oh!'

She touched her cheek and blushed. It was a long time since a handsome man had kissed her, and this tall American was definitely handsome. Esme's romantic heart went pitter patter in her skinny chest. At the same time, she reminded herself that Lisa wouldn't have left without a good reason but Edie said it was OK to tell him where to find Lisa, so she gave Dan directions to the café.

Once again Dan wanted to kick himself when he discovered Lisa was working at the café at the garden centre. Why hadn't it occurred to him to look there? God knows she'd spent enough time at the place rescuing the neighbours' plants.

'I'll be keeping my eye on you,' Esme quavered. 'So no funny business.'

'Absolutely not, Mrs Moody.'

Dan wondered how she planned to extract retribution if he didn't hold up his end of the bargain. Attack him with her walking frame?

He loped the short distance to the garden centre, the smile gradually leaving his face as he wondered why Lisa hadn't contacted him.

✮

Lisa was depressed *and* worried. She was depressed because her period had started. It was good news, a relief, or so the logical part of her brain tried to tell her. But the logical part hadn't been able to stop her from crying herself into an exhausted sleep again last night. She was *really* tired of crying all the time.

Dan's baby would have been something she would have had of him. It would have been a reason to let her feet follow her heart back up the coastal road to the house on the cliff and tell him he was going to be a father. He'd want to know about his child, and she wouldn't dream of keeping it from him. What progress they could have made with the insurmountable problem of his refusal to accept that she wasn't Linda was something Lisa didn't have an answer for, but a child would have been enough of a reason to try to work things out. Dan might not want *her*, but she knew he'd want his son or daughter.

She was worried because her father hadn't shown up for work that day. The only time Lisa could recall Brian taking time off was when he had an operation on his varicose veins two years ago, and even then he'd defied doctor's orders by returning to work a couple of days after he was discharged from the hospital and still hobbling around in elastic support stockings. Jill was furious.

By mid-morning Lisa was concerned enough to consider walking to her old house and knocking on the door to ask where he was. Instead, she called Sherry's cellphone and was frustrated to get her voicemail.

'Do you know if Brian from the garden centre is sick?' she asked Anton and Starr.

They shook their heads.

'Why?' Starr asked. 'Did somebody tell you he was?'

'No. But he hasn't arrived for work today.'

Starr exchanged a puzzled look with Anton. 'He's the manager; he might have gone to see a supplier or something.'

'No,' Lisa insisted. 'He always does that in the afternoon.'

Starr's brows rose.

Lisa popped her head into the garden shop to ask Kaylene and Lianne if they knew where Brian was.

'He phoned in this morning to say he'd be coming in late today. Why did you want to see him?' Kaylene asked. 'If it's another one of your rescue plants, I could have a look at it for you.'

'No,' Lisa forced a smile. 'But thanks for the offer.'

She was taking an order inside the café when she sensed something was different. The people sitting at the table she was serving had turned their heads and were staring at the doorway. The fine hairs on the back of Lisa's neck stood up as if she'd been stroked by an unseen hand. She looked up and saw Dan standing just inside the doorway to the café. She grabbed the edge of the table to steady herself.

His hair needed a comb and his khaki chinos and caramel-coloured shirt needed ironing. He looked tired and gorgeous. Lisa felt like a dowdy peahen in her shapeless black skirt and T-shirt. She couldn't afford a trip to the hair salon, so her nice new haircut was scraped back again into two scrawny pigtails that stuck out at right-angles above her ears. Her heart and stomach did a somersault of joy. She thought she saw Dan's eyes light up, but decided she'd imagined it when he glowered at her.

Starr and Anton took one look at Lisa's expression and the large man scowling at her and decided he must be the cause of her misery. They headed across the café to run interference.

Starr had to tip her head back to look up at the giant, her lavender eyes flashing a warning. 'Can I help you?'

Dan tore his gaze from Lisa to the tiny waitress with fairy eyes and a silver nose stud and wondered what it was about him that made little women so prickly. He guessed she was another one of Lisa's champions, and damned if there wasn't another one right behind her, a guy in his thirties wearing an apron over his jeans and carrying a very young baby over one shoulder.

'I'm here to see Lisa,' Dan explained, glancing across at her.

She looked as if she wanted to burst into tears or make a run for it, which didn't fit with the beautiful smile she gave him when she first saw him.

'She's busy,' the fairy said curtly.

'Fine,' Dan replied. 'I'll have a coffee instead.'

That threw the Lavender Fairy. She glanced at her wingman who looked as if he was considering trying to throw Dan out but didn't rate his chances because he was at least six inches shorter. He might have changed his mind if he knew Dan had been successfully manhandled out the door by a woman a couple of nights ago. One thing was certain; Lisa's friends were ready to go into battle for her.

The other customers were watching the show with interest.

Lisa seemed to come to life. She hurried over and put a placating hand on the man's arm. Dan clenched his jaw at the jealousy her action ignited in him.

'It's OK, Anton. Really, it's OK,' she said.

Anton regarded Dan suspiciously. 'Are you sure?'

'Yes, really,' Lisa turned to the Lavender Fairy. 'I'll be fine, Starr.'

How apt, Dan thought, the fairy's name was Starr. The cavalry reluctantly returned to their posts.

Lisa looked up at Dan and twisted a corner of her apron around her index finger. 'Come outside.'

She showed him to one of the wooden tables shaded by umbrellas in the outdoor area. When Dan had taken a seat, Lisa remained standing and took out her notepad and pen. 'Was it just a flat white?'

He stared. 'Are you serious?'

'Yes. I work for Anton and he's running a business.'

Apart from that heavenly smile, this was not how he'd imagined their reunion. 'Fine! I'll take a flat white and ... and ...'

The menu chalked on the big blackboard behind the counter hadn't been high on his list of priorities when he walked in the door.

Lisa scribbled on her notepad. 'And two chocolate muffins.'

Dan watched in amazement. 'You're writing down orders?'

She looked up and smiled briefly. 'Yes. Anton's dyslexic too, so we have a system.'

She left to place his order. When she returned, she was carrying a tray with Dan's muffins and coffee and a small bottle of Sprite with a straw. She placed it on the table before turning to head back into the café again.

Dan reached out and caught her wrist to stop her. She gasped as the familiar spark of awareness leapt between them. 'Lisa, we need to talk.'

She stared at his fingers wrapped around her wrist and

nodded. 'I know. Anton said I can take my break. I've got one more thing I need to get.'

He reluctantly let her go.

She surprised him by returning carrying the baby over her shoulder and pushing a bright-green baby buggy covered in yellow chickens.

Dan scrambled to his feet to take the buggy from her and pull out a chair. He watched as Lisa transferred the baby to the crook of her arm, picked up the lemonade bottle and sucked on the straw. The sight of her holding the baby and sucking on the straw made him forget what he wanted to say.

She placed the bottle on the table and turned the baby to face him. 'This is Joey. He's Anton and Susie's baby, they're the owners of the café. He's six weeks old today.' She lifted the baby into the air and smiled into his tiny, pink face. 'Aren't you, Joey? And you know how to smile!'

Joey obligingly displayed a set of pink, toothless gums.

Lisa kissed him and returned him to the crook of her arm.

Dan burned to ask if she was pregnant but wasn't sure how to bring the subject up. Did he just blurt it out? Was bringing Joey along her way of introducing the subject?

'Joey's my chaperone.'

'Your...what?'

'Anton would only let me come and talk to you if I brought the baby with me.'

Dan's brows shot up. 'Why?'

'He thinks everybody behaves well around a baby - poor deluded man - but Starr said you were OK. She's training to be a midwife and you came to see the newborn baby of one of her clients. She said anybody who was as gentle as you were with that mother and her baby wouldn't lose his temper around Joey.' She stroked Joey's cheek with her finger and watched Dan.

He raked a hand through his hair. She wasn't the only who needed a haircut. 'What do they think I'm going to do? Beat you to death with a chocolate muffin and bury you in the pansy display?'

She smiled properly for the first time, which accentuated the hollows beneath her cheekbones and the shadows under her eyes. Dan hated how thin she was.

'If you'd seen your face when you first came in, you'd understand why Anton and Starr were worried. You're hardly little and you were glowering like a chook with haemorrhoids.'

'A chook with *haemorrhoids?*'

'A chook is a chicken – '

'I *know* what a chook is,' Dan scowled. '*And* haemorrhoids.'

'You know what I mean.'

'I have every right to look pissed, Lisa!'

'Dan!' She hugged Joey closer. 'Mind your language.'

'Sorry, Joe. But I think most people would agree I've got good reason to look *annoyed*, Lisa. I'm *annoyed* at the way you ran out without so much as a word as to where you'd gone.'

'I didn't run out, I *left*.'

'Whatever,' Dan replied impatiently. 'You still could have told me where you were going.'

'No, I couldn't! You think I'm Linda, which means you think I'm a liar—'

'I don't! You're not a liar ... just . . .'

'What? Deluded? A spinner of tales? *Bonkers?*' Lisa

demanded. Joey began to wave his arms anxiously. 'Sorry ... sorry, sweetheart,' she soothed.

Dan watched her comfort the baby and wondered how he'd let the conversation get away from him and how he was going to ask why she'd been to see a doctor.

'Esme said you've been sick,' he began tentatively.

'Don't change the subject,' Lisa said resentfully. 'You and Craig and your damned facts and research. I don't care how many medical degrees and years of experience you have between you, neither of you have ever died, *I'm* the expert about that . . .'

She trailed off as Brian Jackson came out of the entrance to the garden shop carrying a tray of plants. Her face lit up. 'Dad...'

Dan looked at Brian and gritted his teeth.

Brian smiled at Lisa when she waved to him. He shifted his attention to Dan. They exchanged a nod.

Dan held his breath and watched Lisa from the corner of his eye.

She looked at him accusingly. 'You two *know* each other?'

'We've met,' he hedged. 'Once.'

Where?' she demanded, storm clouds gathering on her face. '*Where* did you meet my father?'

'At your sister's.'

'At *Sherry's?* What were you doing at Sherry's?'

'Trying to find you.'

Lisa gasped. 'I can't believe Sherry told you where I was! Is that how you found out?'

He narrowed his eyes. 'Do you mean Sherry *knew* where you were?'

'Of course she did. She's my sister.'

In deference to Joey, Dan swore soundlessly. 'Your damned sister should take up poker.'

'You mean she *didn't* tell you?'

'No. Your parents arrived and she threw me out of the house.'

'My parents? You mean you've met my father *and* my mother?'

'Only briefly,' Dan shook his head. 'I still don't know how she did it. I mean she's tall for a woman and she's strong, but I still can't figure out how she managed to get me out the door.'

Lisa shrugged. 'She's used to it,' She returned her attention to her father. 'There's a lot of bees flying around those plants. Dad's allergic to them.'

Dan wasn't listening. 'Lisa, why did you visit a doctor?'

She looked at him sharply. 'How did you know I'd been to see a doctor?'

'Your mother told me.'

'My *mother* told you?'

One of the glass doors leading to the café opened behind them and Jill Jackson stepped through. Dan dropped his forehead into his palm and sighed.

Lisa gazed at her mother in shock.

'I want to speak to you,' Jill said in an ominous tone.

'Aw, hell . . .' Dan muttered and grabbed the baby from Lisa's suddenly limp hands.

Nobody noticed Kaylene walk by with another tray of plants. But they all heard her scream. She came running from behind the potting tables where Brian had been stacking the plants and shrieked, 'He's been stung by a bee!'

When they reached Brian, he was gasping for breath on the ground behind one of the potting tables and his face was beginning to swell.

Dan shoved the baby into Jill's arms, dropped to his knees and prised Brian's hands from his throat so he could loosen his clothing. He turned to ask Jill if they had an anaphylaxis kit, but Lisa had already taken off towards the garden shop with Jill following close behind. Lisa quickly returned holding a small adrenaline kit in her hands. Dan watched in amazement as she grabbed the syringe, yanked up Brian's sleeve and injected him.

'It's okay, Dad. You'll be alright in a couple of minutes.' She sank back on her heels while Jill hovered behind her holding Joey.

Brian's breathing began to ease. Dan checked his pulse and told Kaylene to call an ambulance. She looked pale and shaken. He smiled reassuringly. 'Do you think you can do that?'

She nodded jerkily. 'Yes ... yes. I'll do that.'

Jill stared at Lisa. 'How did you know where to find it?' she whispered when Kaylene had gone.

As Dan watched them, the awful prickling in his scalp started, making him feel like he was the one who'd been attacked by bees.

Lisa stroked her father's knee through his trousers. 'It's in his old brown leather bag, the one that's like a doctor's bag and he's got a kit in the car in the glove compartment. I've always been better at giving the injections than anybody else, even though you work at the medical centre. The sight of blood makes Ben feel faint and Sherry would rather have an injection than give one.'

Kaylene returned along with Anton, who took the baby from Jill.

'Anton, I'm sorry but can you . . .' Lisa began.

'It's OK. You go do ... whatever it is you have to do,' Anton glanced around the circle of frozen faces. 'Kaylene told me what happened. Susie can cover for you.'

Lisa tried to smile. 'Thanks.'

'Oh, I forgot to tell you,' Anton continued apologetically, 'Susie asked me to pass on a message that Mrs Moody got from your sister yesterday. She said to tell you that your mother is on the warpath.'

Jill made a noise like she was gargling stones.

Anton realized he'd just put his size ten shoe in his mouth, made his excuses and left.

'I need to talk to you,' Jill repeated in a very different tone to the one she'd used when she stepped out of the café.

Brian took Lisa's hand and squeezed it.

'I want to talk to you, too,' she told Jill. 'But can you give me a moment with Dan first?'

Lisa led Dan to where the trays of annuals were kept beneath wide green awnings. 'Thanks for helping my father.'

'I didn't do much. You were great.'

She pressed some soil more firmly around a potted pansy. 'I just realized why you came to see me.'

'What do you mean?' Dan asked warily.

'You wanted to know if I was pregnant, didn't you?' she asked quietly.

He hesitated. 'Yes, but that wasn't the only rea—'

'I'm not. I got my period a couple of days ago. So that's one less thing you have to worry about.'

'Yes,' Dan agreed hollowly.

When the ambulance arrived, Lisa went outside with her mother and father.

It wasn't until she'd gone that Dan realized that the

entire time he'd been speaking to Lisa he'd referred to Sherry, Brian and Jill as her sister, father and mother.

Chapter 24

Lisa stepped inside her old home for the first time in more than three months. Sherry was with her. Their mother had called her and asked if she'd take Lisa back to their house while she accompanied Brian to the hospital.

'He should be discharged later today, once they're happy the swelling has gone down and his breathing is alright,' Jill said before the ambulance left the garden centre.

'I know,' Lisa answered.

Her response clearly perplexed Jill.

'Would you mind waiting for us?' she asked politely.

'No, I don't mind,' Lisa replied woodenly, hating the way her mother was treating her like a stranger.

'Thanks,' Jill hesitated. 'I'll call Sherry if they plan to keep Brian in.'

Brian, Lisa noted, not *your father* but *Brian*.

The paramedics loaded Brian into the back of the ambulance. He looked pale but smiled at Lisa from behind his oxygen mask and wiggled his fingers. She mouthed *Behave yourself* and he mouthed back, *See you later*.

At the house, Sherry watched Lisa wander from room to room, touching familiar objects.

'Everything looks the same.'

Sherry nodded and swallowed the lump in her throat as she watched the expressions on Lisa's face. Joy, relief, sadness.

'What about my room?'

'Oh... yeah,' Sherry's voice cracked with emotion. 'That's *definitely* the same. In fact, it's like a shrine. Mum finally washed the sheets a few weeks ago, not that she'd let anybody sleep in there.'

The Jackson house had been added onto by Brian a bit at a time without any great thought to planning. Lisa's bedroom was at the very end of the hallway, but the quickest way to it was through the lounge and dining room and she unerringly took the shorter route.

She wandered about slowly, touching things, opening the drawers in the dressing table beneath the window, and looking in the wardrobe before going to sit on the bed. She smoothed her palm across the pale turquoise bedcover she'd bought last summer when Brian and Ben redecorated the room for her and frowned. 'Where's Fish?'

Fish was a stuffed toy that had been her companion through countless trips to the hospital as a child, and later when she lay in bed clutching a hot-water bottle to soothe the pain caused by endometriosis. Fish was orange with hideous yellow lips and a missing eye. Jill and Brian couldn't recall who had given him to Lisa when she was little.

Sherry shifted uncomfortably. 'We ... um. . . we . . .'

'You what?'

'We buried him with you.'

'*You what?*'

Sherry squirmed. 'Mum wanted to. It made her feel better.'

'It doesn't make me feel any better at all!'

She pressed a palm against her forehead. 'How could we be so stupid? We never thought to ask.'

Lisa shuddered. 'Poor Fish!'

Sherry felt a bubble of laughter work its way into her throat and turned it into a cough.

'It's not funny!'

She snorted and doubled over with laughter.

Lisa threw a pillow at her and missed. 'You're a heartless cow!'

Sherry laughed harder. At least the outburst had lessened some of the awful tension.

'You're supposed to be nice to me,' Lisa complained. 'I'm back from the dead.'

'I've been an absolute bloody angel to you, you thankless tart. Not only have I been pleading your case with Mum, Dad, and Ben, I've also been running interference between you and Dan Brogan.'

Lisa wrapped her arms around her waist and looked away.

'What's up with you and the good doctor, Lees?' Sherry asked gently. 'Mum said he was with you at the garden centre and he was a big help when Dad got stung. How did he find out where you were? Did you tell him?'

Lisa concentrated on pleating the edge of the bedcover. 'No. Esme's sister Edie told him. She lives next door to him.' She smiled faintly. 'He was annoyed when he found out you knew where I was and hadn't told him and he can't figure out how you threw him out of your place.'

Sherry rolled her eyes. 'It's not how big you are but how you handle yourself.'

Lisa moved on to folding the edge of the pillowcase. 'You know why he came to see me? To find out if I was pregnant.' She looked up at the sound of Sherry's indrawn breath. 'It's OK, I'm not.'

'I knew there was something more to it when you told me you were leaving him because he wouldn't believe you weren't Linda,' Sherry replied grimly. 'He ... didn't force you, did he Lisa?'

'Force me?' Lisa closed her eyes and shook her head. 'Sherry, I didn't know sex like that existed. I couldn't get enough of him. He was wonderful. No, he was *amazing.*' She pulled a face. 'I admit the first time I had my doubts about it being feasible because the guy is six feet five inches tall—'

'I get the picture.' Sherry interrupted dryly.

Lisa reddened.

'So if you were having so much fun, why did you leave?'

'I left because *I* was making love to Dan whereas *Dan* was having sex with his unfaithful wife, Linda.'

Sherry arched a brow. 'She was unfaithful to him?'

'Yes,' Lisa hesitated. 'And pregnant to some guy called Jack Millar. She ... no, *I* had a miscarriage in the hospital.'

'Bloody hell!'

'Yeah, bloody hell.' Her face crumpled. She buried it in her hands.

Sherry felt like crying, too. How much more emotional pain could Lisa withstand without breaking? She sat on the bed and gathered her sister into her arms.

'Mum doesn't believe me!' Lisa sobbed.

'Neither did I at first, but you've convinced me,' Sherry soothed. 'And Mum is halfway to believing you or she wouldn't have asked you to wait for her and Dad.'

'You should have been ... the ha-hardest one to convince because you're such a cynical old bag and ... and Mum and Dad and Be-hen should be the ones who believe me because they're kind and gentle and not so ha-hard-boiled—'

'Gee, thanks.'

'You-hoo know ... what I mean!' Lisa gulped. 'Everything's such a me-hess! Bugger George!'

'George?'

'The angel!'

'Oh yeah ... George.' Sherry couldn't believe she was having this conversation. 'So you'd rather be in heaven or wherever the hell — pardon — I mean, wherever you *were* and have missed out on all that great sex with Dan Brogan?'

Lisa gulped again and considered. 'No.'

'I rest my case.'

'You make it sound sordid.'

'No, I'm not. If I'd got laid for the first time in three years by a man who was great in bed and hung like a hor—'

'Sherry!'

'What?' Sherry asked innocently. 'What did I say?'

She really didn't give a damn about the size of Dan Brogan's dick, but it was a great way to refocus Lisa. She picked up the box of tissues from the nearby dressing table and held them out.

Lisa snagged a couple and blew her nose loudly.

'So tell me, Lisa, is Dan an only child?'

'No, he's got a younger brother called Glenn.'

'Really?' Sherry arched a brow. 'And is Glenn married?'

Lisa gave a watery chuckle. 'No. He used to be a professional basketball player, but now he coaches. Dan said he's even taller than he is.'

'He is?' Sherry pressed a hand to her heart. 'As soon as we have you back in the fold, so to speak, we'll work on getting Dan Brogan straightened out about the differences between you and his slapper wife.'

'I wouldn't get your hopes up on that score,' Lisa said bleakly. 'I've been trying to do that for the past three months without any success.'

Sherry stroked her back. 'I showed him a photo of you

when he came to my place. He didn't give it back.'

Her eyes widened. 'Dan took a photo of *me*?'

'Yes, the little thief or should I say, big thief?'

'I wonder why he did that.'

'Yeah,' Sherry drawled. 'I wonder why.'

When Jill and Brian returned from the hospital later that evening, Lisa was curled up asleep on her old bed. The sight of the stranger with the dark hair and beautiful face lying on her dead daughter's bed upset Jill and made Brian smile.

Jill looked accusingly at Sherry. 'You shouldn't have let her go in there!'

'Would you like me to kick her out, Mum?' Sherry enquired.

As Jill hovered in the hallway looking into to Lisa's darkened bedroom, Brian watched over her shoulder and smiled at the figure snuggled beneath the bedcovers. For the first time in months, there was peace in his heart.

'And by the way,' Sherry continued, 'she's got the pip.'

'*She's* got the pip?' Jill hissed. 'About what?'

'Fish. She's really upset he's gone.'

Jill pressed her hands against her cheeks. 'This can't be happening.'

Reaching around them both, Brian closed the bedroom door. 'We'll figure it out in the morning.'

★

Next morning, Dan phoned to find out how Brian Jackson was and was surprised when he answered the phone. Brian thanked Dan for his help at the garden centre and they exchanged stilted chitchat until Dan finally broached the real reason for his call.

'I called Mrs Moody, but she said Lisa didn't come home last night.'

'She stayed here last night and slept in her own bed.'

Brian couldn't have made his feelings any plainer. The Jackson family seemed to have accepted Lisa as their daughter.

Dan felt dazed. He couldn't recall ending the conversation, but he did remember telling Brian that Lisa walked in her sleep.

'Yes, I know,' he replied gently. 'She's done it since she was a little girl.'

Clearly, Lisa didn't need him anymore. She was no longer his responsibility. She was back with her family, with the people who loved her.

Dan felt numb.

His wife was dead.

Linda was dead.

He went to her wardrobe, opened the jewelry box, and looked at the platinum wedding band and diamond engagement ring lying on the black velvet interior. He vividly recalled the day he gave Linda the engagement ring and the day he put the wedding ring on her finger. He remembered how she looked in the long, ivory dress he'd bought for her and the tiny, white cap on her inky black hair, with the white veil trailing behind her. She had been radiant and so beautiful that it hurt to look at her.

Dan put the rings in his pocket and drove to Long Bay beach.

It was a cool, blustery winter's day which somehow seemed appropriate. He walked the length of the beach, a lone figure on the deserted sand, his hands tucked into his jacket pockets, the rings pressing into his palm.

The water was a metallic grey topped by whitecaps. Across the channel, the dormant volcano of Rangitoto

Island was cloaked in dirty clouds that threatened rain. Dan thought about Linda's childhood, imagining the sweet, bright little girl struggling to do her homework in her bedroom while her alcoholic, abusive mother entertained men downstairs. He recalled the look on Linda's face the day they went to the hospital to see Betty Mulholland and watching her fragile confidence disintegrate in her mother's presence.

Dan stood on the beach watching the waves toss and churn and cried for the sweetness and ability to trust that had been purged from Linda by her mother and poverty and ignorance. She hadn't deserved her childhood. And she hadn't deserved to die the way she did, miserable and frightened and lonely, convinced she was nothing more than a beautiful face and body.

He finally understood that his reasons for marrying Linda hadn't been entirely selfless; he'd wanted to rescue her, to make things better. He'd believed he could make her whole and had played an equal part in the failure of their marriage which had died a long time before Linda began her affair with Jack Millar.

'I'm sorry, Linda. I'm sorry you were so sad.'

Taking the rings from his pocket, Dan looked at them one last time. He made a fist, pressed his lips to the circle created by his thumb and index finger and threw them far out into the boiling sea.

The wind dried the tears on his cheeks. His heartbeat slowed.

Although the last few months had been extraordinarily difficult, he'd come to know what true happiness felt like and briefly lived the kind of life he'd always wanted.

It was time to forgive himself and move on. He just

hoped he hadn't left it too late.

☆

Lisa only spent one night in her old bed before returning to Esme's.

Going home hadn't been the joyous, positive experience she'd imagined. For a start, her mother had grilled her like a Gestapo commandant — all that was missing was a bright light shone into her eyes. Lisa couldn't really blame her; it wasn't every day your dead daughter returned in the body of a total stranger.

She sat at the dining room table opposite Jill and patiently answered every one of the questions fired at her, but despite getting everything right — and in several cases *correcting* her mother when she'd forgotten certain details — Jill only seemed to grow more determined to catch her out. Lisa wasn't sure what was more upsetting: her mother's efforts to trip her up with a lie or the cigarettes and lighter on the table beside her. Several times her mother reached for the packet, but each time she thought of something else to ask Lisa and took her hand away again.

Lisa finally snapped. 'Do you want to know what colour knickers I wore on my first day to school?'

'Why? Do you remember?'

She flung up her hands. 'Are you serious?'

Unfortunately, her mother clearly was.

'I forgot to wear any knickers to school on my first day! You had to come to school and bring me a pair!'

Hearing Lisa shout brought Brian running. They watched in horror as Jill's face crumpled and she fumbled for a cigarette.

Lisa snatched up the cigarettes and lighter and waved them in her mother's face. 'I did not smoke all those cigarettes for fun, Mum! How dare you start smoking again!'

Marching to the front door, she wrenched it open and threw the items into the front garden — and straight into the startled face of her brother Ben, who was on his way up the steps.

Lisa was overjoyed to see him. She launched herself at him. '*Ben!*'

Ben pushed her away, his face a mask of fury. '*Back off!*'

Brian had followed Lisa to the door. He caught her by the elbows and felt her trembling. The violence in his son's eyes and voice shocked him. 'Ben!'

Jill pushed past Lisa and Brian. 'I can't believe what I just saw! You could have hurt Lisa!'

Ben was dumbfounded. 'Don't tell me she's got you suckered, too?' His gaze shifted between his mother and father. 'Aw, Dad . . .not you, too?' He turned on Lisa, who shrank back against her father. 'How the hell do you do it, lady? First you get — *Sherry*, for God's sake! — to believe your bullshit and now our parents. How could you to do this to us?'

'Ben, please don't . . .' Lisa implored. 'Please believe me!'

He wasn't listening.

'Sherry said you stayed last night in Lisa's bed. Do you get some kind of kick out of pretending to be a dead woman?' He pointed towards the road beyond the gate. 'My sister is *dead*! She's buried in a box at Schnapper Rock Road cemetery feeding the worms!'

Jill and Lisa moaned in distress.

'That's enough, Ben!' Brian barked. 'Go home! Come back when you can keep a civil tongue in your head.'

'Dad! You can't believe this!'

'No! No, I'll go.' Lisa pulled away from her father and hurried down the steps past Ben. 'This was a mistake.'

'*Lisa!!*'

Lisa stopped and looked back at the three of them. Despite the horrible things Ben had said, her heart lifted. She loved them.

She would *always* love them.

Ben sucked in a breath when she suddenly smiled at them the way Lisa used to smile, her entire face getting in on the act. 'It's OK, I'm only down the road,' she said to her mother.

'Remember to get your adrenaline kit replaced,' she told her father.

Lisa looked at Ben. 'Marrying Brenda is a really dumb idea, Ben.'

The look on his face made her bolt for the front gate. As she ran awkwardly along the pathway, Lisa heard her mother snap, 'Ben! I want to talk to you.'

☆

Later that night, Ben Jackson knocked on Dan's front door.

Dan recognized him from the photo he'd taken from Sherry's house.

'Are you Dan Brogan?'

He nodded.

'You don't know me. I'm Ben Jackson and I really need to talk to you.' Ben's calm tone belied the seething anger in his eyes.

Dan opened the door wider. 'You'd better come in.'

Ben refused the offer of a seat, a beer or coffee, preferring to conduct their conversation standing in the middle of the kitchen.

'This isn't a social visit. I'm here to ask you to get your wife to leave my family alone.'

On the few occasions Dan had allowed Lisa to talk about her family, she'd spoken of her brother as a gentle, easy-going guy who used to write songs and played in bands in his spare time until he met his girlfriend, Brenda.

'Then everything changed. He stopped writing songs, left the band, and gave up sport to become a couch potato. He put on weight and chased the almighty dollar for Brenda bloody Buckner.'

Dan studied Lisa's brother. 'She isn't my wife.'

Ben's mouth twisted in frustration. 'I don't believe this.'

Dan felt a pang of sympathy. He'd spent the past few months feeling the same way.

'What you mean is, you can't control your own wife!'

'Damned right I can't. What do you think she is, Jackson? A remote-controlled car? She's a person *and she isn't my wife.*'

Ben shook his head. 'You've all gone fucking nuts.'

Dan took pity on him.

He took two beers from the fridge and placed them on the kitchen table. 'You might as well sit down and have a beer, because believe me you're going to need one when I'm done.'

Just after midnight, Ben blearily surveyed the empty beer cans littering the surface of Dan Brogan's kitchen table. 'I still think it's ... a load of bullshit.'

Dan gazed morosely at the beer can braced on his belly and gave it a clumsy shake to gauge how much was left. 'I wish.'

That wasn't entirely true. Given a chance, he'd like to shake George the angel by the hand.

'People don't get . . .' Ben twirled a finger in the air '. . . put back into other people's bodies by fucking angels.'

'How d'you know? You ever died?'

Ben's mouth open and closed several times. 'You're a fucking doctor, for God's sake!'

'Will you stop saying that? I know about live people, not dead ones.'

Ben's cellphone went off for what seemed like the hundredth time since he'd arrived.

'You gonna answer that?'

He shook his head slowly from side to side. 'It'll be Brenda wanting to know if I'm out spending money and having fun.'

'Your fiancée?'

Ben nodded moodily.

Dan grunted. 'Lisa said she's a pain in the ass.'

'Aww ... she's alright.'

'And she said you always say "Aww, she's alright" whenever anybody says Brenda's a pain in the ass.'

'Her and Sherry,' Ben mumbled irritably. 'They've got too much to say for themselves.'

Dan nodded, 'Uh huh.' He placed his beer can carefully on the table. 'Do you love her?'

'Who?'

'Brenda, you dope.'

Ben was so surprised by the question he sat up straight in his chair. It was not the kind of thing guys talked about, not the kind of thing they would ask one another, drunk or sober. But then he figured the situation was hardly normal, so the usual rules didn't apply. Nonetheless, the question made Ben uncomfortable, because he wasn't sure how to answer it. The big American watched him across the table, waiting patiently for a reply. Ben guessed that if he decided not to answer Dan Brogan wouldn't hold it against him.

'I don't know,' he finally admitted.

Dan nodded thoughtfully.

Ben liked him. In different circumstances he would have enjoyed the other man's easy-going company and sense of humour. In fact, he was just the kind of guy Ben would like one of his sisters to marry. He was certainly tall enough for Sherry, although Ben doubted the man existed who could handle his stroppy, razor-tongued sister. He reminded himself that Dan Brogan was *Linda Brogan*'s husband, the same Linda Brogan who was running around town pretending to be Lisa and upsetting his family.

'What about you, Brogan?' he demanded. 'Do you love your wife?'

'My wife's dead.'

Ben slammed his palms on the tabletop in frustration, making the empty cans jump and fall over. 'Alright then! *Did* you love your wife?'

It was Dan's turn to struggle to find an answer. 'To begin with.'

'What sort of an answer is that?'

'The truth.' Dan frowned and picked up one of the cans and scratched at the metal surface. 'Things change. Time makes changes you don't always see or want to see. People don't stay the same.'

His honesty and words struck a chord deep inside the part of Ben, he refused to explore. 'Do you love Lisa?' he asked gruffly.

The corner of Dan's mouth lifted in a crooked smile. He nodded and smoothed his thumb across the beer can.

'Yes,' he said quietly. 'I love Lisa.'

Chapter 25

Lisa woke up on the morning of Ben's wedding telling herself she had no right to interfere, that it wasn't her *place* to interfere. But as the day wore on and she imagined the rest of the family getting ready to go to the church, she realized that what was right and what was necessary were two different things.

She'd never gate-crashed a wedding before. What did a gatecrasher wear to a wedding? Did she dress up like a regular guest? Or was it better to keep a low profile and look like somebody who'd slipped in off the street to get a closer look at the bride? Eventually she settled for the undercover look — dark jeans, dark T-shirt, and black sports shoes (essential if she pissed Ben off so much that she had to make a run for it). She completed the look with a black baseball cap worn low over a pair of black shades.

A look in the mirror made her shudder. She looked like a robber about to drive the getaway car.

After checking her watch, she scurried out the doorway and off in the direction of the church at a brisk trot. She would have run but doubted that her ankle was up to an all-out sprint just yet, so she paid one of the neighbour's kids to loan her his bicycle.

'I'll have it back by the end of the day.'

'The end of the day?' Her pint-sized business partner screwed up his face and scratched beneath his metallic-burgundy safety helmet. 'Then it'll cost you extra.'

Lisa scowled. 'I've a good mind to speak to your mother!'

'That's my new bike. If my mother finds out I gave it to

you she'll ground me for a month.' He scratched harder. 'And I don't know *what* she'll do to you.'

Lisa coughed up the extra cash and quit the scene in case his mother decided to put in an appearance. He'd offered to loan his helmet for an extra three dollars, but all that scratching had put her off.

It was a lousy day, grey and overcast and threatening rain. Who else but Brenda would choose to get married in the middle of winter, Lisa thought irritably as she pedaled down the road towards the church, hunched over the too-small bike. She bet Brenda had chosen the July date because she wouldn't have to pay top dollar to hire the reception hall like she would in spring or summer. The thought helped shore up Lisa's wavering confidence that she was doing the right thing, that and missing out on the opportunity to see Sherry in all that sickly green satin.

☆

Dan had been called into the hospital to see one of his patients early on Saturday morning. Ever since Ben Jackson mentioned he was getting married on the weekend, Dan had been feeling uneasy. Lisa was vehemently opposed to the wedding and, remembering how she'd been with her father and mother at the garden centre, clearly wouldn't hesitate to do whatever she thought was necessary to keep her family happy. The bad feeling grew until it sat on Dan's shoulder like a gremlin grinning and pounding him on the head.

He was pulling up to Esme Moody's when he spied Lisa riding across the road on a kid's bike, pedaling for all she was worth. Dan watched in disbelief as she wobbled off along the road before snapping out of his trance and heading after her.

He got behind her, tapped the horn gently and sucked in

a breath when Lisa jerked and nearly fell off the bike. She looked over her shoulder angrily, her face slackening in shock when she saw his car. Her wide eyes rose to his scowling face. He saw her mouth his name before she reluctantly pulled to the side of the road.

Dan pulled alongside her and lowered the passenger window. 'What the hell do you think you're doing riding a bike without a helmet on?' he yelled. 'And whose bike is it anyway?'

Lisa's expression turned stubborn. 'I borrowed it, and I haven't got a helmet because I think the owner has nits. Now if you don't mind buggering off, I have things to do.'

She took off before Dan could stop her.

He chased her down the road, trying not to get too close and frighten her, and at the same time not hold up the traffic behind him. Lisa kept looking over her shoulder at him. Suddenly, she pulled onto the pavement and disappeared down an alleyway between two houses.

Dan was cursing a blue streak when he finally found the church where Ben's wedding was being held. It was the third one he'd visited, and the only one with a bright-blue kid's bike propped beside the church steps.

He was pulling into the kerbside, when Lisa come racing out of the church doors, closely followed by Sherry Jackson wearing a green satin bridesmaid's dress hiked above her knees to display red fishnet stockings and garters. Ben Jackson burst out of the doors behind Sherry, dressed in a dark-blue suit with a corsage pinned to the lapel, and looking angry as hell.

Dan had a horrible idea he knew what Lisa had done. He jumped out of the car and sprinted towards them.

Lisa pounded down the steps and skidded to a halt when

she saw him.

'What the hell have you done, Lisa?' Dan cried as the wedding guests spilled from the church to stand at the top of the steps and watch the show.

'Nothing I'm ashamed of!' she declared defiantly until she glanced over her shoulder and saw Ben bearing down on her with murder in his eyes. She shrieked and ducked behind Dan.

Sherry grabbed Ben's arm to stop him but hindered by high heels and yards of satin skirt, he gave her the slip. 'Don't you *dare* hurt her, Ben! I wish I'd thought of it!'

Ben stopped in front of Dan and snarled, 'Get out of the way, Dan!'

Lisa clutched Dan's shirt and buried her face in his back.

Dan sighed. 'I can't do that, Ben.'

'I'm going to kill her!'

'I know how you feel, I've felt like that once or twice myself, but I still can't get out of the way.'

Lisa gasped indignantly against Dan's back.

'Do you know what she did?' Ben roared. 'When the minister asked if there was any reason why the marriage couldn't take place she stood up and said I couldn't marry Brenda because she buys my birthday presents from the two-dollar shop!'

'It's true,' Lisa mumbled.

Ben's eyes bulged. He tried to lunge around Dan, but Dan turned so he remained between brother and sister.

Sherry began to laugh.

Brian and Jill Jackson came down the steps.

Brian grabbed Ben's shoulder. 'I know you're angry, but this isn't the time or the place, Ben.'

'Lisa! *What* were you thinking?' Jill shouted at the

middle of Dan's chest.

'I wish I'd thought of it,' Sherry repeated.

'Shut up, Sherry!' Ben and Jill snapped.

'Bennn! Are you going to come back in?' Brenda wailed from the top of the steps. 'The minister said there's still time if we hurry. There's another wedding in half an hour.'

Dan felt Lisa hold her breath and clutch his back more tightly, while Sherry, Brian and Jill looked apprehensively at Ben.

He stared at Dan's chest for several long moments, his throat working and his blue-grey eyes unfocussed. He turned and looked up at Brenda in the wedding dress and veil her mother had made for her to save money, even though he'd offered to buy her a gown.

Ben slowly shook his head.

Lisa was peeping around Dan's side. She let out a shuddering breath and slumped against his back. Sherry closed her eyes and smiled.

Brenda burst into noisy tears. 'I hate your sisters! *I hate them!*'

'There, there!' Raylene Buckner soothed. 'They were always stuck up, those Jacksons. Thought they were too good for us, and they couldn't cook to save themselves.'

The Jackson women stared incredulously at Ray's departing beanpole figure.

'The cheeky bitch!' Jill fumed. 'She doesn't even know how to work an oven!'

'No need to waste the tucker at the reception, is there?' Denny's voice drifted back to them as his side of the family headed back inside the church. 'We might as well go and enjoy it. It's all paid for.'

'That woman was right, you know,' Jill's Auntie Violet

shouted as she made her way slowly down the church steps on Cousin Sandra's arm. 'Brenda is as tight as a duck's bum. Wish I hadn't wasted money on that nice ashtray for their present.'

'*Mum!*' Cousin Sandra hissed.

Ben went to find Brenda.

Jill and Brian put their arms around Lisa and hugged her tightly. She hugged them back hard while Sherry and Dan watched and cleared their throats.

Jill gave Dan a watery smile. 'Thank you for looking after her and for saving the day again. Dan, is it?'

'Yes.' Dan shook Brian's hand and hugged Jill back when she embraced him. 'It's nice to meet you both,' He surprised Lisa by asking, 'Could I talk to you for a moment, Mr Jackson?'

Brian's greying brows rose. 'Of course.'

Dan gestured towards some trees on the other side of the churchyard and the two men walked away together.

'What's all that about?' Lisa asked.

Sherry shrugged.

Lisa looked her up and down. 'You look like a gallstone.'

'You look like you should be driving the getaway car.'

'What's with the fishnet stockings and garters?'

Sherry smiled smugly. 'Aren't they great?'

'They are *not* great,' Jill smeared her makeup as she tried to dry her eyes. 'They're totally inappropriate.'

'I figured if Brenda was going to make me wear a hooker's dress I might as well wear hooker's underwear.' Sherry looked at the church. 'I s'pose I'd better go and see how Ben is.'

'Do you think he'll ever forgive me?' Lisa quavered.

Jill put her arms around her again.

'Of course, he will,' Sherry said. 'Sometime in the twenty-fifth century he'll have forgotten all about it.'

She headed up the steps.

Dan and Brian returned. Brian was smiling. Lisa thought Dan looked nervous.

Brian extended an arm to his wife. 'Come on, let's get home.'

'What was all that about?' Jill asked.

'None of your business,' He replied crisply.

She looked at Lisa. 'But—'

'You'll see Lisa soon enough. Dan wants to talk to her alone. He can bring her home later.'

When they'd gone, Lisa looked up at Dan in confusion. 'Why did you send them away?'

He looked so serious her concern grew.

'I really like your family, Lisa.'

Lisa wondered if she'd heard right. Had he just called them *her family?*

'You do?'

He nodded. 'But I'm only asking one of them to marry me.'

Lisa simply stared up at him. Slowly she smiled, her whole face lighting up. 'You believe me? *You believe me!*'

'Is that a yes?'

'*It's a yes!*'

Dan opened his arms and Lisa threw herself against him, wrapping her arms around his waist and holding on tight. He rested his chin on top of her head and said softly, 'I know Linda's dead. I've known it for a long time, but I couldn't allow myself to believe it — to believe *you*.'

He felt Lisa nod against his chest. She tipped back her head and looked up at him. 'I *totally* understand.'

'I love you,' Dan mouthed, the lump in his throat making it impossible to get the words out. He swallowed and tried again. 'I love you, Lisa Louise Jackson.'

'Got you the first time.' She went up on tiptoe to hook her arms about his neck. 'That was a *really* good bit!' she said. 'Now get to the other good bit!'

He frowned. 'Huh?'

Lisa raised her chin and parted her lips.

'Oh! *That* good bit! Oh yeah ... I can do that. . .'

☆

Dan told Lisa that the reason he asked to speak to Brian in the churchyard was to get his permission to ask her to marry him.

Lisa was touched he'd thought to do it. 'It will mean a lot to my father.'

When they made love later that day, Lisa stopped Dan when he reached for a condom and asked him quietly, 'Do we have to?'

He looked at her closely. 'Are you sure?'

She nodded. 'Yes, *very* sure.'

Dan grinned crookedly. 'You're just worried about having to front up to that little checkout girl again, aren't you?' He sank back against the pillows and let her climb astride him.

'Found me out,' Lisa sank down on him, closed her eyes and smiled. 'Found me out.'

Sherry Jackson walked slowly across the arrivals area at Auckland airport. It was early in the morning and three flights had just arrived. The area was jam-packed with weary travelers eager to get through passport control and customs and outside to meet their relatives and begin their holidays.

Despite managing to pull a relieving duty at the airport, Sherry was in a very good mood, had been ever since Ben's wedding day. Ben felt bad about jilting Brenda at the altar and didn't have a lot to say to Lisa, but Sherry was confident he'd eventually come around. He had a heart the size of the Pacific Ocean and watching the way Lisa interacted with the family just like the old Lisa used to had put a stop to his protests she was a fake.

Lisa and Dan were getting married next Saturday on Waiake beach if the weather co-operated, or in Jill and Brian's living room if it didn't. Sherry was going to be Lisa's bridesmaid. They planned to wear simple silk sheath dresses; Lisa's was white and Sherry's a deep blue. Sherry got a lump in her throat every time she saw Lisa and Dan together. They overflowed with happiness, making everybody around them feel happy too. Even better, they weren't sickly about it. That would have been a step too far for Sherry's unromantic soul.

She was curious to see how Dan's family would react when they met Lisa. It was going to be particularly hard for them because they had known Linda Brogan, and from what Lisa had told her they hadn't liked Dan's first wife very much.

Lisa said that Dan had told his mother, father and brother what had happened to her after the accident.

'What did they say?'

'Dan said his mother had spoken to her priest about it and basically said something along the lines of God moves in mysterious ways, and his father is happy as long as Dan's happy.'

'And the brother?' Sherry prompted.

Lisa chewed her lip. 'Dan said the same pretty much goes for Glenn, but I get the feeling he might not be so accommodating, and I guess you can't blame him — look at how you and Ben acted when you thought I was Linda.'

Sherry didn't intend to be so impartial or forgiving. If Glenn Brogan upset Lisa, he'd regret it.

As she strolled past the x-ray machines processing the hand luggage, she heard raised voices. Sherry drifted closer to the long tables where the Ministry of Agriculture and Fisheries officers examined any suspicious-looking luggage. Her steps faltered when she saw the man making all the noise.

He was huge, at least six feet seven or eight, with the body of an athlete and the face of a movie star. Her expert gaze recognized his jeans and the teal-coloured shirt he wore over a black T-shirt as designer labels, and that the heavy black boots on his massive feet must be custom made. He had black, wavy hair and a face that was all angles and planes, the jut of his cheekbones sharp, his brows an angry black slash above a straight, arrogant blade of a nose.

'It's a *banana!*' he protested in an American accent, the words rumbling up from deep inside his impressive chest. 'So sue me!'

Wayne, the customs officer, looked pissed off, which was unusual because he wasn't easily ruffled. The banana seemed to have arrived inside one of the pockets of the big American's golf bag and he wasn't reacting well to the situation.

'It's a breach of biosecurity, sir,' Wayne said shortly. 'You were supposed to declare any food or animal products you were carrying on your declaration card.'

'How could I declare it if I didn't know it was in there?'

Movie Star Man demanded. 'Look at the damned thing! It's rotten!'

'We don't tolerate verbal abuse, sir.'

Sherry wandered closer and smiled sympathetically at Wayne. 'Anything I can do to help?' she asked, taking care to keep her tone even and non-confrontational.

The American turned quickly and stared. His eyes were an astonishing shade of golden-brown. They slowly swept Sherry from head to toe. His mouth curved in a smile, making the cleft in the middle of his chin deepen.

Sherry felt as if her lungs had seized. He was gorgeous. And he knew it. She loathed his dimpled chin and cocky I'm-God's-gift-to-women smile. Her blood began a slow boil.

'You're a *cop?*' he asked incredulously.

'That's what it says on my badge. What seems to be the problem?'

'The *gentleman* doesn't seem to appreciate how serious it is to bring food or animal products into the country,' Wayne said flatly.

God's Gift spread his hands and scowled. 'It's a *banana*, for crissakes!'

She itched to tell him where he could put his banana. 'It's a breach of New Zealand biosecurity, sir. The infringement carries a fine of two hundred dollars.'

He laughed. He actually *laughed*. Sherry almost expected him to bend over and slap his knee. 'You're going to fine me two hundred dollars for a banana? Damned expensive banana!'

'Isn't it?' she replied silkily. 'If you don't have the necessary funds in New Zealand money, Amex and Visa are quite acceptable.'

She was handling things all wrong, but the guy made her

fume. It was satisfying to see the smile slip from his face.

'I'll pay the fine! Take the damned banana and throw it in the trash!' He turned his back on Sherry and looked expectantly at Wayne. 'Can I have my golf clubs back? Please?'

'Certainly, Mr Brogan.'

Sherry's mouth dropped open.

Surely not? This couldn't be Dan's brother. Greg or whatever his name was. She worried her bottom lip with her teeth. Brogan wasn't a common name - except in Ireland - and he was extraordinarily tall.

It had to be.

Shit!

Just her luck.

Dan's brother paid the fine, wrenched his golf clubs from the bench and slung them over his shoulder as if they were a bag of driftwood instead of a full set of Pings.

'Thanks for the welcome,' he told Sherry sarcastically and strode away.

'Here to serve, sir,' Sherry said sweetly.

'Dickhead,' Wayne muttered.

Chapter 26

The weather cooperated.

Lisa and Dan were married on Waiake beach on Saturday afternoon watched by the Jackson and Brogan families and a small group of friends, including Edie, Norm, Simon and Esme. Anton, Susie and Starr came from the café. The ceremony was simple and moving. As far as the celebrant was aware, Lisa and Dan were renewing their marriage vows; but their families understood that for them this was their wedding day.

Jill cried and Brian's eyes were suspiciously bright when he placed Lisa's hand into Dan's. Lisa looked lovely in her simple white dress. She carried a spray of white gardenias and two more pinned in her short black hair. Her feet were bare, and her smile was huge.

Glenn stood up for his brother and Sherry for her sister. They avoided making eye contact during the entire ceremony.

Glenn couldn't believe it when Sherry walked through the door of the Jackson household the day before the wedding and was introduced as Lisa's sister. Out of her uniform she was even more stunning. She wore a pin-striped trouser suit, black spiky-heeled boots. Her black hair fell to her shoulders like a waterfall and her breasts swelled provocatively above the top button of her jacket. He just about swallowed his tongue.

When he managed to recover use of it, he pointed and barked, '*You!*'

Sherry raised her brows, curled her lip and murmured,

'What a *pleasant* surprise.'

Dan had heard about Glenn's run-in at the airport with a drop-dead gorgeous cop, and swiftly made the connection. When Glenn first described the woman to him, he'd asked Lisa if Sherry was working at the airport.

Lisa laughed and shook her head. 'Sherry hates pulling airport duty almost as much as she hates working with schoolkids.'

Glenn decided Lisa's sister sounded like a ballbreaker.

He hadn't been able to get the airport cop out of his head. He'd become used to women throwing themselves at him during his years playing in the NBA. There were a lot of beautiful women in the world, but that didn't mean they were special. The airport cop was. Her body alone was worthy of a second or third look, but her face was what made her truly different. Even without a scrap of makeup on and her hair pulled back in a ponytail, her extraordinary bone structure and challenging dark blue stare made her compelling. She had a sexy little mole right beneath her left eye that Glenn imagined painting with the tip of his tongue. He was sure he hadn't imagined the flare of attraction in her eyes when she'd first looked at him. She'd definitely liked what she saw, but she sure as hell didn't like *him* one bit.

Glenn knew he'd acted like an asshole at the airport. He was tired and his knee was killing him after the long flight. Since he'd quit playing professional basketball, he'd been feeling increasingly disenchanted with his life and didn't know what the hell to do about it. He was bored and restless. Sometimes he felt like a stick of dynamite waiting to go off.

He was worried about his brother. Dan didn't deserve any more shit in his life. Glenn was dumbfounded by the story Dan told him about Linda, who was now *Lisa*. His brother, who was the calmest, most sensible person he knew, believed his wife was dead and another woman was living in her body; a woman, furthermore, he claimed he loved.

Glenn didn't buy the reincarnation theory, or whatever you wanted to call it. He admitted Lisa was different to Linda. She even looked different, her hair cropped short and always slightly messy, one strap of her wedding dress slipping off her shoulder, and she laughed — *laughed* — when she stepped too close to the water and got her feet and hem soaked.

Dan hooked an arm around her and swung her out of the waves, smiling the way he did when he was really happy. In the past, Linda had tried to flirt with Glenn, which he hadn't appreciated from his sister-in-law. Lisa had nothing more than a joke and smile to offer him. She only had eyes for her husband.

'What do you make of her?' Glenn asked his father as they headed up the beach for the ride back to the wedding banquet at the Jackson house.

'Don't know what the hell to make of her,' Kell replied quietly so his wife, Molly, wouldn't hear. 'If I'd met her for the first time today, I'd be extremely happy to welcome her into the family.'

The photographer called them back for a few final shots. 'I think the weather will hold just a little longer. But we need to hurry.'

Lisa was shivering, so Dan put his jacket around her shoulders. Sherry Jackson had goosebumps too. Glenn would have offered her his jacket, but she lifted her nose in the air and borrowed her brother's instead. He noticed Ben Jackson didn't look nearly as thrilled with the proceedings as the rest of the Jackson family. He remained aloof and seldom smiled.

'Poor lad,' the little old lady with the walking frame said when Glenn went to dig her out of the sand. 'He's just been jilted at the altar, you know.'

'Gee,' Glenn said. 'Bad luck.'

More like a lucky break. What idiot would willingly consign himself to a lifetime with the same woman? His brother excepted, of course.

'He wasn't the one who was jilted, Mrs Moody,' a tiny, young woman with stunning lavender eyes and cropped red hair said. 'He was the one who jilted her.'

Glenn studied Ben Jackson with renewed respect.

Mrs Moody gasped. 'But he seems such a nice young man! All of Lisa's family seem nice.'

Glenn agreed. They did seem nice, apart from her big sister.

The photographer moved them around, taking shots of them sitting on the rocks on the beach or under the trees that Lisa said were called pohutukawa trees and had red flowers at Christmas.

'They're known as the New Zealand Christmas tree,'

Weird. Very weird. How did a native Californian who couldn't read suddenly become a walking New Zealand guidebook?

The wind kicked up making Lisa shiver inside Dan's jacket. 'Come on! Off with it! We won't be able to see your lovely dress!' the photographer called.

'But it's a lovely jacket,' Lisa teased, snuggling into Dan's over- sized jacket before reluctantly relinquishing it to his mother, Molly.

Glenn had to grin. He stopped smiling when he was

asked to pose beside Sherry Jackson on one of the rocks.

'Closer! Can you sit closer together?' The photographer was crawling around on the sand to get the right angle. 'And can you take your jacket off, dear?'

Sherry removed her brother's jacket giving Glenn, who was sitting behind her, a clear view straight down her beautiful cleavage.

She stared at the photographer adjusting the lens on his camera. 'Put your eyes back in their sockets, Glamour Boy,'

His lip curled. 'You should be so lucky, Attila.'

'Smile!'

They bared their teeth for the camera.

Sherry looked over her shoulder. 'Lucky? Lucky would be you getting caught in the surf and washed all the way back to America.' She glared at him. 'I've seen the way you look at Lisa, so I'm warning you, do *not* upset my sister. She's been through enough.'

'I haven't got a beef with your sister — well, not much — provided she treats my brother a damned sight better than she did when she was Linda. He's had enough shit to last a lifetime.'

She eyed him with distaste. 'Your parents must have given all the nice qualities to your brother. There was obviously nothing left over for you. What a relief they didn't have a third child.'

'Yeah. It probably would have been a girl.'

☆

'I don't think my sister and your brother like each other,' Lisa told Dan when they were dancing in her parents' living room after the wedding banquet.

The furniture had been taken out and the doors to the adjoining deck thrown open to make room for dancing. Ben had managed to get his old band back together and they were providing the music from the deck.

'Maybe,' Dan replied.

'What do you mean maybe? They won't even look at each other.'

'Only when they think the other one can see.'

Jill was dancing with Kell, clinging to his six-feet-four-inch frame, and chatting up a storm as he smiled and guided her around the makeshift dance floor. Molly and Brian were parked on one of the sofas looking at horticultural books, having discovered a shared passion for gardening.

Edie and Norm had come dressed in their kilts and frilled shirts, complete with tartan bonnets. They'd commandeered one corner of the room and were leaping about with their arms above their heads, somehow managing to keep in time to the band and perform a Scottish reel.

Norm had been delighted to discover Starr was a student midwife. 'They almost lost me in the hospital, you know,' he told her.

'They *did* lose me! For over an hour!' Esme piped up, stealing his thunder.

'You were stuck in an elevator! It's not the same thing!'

Starr was trying to teach Slade how to rock and roll, tripping lightly under his arm like a pretty little water sprite in a dress of deepest purple.

Dan noticed Ben's eyes kept straying to her where he stood at the microphone playing lead guitar and singing. 'Your brother's really good.'

Lisa smiled proudly. 'I know.'

She wished Ben would unbend towards her just a little, but guessed she'd just have to be patient.

'Give him time, Lisa,' Dan said against her ear.

She looked up at him. 'Somewhere amongst the wedding presents there's a really ugly ashtray. It's a present from Ben.'

'Why? Neither of us smoke.'

Lisa stroked his back through his suit jacket. 'It's a bit of family tradition. I'll tell you about it later.'

She lifted her face for his kiss.

Whatever their views about the wedding and the strange beginnings of Dan and Lisa's relationship, there wasn't a person in the room who didn't smile a little when they saw Dan kiss her.

Lisa suddenly pulled away. 'Hang on!'

She rushed onto the deck and spoke to Ben. He nodded. She skipped back to Dan and into his arms.

Ben finished the song. 'The next song is a special request from the bride for the groom.'

He closed his eyes and strummed his guitar. Behind him the electric organ purred, and the drummer picked up the beat of Matchbox Twenty's hit 'Unwell'. Ben put his lips to the microphone and began to sing about how right now he wasn't crazy, just a little unwell, and soon they would all see a different side of him and how he used to be.

Somebody began to clap. Everybody joined in and began to dance, some hooking arms and whooping about the room, while Norm and Edie gave a particularly energetic display in their corner.

Dan looked down at Lisa and laughed. 'You little minx.'

She let out a shriek when he wrapped his arms about her hips, lifted her off the ground and swung her around. Lisa lifted her arms above her head and laughed out loud.

★

Moira and George watched the proceedings, invisible unseen guests.

George clapped along with the music. 'I do love a good party.'

Moira tapped her foot sedately.

'See?' he grinned and nudged her gently with his elbow. 'Told you it'd be alright.'

Acknowledgements

For Les, McKenzie and Fleur -
couldn't have done it without you.
And in memory of George (1922-2001)

About the Author

Introducing Michelle Holman, the witty wordsmith from the lush landscapes of New Zealand, whose enchanting tales of romance and laughter have captured the hearts of readers worldwide. With

a pen as her compass and humour as her guide, Michelle weaves stories that transport readers to a world where love conquers all.

From her debut novel, "Bonkers," to her latest masterpiece, Michelle's writing sparkles with warmth and charm, inviting readers on a journey filled with unforgettable characters and heartwarming moments. Her novels are a celebration of love, friendship, and the joy of finding laughter in life's unexpected twists and turns.

As a nurse turned author, Michelle infuses her writing with the same compassion and empathy that defined her career in healthcare. Her characters leap off the page with authenticity, their struggles and triumphs reflecting the universal experiences of the human heart.

For details about all Michelle's books, including upcoming titles and work in progress, please visit:

@michelleholmanauthor
www.michelleholman.com

www.ingramcontent.com/pod-product-compliance
Lightning Source LLC
Chambersburg PA
CBHW020415010526
44118CB00010B/269